posh logic

100 PUZZLES

The Puzzle Society™
puzzlesociety.com

Andrews McMeel
Publishing, LLC
Kansas City · Sydney · London

09 10 11 12 13 LEO 10 9 8 7 6 5 4 3 2

ISBN-13: 978-0-7407-8556-6
ISBN-10: 0-7407-8556-7

www.andrewsmcmeel.com
www.puzzlesociety.com

All puzzles supplied under license from Puzzler Media Ltd.—
www.puzzler.com

Illustration by Brie Harrison—www.briedee.com

ATTENTION: SCHOOLS AND BUSINESSES
Andrews McMeel books are available at quantity discounts
with bulk purchase for educational, business, or sales
promotional use. For information, please write to: Special
Sales Department, Andrews McMeel Publishing, LLC,
1130 Walnut Street, Kansas City, Missouri 64106.

solving tips

The next few pages have all the instructions you'll need to tackle the puzzles in this book. They may look a little complicated but you'll soon get the hang of things.

Logic Problems

With each standard problem we provide a chart that takes into account every possibility to be considered in the solution. First, you carefully read the statement of the problem in the introduction, and then consider the clues. Next, you enter in the chart all the information immediately apparent from the clues, using an ✗ to show a definite **no** and a ✓ to show a definite **yes**. You'll find that this narrows down the possibilities and might even reveal some new definite information. So now you re-read the clues with these new facts in mind to discover further positive/negative relationships. Be sure to enter information in all the relevant places in the chart, and to transfer newly discovered information from one part of the chart to all the other relevant parts. The smaller grid at the end of each problem is simply a quick-reference chart for all your findings.

Now try your hand at working through the example below—you'll soon get the hang of it.

EXAMPLE

Three children live on the same street. From the two clues given below, can you discover each child's full name and age?

Clues

1. Miss Brown is three years older than Mary.
2. The child whose surname is White is 9 years old.

Solution

Miss Brown (clue 1) cannot be Brian, so you can place an ✗ in the Brian/Brown box. Clue 1 tells us that she is not Mary either, so you can put an ✗ in the Mary/Brown box. Miss Brown is therefore Anne, the only possibility remaining. Now place a ✓ in that box in the chart, with corresponding ✗'s against the other possible surnames for Anne.

If Anne Brown is three years older than Mary (clue 1), she must be 10 and Mary, 7. So place ✓'s in the Anne/10, Brown/10 and Mary/7 boxes, and ✗'s in all the empty boxes in each row and column containing these ✓'s. The chart now reveals Brian's age as 9, so you can place a ✓ in the Brian/9 box. Clue 2 tells us that White is 9 years old too, so he must be Brian. Place a ✓ in the White/9 box and ✗'s in the remaining empty boxes in that row and column, then place a ✓ in the Brian/White box and ✗'s in all the remaining empty boxes in that row and column. You can see now that the remaining unfilled boxes in the chart must contain ✓'s, since their rows and columns contain only ✗'s, so they reveal Green as the surname of 7-year-old Mary.

Anne Brown, 10.
Brian White, 9.
Mary Green, 7.

	Brown	Green	White	7	9	10
Annie	✓	✗	✗	✗	✗	✓
Brian	✗			✗		✗
Mary	✗			✓	✗	✗
7	✗					
9	✗					
10	✓	✗	✗			

	Brown	Green	White	7	9	10
Annie	✓	✗	✗	✗	✗	✓
Brian	✗	✗	✓	✗	✓	✗
Mary	✗		✗	✓	✗	✗
7	✗	.	✗			
9	✗	✗	✓			
10	✓	✗	✗			

The solving system for the puzzles that don't have grids is very similar. Read through the clues and insert any positive information onto the diagram. Then read through the clues again and use a process of elimination to start positioning the remaining elements of the puzzle. You may find it easier to make a few notes about which elements of the puzzle you know are linked but that cannot yet be entered on the diagram. These can be positioned once the other examples of those elements are positioned. If you find it difficult to know where to begin, use the starting tip printed at the foot of the page.

Logi-5

Start by looking at the intersection of columns and rows that contain at least two starter letters, preferably more, and then use the "shapes" to further eliminate possible letters from that intersection square. You may well find that you can now position at least one letter exactly. There is one more "trick" to help: If, in your eliminating, you find two squares in a row or column each of which must contain one of the same pair, then the other squares in the row or column cannot contain those letters and can be eliminated.

Battleships

Before you look at the numbers around the grid, there are a number of squares you can fill in from the starter pieces given. If an end piece of a ship is given then the square next to it, in the direction indicated by the end must also be part of a ship. If a middle piece is given then the pieces either side must also be ship parts; in this instance, you need some more information before you can decide which way the ship runs. Also, any square that is adjacent to an end piece (apart from those squares in the direction of the rest of the ship), any square touching the corners of a middle piece, and all squares around destroyers (one-square ships) must be sea.

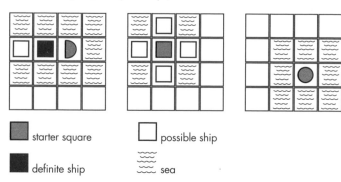

■ starter square

□ possible ship

■ definite ship

~~ sea

Now, look at the numbers around the grid and eliminate rows and columns in which the large aircraft carrier might be. Either from this or by looking at the next consequences of the remaining possibilities, you should be able to position this ship. Now fill in the sea squares around the carrier and move on to the smaller ships.

ABC

Start by looking at the rows and columns that have letters, numbers, and arrows at both ends. From that information you should be able to work out the order of the letters within those rows and columns. This will give you a few possibilities within the grid to place your first letter. Work through these possibilities and the solution will eventually appear.

Five-Star Problem

The twelve small boxes that compose the "5" in the diagram each contain one of the multiples of 5 between 5 and 60 inclusive. From the clues given, see if you can place the correct number in each of the boxes numbered 1 to 12.

Clues

1. You will not be surprised to learn that no box contains the product of its own multiplication by 5.

2. The sequence 15, 40, 55 appears in successive boxes in ascending order somewhere in the layout.

3. The 5 can be found in an odd-numbered box.

4. The number in box 6 is larger than the one in box 8, which differs by 5 from the one in box 7.

5. The number 20 appears in box 2.

6. The number in box 5 ends in a zero.

7. The figure in box 4 is twice that in box 12.

8. The 25 is in a box numbered two lower than the one containing the 35.

Numbers to be placed:

5; 10; 15; 20; 25; 30; 35; 40; 45; 50; 55; 60

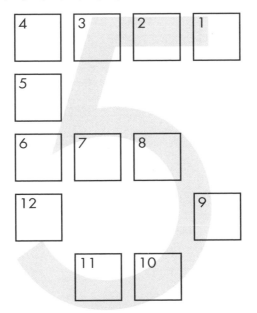

Starting tip: Work out first the number in box 4.

Amateur Athletics

Four of the ladies participating in this year's Clayshire Amateur Athletics Championship not only won their events but also achieved personal best performances. From the clues below, can you work out each woman's normal occupation, where in the county she's from, and the event in which she was a winner?

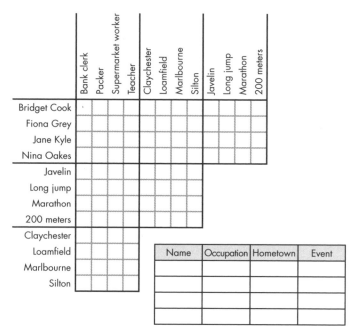

Clues

1. The Claychester athlete who won the 200 meters was neither Nina Oakes nor the woman who works as a packer in a factory producing medical glassware.

2. Bank clerk Jane Kyle is neither the woman from Silton nor the javelin thrower.

3. The supermarket worker who won the long jump event was neither Fiona Grey nor the woman from Loamfield; neither of the latter pair ran in the marathon.

Poker Hands

Our diagram shows four cowhands playing poker in the bar of the Crazy Horse Saloon. From the clues given, can you fully identify the occupant of each seat at the poker table, and work out which hand he holds on the deal in question?

Clues

1. Billy is directly opposite a player holding a pair.

2. Hank has O'Callaghan as his left-hand neighbor at the table, and the man with a pair of 6s immediately to his right.

3. Seat 4 is occupied by Cameron, who does not hold a flush, and whose first name is not Jeff.

4. The full house has been dealt to player number 3.

5. Chuck Lafayette is one of the regular poker players who frequent the Crazy Horse Saloon.

First name: _____   _____
Surname: _____   _____
Hand: _____   _____

First name: _____   _____
Surname: _____   _____
Hand: _____   _____

First names: Billy; Chuck; Hank; Jeff
Surnames: Cameron; Lafayette; O'Callaghan; Russell
Hands: pair of 6s; pair of kings; flush; full house

Starting tip: Begin by working out Hank's surname.

3

The Tedd Family

The Tedd Family is a popular children's TV series about a family of lovable teddy bears, which has been running for about eight years now. It's made as live-action, with actors in all-enveloping costumes playing the parts of Timothy and Tessie Tedd and their children Tina and Tommy. From the clues below, can you work out the full names of the four performers currently appearing in the series, the name of each one's character (which isn't necessarily of the same gender as the performer), and how long they've been in the cast?

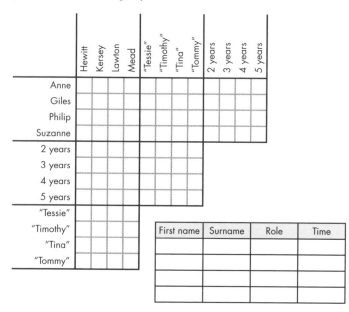

First name	Surname	Role	Time

Clues

1. If you add together the lengths of time that Anne and Giles have been in the series, they come to the same number of years as the total of the periods for which Philip and Suzanne have been playing Tedds.

2. Mead's first name appears in the alphabetical list immediately ahead of that of the man who plays "Tessie Tedd."

3. Ms. Lawton, who plays "Tommy Tedd," hasn't been in the cast of the show as long as the person who plays "Tina Tedd."

4. Giles, who plays one of the male Tedds, has been in the program for an odd number of years.

5. Hewitt's first name appears in the alphabetical list immediately before that of the person who joined the cast most recently.

Battleships

Do you remember the old game of battleships? These puzzles are based on that idea. Your task is to find the vessels in the diagram. Some parts of boats or sea squares have already been filled in, and a number next to a row or column refers to the number of occupied squares in that row or column. The boats may be positioned horizontally or vertically, but no two boats or parts of boats are in adjacent squares—horizontally, vertically, or diagonally.

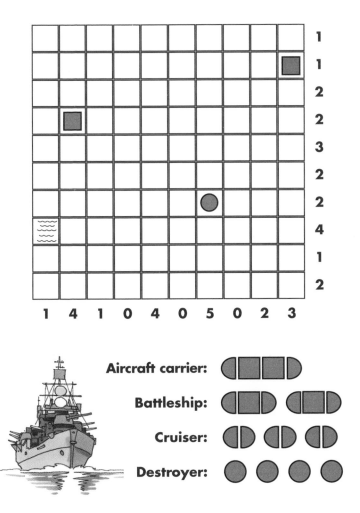

Unfancied Dress

Giggles Ltd. rent out fancy dress costumes in Storbury, and Halloween is one of their busiest times of the year; in fact, last year they were so rushed that the packer got confused and sent out the wrong costumes to five customers who had booked to have their outfits delivered. From the clues given, can you work out each man's name, where in Storbury he lives, what costume he had ordered, and what costume he actually received?

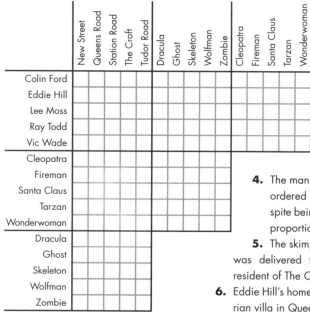

Clues

1. Instead of the costume he had expected, which wasn't the Count Dracula outfit, Ray Todd received one of Giggles' "Sexy Fireman" outfits, with its rip-off Velcro fastenings.

2. The man who had ordered a ghost outfit received a Santa Claus suit.

3. The costume Colin Ford had ordered and the one ordered by the man from New Street, who did not receive the Tarzan outfit, were both either Dracula or the Wolfman.

4. The man from Tudor Road had ordered a skeleton outfit, despite being of less than skeletal proportions.

5. The skimpy Cleopatra costume was delivered to the rugby-playing resident of The Croft.

6. Eddie Hill's home is a rather nice Victorian villa in Queens Road.

7. Lee Moss, who had expected Giggles to send him a zombie outfit, doesn't live in Station Road.

8. It wasn't Vic Wade who took delivery of the Wonderwoman costume.

Dresser	Address	Right dress	Wrong dress

Logi-5

Each line, across and down, is to have each of the letters A, B, C, D, and E, appearing once each. Also, every shape—shown by the thick lines—must also have each of the letters in it. Can you fill in the grid?

		A		E
				D
B			C	

Each line, across and down, is to have each of the letters A, B, and C, and two empty squares. The letter outside the grid shows the first or second letter in the direction of the arrow. Can you fill in the grid?

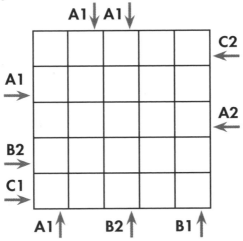

On the Catwalk

Four husbands were "persuaded" to attend an amateur fashion show staged for charity, in which their wives were taking part. We see them seated facing the catwalk on which their respective wives are displaying some of the outfits on show. From the clues given, can you name husbands 1 to 4, and match them with the names of their wives, and the latters' positions on the catwalk?

Clues

1. Jim's seat does not bear an odd number.

2. As you look at the catwalk, Pauline is immediately to the right of Arnold's wife.

3. Tony is seated farther left than the man who is married to Nicole.

4. The man in seat 2 and the woman in position A are husband and wife.

5. Reg and Sally's husband are separated from each other by the man married to the woman lettered D on the catwalk.

Husbands: Arnold; Jim; Reg; Tony
Wives: Laura; Nicole; Pauline; Sally

Husband:	_____	_____	_____	_____
Wife's name:	_____	_____	_____	_____
Wife's letter:	_____	_____	_____	_____

Starting tip:

Start by working out where the husband of wife D on the catwalk is sitting.

Battleships

Do you remember the old game of battleships? These puzzles are based on that idea. Your task is to find the vessels in the diagram. Some parts of boats or sea squares have already been filled in, and a number next to a row or column refers to the number of occupied squares in that row or column. The boats may be positioned horizontally or vertically, but no two boats or parts of boats are in adjacent squares—horizontally, vertically, or diagonally.

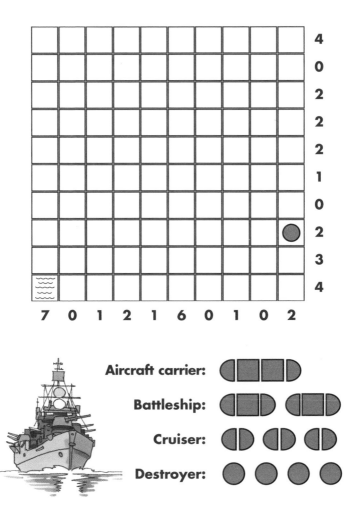

The (Old) Day Job

In the latest edition of *U.S. Writer*, a quarterly American magazine for writers, the authors of five recent best sellers reminisce about the jobs they held before becoming full-time professionals. From the clues below, can you work out each one's full name, in which genre they write, and what occupation they used to follow?

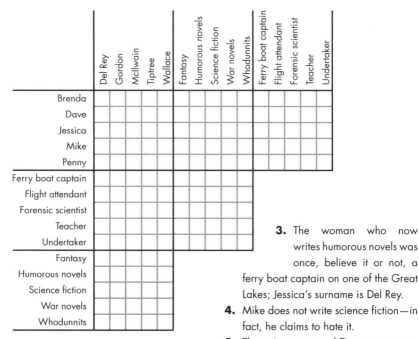

Clues

1. Brenda isn't the author of war novels surnamed Wallace, who is not the person who once worked as a forensic scientist for the Cleveland, Ohio, police department; neither Brenda nor Dave is called Gordon.

2. Penny, who writes whodunnits, isn't McIlwain; McIlwain's first name appears later in the alphabetical list than that of the fantasy writer.

3. The woman who now writes humorous novels was once, believe it or not, a ferry boat captain on one of the Great Lakes; Jessica's surname is Del Rey.

4. Mike does not write science fiction—in fact, he claims to hate it.

5. The writer surnamed Tiptree was once a flight attendant with a major international airline.

6. Dave was a teacher, the profession in which both his parents spent their entire working lives.

First name	Surname	Genre	Former job

Zongs

On the strength of rumors that a new state-of-the-art special effects movie is to be made about Zong, the giant orangutan, a cinema magazine has published an article about the men who wore the orange monkey suit in the four earlier, low-tech versions of Zong's story, none of whom were professional actors—and you could tell. From the clues below, can you work out each man's name, his actual occupation, the title of the film in which he appeared, and the year in which it was released?

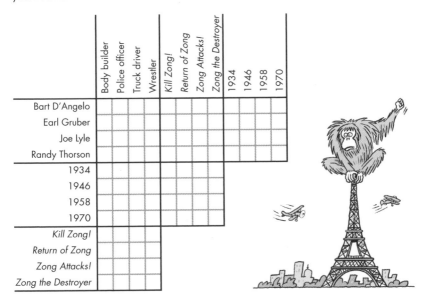

	Body builder	Police officer	Truck driver	Wrestler	Kill Zong!	Return of Zong	Zong Attacks!	Zong the Destroyer	1934	1946	1958	1970
Bart D'Angelo												
Earl Gruber												
Joe Lyle												
Randy Thorson												
1934												
1946												
1958												
1970												
Kill Zong!												
Return of Zong												
Zong Attacks!												
Zong the Destroyer												

Clues

1. Fairly obviously, *Return of Zong* was not the first Zong film to be released.

2. Joe Lyle was a professional body builder and one-time runner-up in the Mr. Galaxy competition.

3. The name of the truck driver who played the main character in *Zong Attacks!* appears in the alphabetical list immediately after that of the man who was Zong in the 1958 movie.

4. The Los Angeles police officer appeared as Zong some time before Bart D'Angelo took the role in *Zong the Destroyer*.

5. *Kill Zong!* came out in 1970.

Name	Occupation	Film	Date

Home, James!

In the days when only the very rich had motor cars, Lady Bountiful of Bountiful Hall employed a chauffeur named James. One week on successive days he drove her to a different one of the locations numbered 1 to 4 on the sketch-map at various times of day, and awaited her Ladyship's return, to be instructed "Home, James!" From the clues given, can you work out for what purpose she visited each of the locations on which day of the week, and work out the time at which James set off to bring her home on each occasion?

Clues

1. It was in the morning that Lady Bountiful went to take coffee with one of her acquaintances, Lady Manners, whose home is south of Bountiful Hall.

2. The wine merchant in the nearby town was visited the day after James set off on the homeward journey at 2:30.

3. The return journey from location 2 started at 10:30 one morning.

4. The convent, which is not in location 1, was visited for charitable purposes by Lady Bountiful on Thursday.

5. James turned east from the entrance gates of Bountiful Hall on the outward journey to Lady Bountiful's dress-maker, where he left for home at the next later time of day than from location 3.

Visits: convent; dress-maker; Lady Manners; wine merchant
Days: Tuesday; Wednesday; Thursday; Friday
Times: 10:30AM; 11:30AM; 2:30PM; 3:30PM

Bountiful Hall

1

2

3

4

Visit: _____
Day: _____
Time: _____

Starting tip:

First work out at what time James drove home from Lady Manners's house.

12

Off the Subs' Bench

A musical revue was going well, attracting almost a capacity audience for every show, but over the weeks of the run a number of the girls in the chorus line either fell ill or sustained an injury, and had to be replaced. From the clues given, can you name the girl who dropped out in each of the listed weeks and her replacement, and say which position in the chorus line each pair occupied?

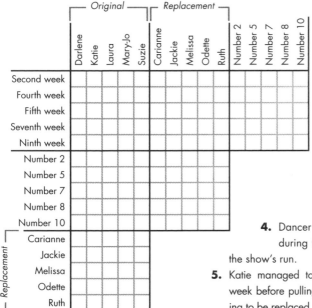

Clues

1. Melissa was the replacement for a girl who had to leave the show later in the run than Laura.

2. Odette took over position number 8 in the line when she was called on to perform, which was in a later week than the one when Darlene dropped out.

3. Ruth's services were called upon in the fifth week of the revue's run, but not for position 10; the previous dropout's position in the line was three lower than Jackie's.

4. Dancer 5 was substituted during the seventh week of the show's run.

5. Katie managed to last until the ninth week before pulling a muscle and having to be replaced.

6. Mary-Jo's replacement was Carianne; this was not the first enforced change in the line-up, in the second week of the show.

7. When the show opened, the girl dancing in position 7 was Suzie.

Week	Original	Replacement	Position

Battleships

Do you remember the old game of battleships? These puzzles are based on that idea. Your task is to find the vessels in the diagram. Some parts of boats or sea squares have already been filled in, and a number next to a row or column refers to the number of occupied squares in that row or column. The boats may be positioned horizontally or vertically, but no two boats or parts of boats are in adjacent squares—horizontally, vertically, or diagonally.

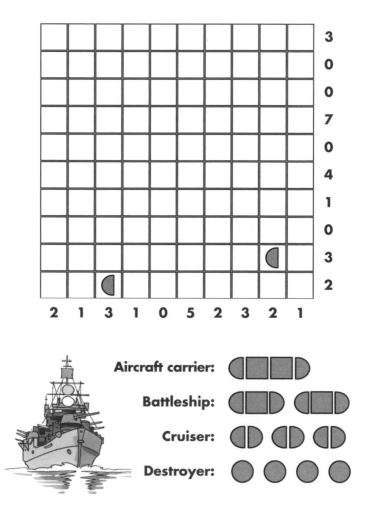

3
0
0
7
0
4
1
0
3
2

2 1 3 1 0 5 2 3 2 1

Aircraft carrier:

Battleship:

Cruiser:

Destroyer:

Party Pieces

The recent show *Party Pieces* invited ordinary people who claimed to have particular talents to perform them in front of a panel of judges on prime-time TV. Among the judges was the infamously rude Silas Fowell, and true to form he dismissed and humiliated several of the "turns." From the following information, can you work out the order in which the contestants appeared, the nature of their act, and Silas's verdict on their performance?

	Guy Benton	Victor Bull	Phil Hart	Ivor Hope	Faith Long	Impressionist	Juggler	Magician	Singer	Ventriloquist	"Abominable"	"No-hoper"	"Utterly talentless"	"Waste of time"	"Worse than useless"
1															
2															
3															
4															
5															
"Abominable"															
"No-hoper"															
"Utterly talentless"															
"Waste of time"															
"Worse than useless"															
Impressionist															
Juggler															
Magician															
Singer															
Ventriloquist															

Order	Performer	Act	Verdict

Clues

1. First up was a performer described by Silas as "abominable"—it wasn't Victor Bull.

2. An act described as "utterly talentless" was next up after Phil Hart and immediately preceded the magician.

3. Impressionist Faith Long immediately followed the performer dismissed by Silas as a "no-hoper."

4. The third act was the singer.

5. Guy Benton's act was described as "a waste of time"; he was neither the ventriloquist nor the singer.

6. The juggler? "Worse than useless," opined Mr. Fowell.

Logi-5

Each line, across and down, is to have each of the letters A, B, C, D, and E, appearing once each. Also, every shape—shown by the thick lines—must also have each of the letters in it. Can you fill in the grid?

ABC (18)

Each line, across and down, is to have each of the letters A, B, and C, and two empty squares. The letter outside the grid shows the first or second letter in the direction of the arrow. Can you fill in the grid?

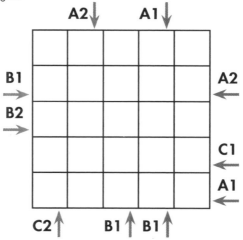

The Diver

Davy Jones is a movie cameraman and a skin-diver, and his skill in both roles means he gets plenty of work, mainly on TV documentaries; last year, he worked on five of them. From the clues below, can you work out which director he worked with in each of the listed months, the ship from which the film unit operated, and the subject of the documentary they made?

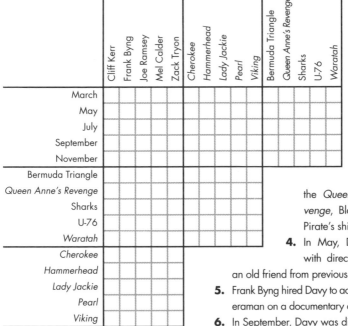

Clues

1. The expedition on the yacht *Hammerhead* to locate the wreck of the World War II submarine *U-76* took place two months before Davy worked with Joe Ramsay.

2. The documentary on the *Waratah*, a liner that mysteriously vanished off the African coast in 1909, was made earlier in the year than the one with which Davy assisted Mel Calder.

3. Davy's trip on the *Pearl* took place later in the year than the making of the film about the search for the wreck of the *Queen Anne's Revenge*, Blackbeard the Pirate's ship.

4. In May, Davy worked with director Cliff Kerr, an old friend from previous assignments.

5. Frank Byng hired Davy to act as lead cameraman on a documentary about sharks.

6. In September, Davy was diving from the converted minesweeper *Cherokee*; the *Viking* was not the ship used by director Zack Tryon and his film crew.

7. The documentary on which Davy worked in July dealt with the fabled—or is the word mythical?—Bermuda Triangle.

Month	Director	Ship	Theme

Comrades in Arms

When Hollywood Studios bought the movie rights to the downbeat, anti-war best seller *Comrades In Arms*, which tells the heart-wrenching story of five young Americans whose lives are ruined by service in the United States Army Air Force in World War II, producer Stanley Angelfisch immediately decided to change the fates of the five heroes. From the clues below, can you work out the full name of each of the main characters, what happens to him in the book, and what is to happen to him in the film?

	Bergman	Greco	Horowitz	Joad	Wilder	Executed by Nazis	Jailed for murder	Killed in plane crash	Loses both legs	Suicide	Awarded Medal	Becomes int. off.	Becomes movie star	Marries duke's daughter	Posted to training unit
Alvin															
Dean															
Glen															
Nelson															
Ray															
Awarded medal											
Becomes int. off.											
Becomes movie star											
Marries duke's d'er											
Posted to training											
Executed by Nazis						
Jailed for murder						
Killed in crash						
Loses both legs						
Suicide						

Clues

1. In the book, Nelson's aircraft is shot down and he is captured by the Nazis, who eventually execute him for his part in a mass escape.

2. In the movie, Lt. Wilder will, instead of suffering the dire fate allocated to him in the book, become an intelligence officer.

3. The surname of the man who, in the movie, is posted to a training unit contains fewer than seven letters.

4. Lt. Glen Bergman is not the man who, in the book, is killed in a plane crash while flying drunk but in the movie will survive to marry the daughter of the duke of London.

5. The man who, in the film, will cap a successful Army Air Force career by becoming a movie star, is not the one who, in the book, returns safely to the USA only to be jailed for the murder of his wife; the latter's surname is either two letters shorter or longer than Dean's.

6. In the book, Lt. Horowitz, unable to face having to fly on operations again, commits suicide.

7. In the film, Alvin will be awarded the Medal of Honor (America's highest gallantry decoration) for a heroic attack on an enemy headquarters.

First name	Surname	Book fate	Movie fate

Battleships

Do you remember the old game of battleships? These puzzles are based on that idea. Your task is to find the vessels in the diagram. Some parts of boats or sea squares have already been filled in, and a number next to a row or column refers to the number of occupied squares in that row or column. The boats may be positioned horizontally or vertically, but no two boats or parts of boats are in adjacent squares—horizontally, vertically, or diagonally.

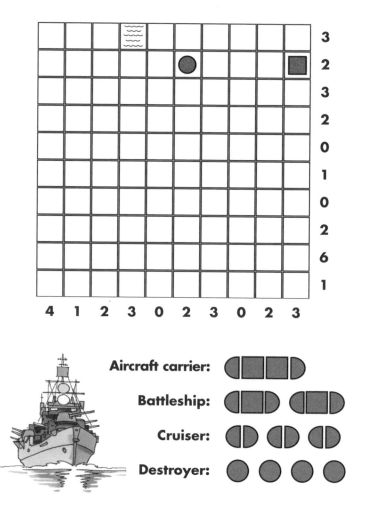

Buccaneers Bay

Buccaneers Bay, on the coast of the Caribbean island of Gran Tortilla, is so named from the four pirate ships that sank there between 1675 and 1765; however, despite the ominous names of the ships and their captains, none was lost in action, and all of the crews survived—in fact, most of the leading families of Gran Tortilla are descended from pirates. From the clues given, can you work out the name of each pirate ship, its captain, the reason why it went down, and the year of its loss?

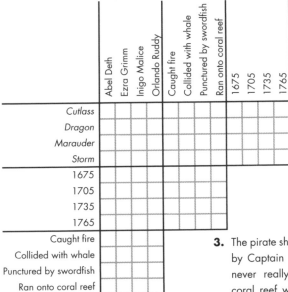

Clues

1. The *Dragon*, which did not sink in 1735, was not Captain Ezra Grimm's ship, which accidentally caught fire and burned to the water line—luckily, while Grimm and his men were all ashore enjoying a beach barbecue.

2. The *Marauder* was the last of the four vessels to go down; the first to sink was not the one that was punctured by an attacking swordfish and sank so slowly that the crew had time to abandon ship in good order.

3. The pirate ship *Storm* was commanded by Captain Inigo Malice; the *Cutlass* never really sank—she ran onto a coral reef where she remained stuck until she eventually fell apart after a few years' exposure to the elements.

4. The ship that went down in 1705 after colliding with a big, clumsy white whale known as Dopy Dick was not the one commanded by Captain Orlando Ruddy.

Ship	Captain	Sunk	Year

All Change

The four girls sitting next to one another in the office, in the positions shown in the diagram, are all going out with young men who work for the same company. Nothing unusual in that, you may say. However, the young man each is currently dating was previously going out with one of the other three! From the clues given, can you name each of girls 1 to 4, and match her with her current and ex-boyfriends?

Clues

1. Andy, who is now with Tina, used to go out with the girl in position 3, who is not currently dating Mike.

2. Daniel's present girlfriend is working somewhere farther to the left than Vanessa.

3. Angie, in position 2, either is or was going out with Mike.

4. Daniel's ex is now the regular companion of Hugo, who was not formerly going out with the girl in position 1.

Girls: Angie; Delia; Tina; Vanessa
Boys: Andy; Daniel; Hugo; Mike

Girl: _____ _____ _____ _____

Boyfriend: _____ _____ _____ _____

Ex: _____ _____ _____ _____

Starting tip:

Start by naming the current boyfriend of girl number 3.

No Checkered Flag

The main event on Saturday at the Brandstone motor racing circuit was a 36-lap race for sports-racing cars; twelve vehicles started, but only eight of them took the checkered flag at the end of the race. From the clues below, can you work out the details of the four vehicles that dropped out—the driver's name, make of car, what happened to it, and the number of laps it completed?

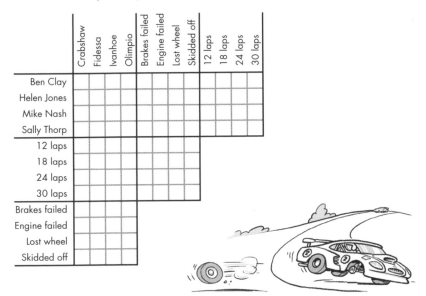

Clues

1. Helen Jones was lucky not to be hurt when her car skidded off the track and slammed into a safety barrier; Mike Nash's Ivanhoe SuperSports was not the car that lost a wheel in the chicane.

2. Ben Clay, who wasn't driving the Crabshaw Crusader, completed 24 laps.

3. The Olimpio's brakes failed and it went straight on at Goodwood Corner, giving the lady behind the wheel an unexpected soaking as the vehicle landed in Brandstone's famous lake.

4. Sally Thorp's car completed more than 12 laps, but not as many as the driver whose car coasted to a stop on the pit straight after its engine failed.

Driver	Car	Incident	Laps

Versatility

Desmond Pout is a prolific writer of novels, but his works are never published under his real name. He uses a different pen name for each of the series of books of different types he produces. From the clues given, can you say in which month last year each of the listed titles was released, work out its genre, and say which pen name appeared on its dust jacket?

	January	March	June	August	November	Espionage	Light romance	Sci-fi	Western	Whodunnit	Austin Dickens	Bentley Wells	Ford Christie	Morris Doyle	Royce Verne
Beyond All Hope															
Dark Journey															
Green Sunset															
Highland Fling															
Shooting Stars															
Austin Dickens															
Bentley Wells															
Ford Christie															
Morris Doyle															
Royce Verne															
Espionage															
Light romance															
Sci-fi															
Western															
Whodunnit															

Clues

1. *Highland Fling*, a light romance set in northern Scotland, appeared next after the book by Ford Christie.

2. The work that hit the bookshops in August was ostensibly written by Bentley Wells.

3. *Dark Journey* was published earlier in the year than *Shooting Stars*, whose subject is not espionage.

4. The title of the book released in March was *Beyond All Hope*.

5. Desmond Pout's pen name when he writes whodunnits is Morris Doyle; the book bearing this author's name was published next after the story of espionage, which wasn't the March offering.

6. Austin Dickens was the name featured on the cover of *Green Sunset*.

7. The western was the first of Desmond Pout's novels to be published last year, but not under the name of Royce Verne.

Title	Month	Genre	Pen name

Rangers

The picture below is a publicity still from the new U.S. TV series *Rangers*, about a quartet of Texas Rangers working out their personal problems while enforcing the law in the Old West. From the clues given, can you work out the first name, nickname, and surname of each of the four leading characters, and the first name and surname of the actor who plays each role?

Clues

1. Randall isn't character D, and Will isn't played by the actor surnamed Modesto.

2. Rusty, a red-haired youngster just re-cruited to the Rangers, is played by Mr. Stamford.

3. Ben's playing the Ranger surnamed Austin.

4. Scott, who has been cast as Chester, is actually a cousin of the man who is ap-pearing as Brazos Lubbock—not such

a coincidence, as both are also related to the boss of the studio that makes the series; neither of the pair is figure B in the picture.

5. Figure A is Abraham.

6. Mr. Lowell, in his role as Houston, is somewhere to the left of Gary, who is playing the ex-Confederate soldier known as Dixie.

Character first names: Abraham; Chester; Randall; Will
Character nicknames: Brazos; Dixie; Rusty; Sarge
Character surnames: Austin; Beaumont; Houston; Lubbock
Actor first names: Ben; Gary; Russ; Scott
Actor surnames: Flint; Lowell; Modesto; Stamford

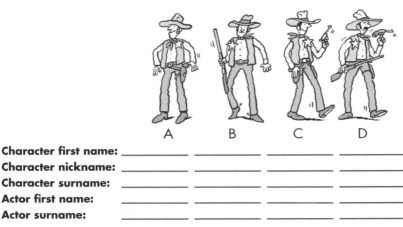

A   B   C   D

Character first name:				
Character nickname:				
Character surname:				
Actor first name:				
Actor surname:				

Starting tip: Work out the nickname of the character Mr. Houston.

The Jay-Birds

The latest all-girl pop group, the Jay-Birds, have done quite well with their first five releases, although they have not yet reached number 1 in the charts. From the clues given, can you name the songs in the order of their release, say which member of the group sang the solo part in each, and work out the highest position in the charts that each song achieved?

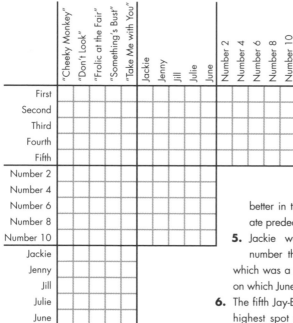

Clues

1. The fourth song did not do as well in the charts as "Something's Bust," which was an earlier Jay-Birds release.

2. Jenny sang the solo part in "Frolic at the Fair," released next before the one featuring Jill.

3. "Take Me with You" did not reach the top four.

4. The second song released by the group was called "Don't Look," which fared better in the charts than its immediate predecessor.

5. Jackie was the vocalist for the number that reached number four, which was a later release than the one on which June was the solo singer.

6. The fifth Jay-Birds number reached the highest spot achieved hitherto by the group.

7. Julie took the leading role on the first song released by the Jay-Birds, which reached a place in the charts denoted by a single digit.

Order	Song	Singer	Position

Battleships

Do you remember the old game of battleships? These puzzles are based on that idea. Your task is to find the vessels in the diagram. Some parts of boats or sea squares have already been filled in, and a number next to a row or column refers to the number of occupied squares in that row or column. The boats may be positioned horizontally or vertically, but no two boats or parts of boats are in adjacent squares—horizontally, vertically, or diagonally.

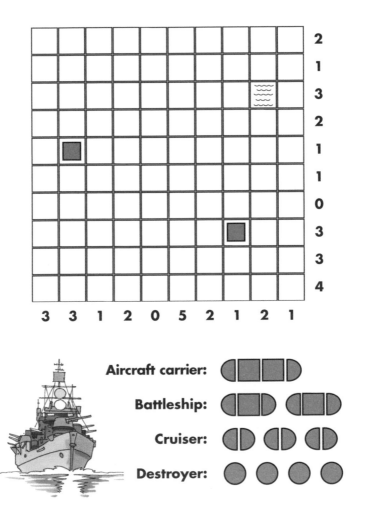

Heading Back East

Many people don't realize quite how recent the days of America's "Wild West" were, but many of the heroes, villains, and ordinary people who had been there lived on well into the 20th century, often making very different lives for themselves. The clues below relate to five men who, having achieved fame in the Old West, did it again in the 20th-century eastern United States; can you work out what each did in the West, what he did in the East, and where in the East he settled?

	Bank robber	Gambler	Texas Ranger	Trail boss	Train robber	Bank robber	Hotelier	Industrialist	Journalist	Politician	Florida	Massachusetts	New York	Pennsylvania	South Carolina
Charlie Dean															
Frank Glaser															
Jake Kovac															
Nate O'Farrell															
Rick Skelton															
Florida															
Massachusetts															
New York															
Pennsylvania															
South Carolina															
Bank robber															
Hotelier															
Industrialist															
Journalist															
Politician															

Clues

1. Nate O'Farrell, who became an industrialist, never visited the state of Florida, nor South Carolina, where one of his contemporaries became a politician; neither the politician nor the man who became a journalist had served as a Texas Ranger.

2. Jake Kovac didn't turn to journalism and wasn't the man who settled in Massachusetts or the former gambler, who didn't go to Massachusetts or take up journalism either; nor was Frank Glaser the gambler.

3. Rick Skelton, who didn't take up journalism, had been a professional thief, back in the Wild West.

4. The man who had made a living in the West by robbing trains settled in New York.

5. The man who had been a bank robber in the West didn't go East until the early years of the 20th century, because he had to wait to be released from the federal penitentiary; in the East, he took up bank robbery again, quite successfully until he came up against the Bureau of Investigation, the fledgling FBI.

6. Charlie Dean achieved fame as one of the last of the great trail bosses and survived a hundred battles with rustlers and Indians, only to die in the *Titanic* disaster at the age of 65.

Name	Western Job	Eastern job	Residence

Cops

Five officers of the police department in the American city of New Bray, on the East Coast, have just been congratulated by their precinct commanders for arresting a much-wanted criminal. From the clues below, can you work out the name of each officer, the number of the precinct he or she belongs to, the name of the district where he or she made the arrest, and the crime for which the arrested man was wanted?

	7th	9th	12th	13th	17th	Belfry Hill	Chinatown	Dysart Park	East Hanway	Kelvin Heights	Bank robber	Burglar	Car thief	Gang leader	Mugger
Gus Hagan															
Jake Lebas															
Mac McRuen															
Rose Silva															
Wes Tanaka															
Bank robber															
Burglar															
Car thief															
Gang leader															
Mugger															
Belfry Hill															
Chinatown															
Dysart Park															
East Hanway															
Kelvin Heights															

Clues

1. Wes Tanaka, a third generation Japanese-American, made his arrest in the middle-class residential district called Kelvin Heights; it was in Dysart Park, the big open space in the city center, that the mugger was apprehended.

2. Mac McRuen serves in the NBPD's 9th Precinct; he wasn't the officer who arrested the leader of a teenage street gang, who came from a lower-numbered precinct than Jake Lebas.

3. Rose Silva, who caught the car thief red-handed in the midst of illegally acquiring a Porsche Boxster, works out of a lower-numbered precinct than the man who made his arrest among the fabulous mansions and luxury apartment blocks of Belfry Hill.

4. The burglar was arrested in the 7th Precinct, which does not cover Chinatown.

5. Veteran patrolman Gus Hagan, who's due for retirement next year, isn't based in the 12th Precinct.

6. East Hanway, in the 13th Precinct, might charitably be described as an inner city district in urgent need of urban renewal.

Cop	Precinct	District	Criminal

Help's on the Way

Four ambulance drivers and their crewmen were called out almost simultaneously the other day to incidents in different directions from the hospital. From the clues given, can you name the crew who headed to each of locations 1 to 4, and say what was the reason for each call-out?

Clues

1. Alan drove his ambulance in the direction diametrically opposite to that taken by the crew who responded to the call-out to a domestic accident.

2. Someone had collapsed in the street at location 3.

3. Bob and Lawrie were aboard one of the ambulances.

4. Steve's ambulance rushed off at high speed to location 2.

5. Joe was in attendance at the road accident, while Andy was driven to location 1.

6. Gerry did not drive his vehicle to the fire.

Driver: _____　　　　　　_____
Crewman: _____　　　　　　_____
Reason: _____　　　　　　_____

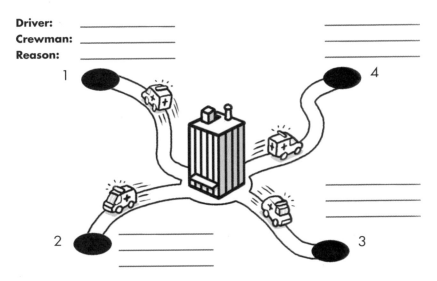

Drivers: Alan; Bob; Gerry; Steve
Crewmen: Andy; Graham; Joe; Lawrie
Reasons for call-out: collapse; domestic accident; fire; road accident

Starting tip:

Begin by naming the driver who headed for location 1.

Secrets of Age

The five oldest residents of The Laurels residential home each claim a reason for their longevity. From the following information, can you work out the age of each of them, their room number in the home, and to what each attributes his or her long life?

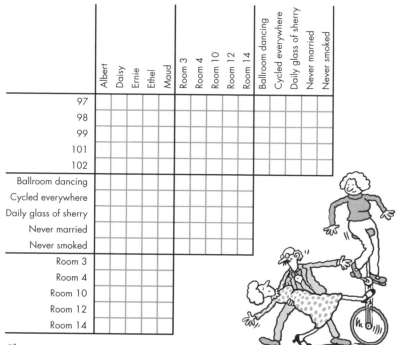

	Albert	Daisy	Ernie	Ethel	Maud	Room 3	Room 4	Room 10	Room 12	Room 14	Ballroom dancing	Cycled everywhere	Daily glass of sherry	Never married	Never smoked
97															
98															
99															
101															
102															
Ballroom dancing															
Cycled everywhere															
Daily glass of sherry															
Never married															
Never smoked															
Room 3															
Room 4															
Room 10															
Room 12															
Room 14															

Clues

1. Maud says she always cycled everywhere, but Daisy, the oldest resident, doesn't attribute her longevity to ballroom dancing.

2. Ernie is a year younger than the occupant of room 12, while Albert is two years older than the resident who says that never marrying has helped him or her to live longer.

3. Ethel is in room 10.

4. The resident of room 14 swears by a daily glass of sherry.

5. The 99-year-old has room 3.

6. The 101-year-old claims to have lived so long through never having smoked.

Age	Name	Room	Secret

Logi-5

Each line, across and down, is to have each of the letters A, B, C, D, and E, appearing once each. Also, every shape—shown by the thick lines—must also have each of the letters in it. Can you fill in the grid?

	D			
C				E
				B
	A			

ABC 34

Each line, across and down, is to have each of the letters A, B, and C, and two empty squares. The letter outside the grid shows the first or second letter in the direction of the arrow. Can you fill in the grid?

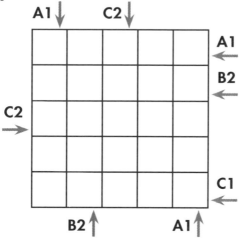

Exercise Can Be Dangerous

Yes, exercise can be dangerous under certain circumstances—if you take it against medical advice, for instance, or if you overdo it, or if—like the people we're talking about here—you happen to be accident-prone. From the clues given, can you work out the full name of each unfortunate, which form of exercise they took up, and what injury they sustained as a result?

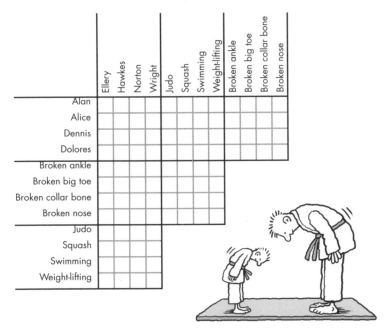

Clues

1. Dr. Hawkes, who had decided to take up swimming but is now reconsidering, has a first name initial the same as that of the person who suffered a broken collar bone in a fall—while still in the changing room!

2. Alan thought it would be a good idea to take up judo, but is now thinking again.

3. The person named Ellery who broke a big toe has a longer first name than the one who took up squash and broke something else.

4. Dennis suffered a broken—indeed, completely flattened—nose; his surname isn't Wright.

First name	Surname	Exercise	Injury

Dark Secrets

Five popular celebrities, frequent guests on TV talk shows and the like, each have a dark secret in their past, which they have been very careful to keep hidden. From the clues below, can you work out each one's full name, what they're famous for today, and the nature of their dark secret?

	Byrd	Chester	Fearn	Stonehall	Wheeler	Naturalist	Novelist	Racehorse trainer	Sports writer	Thriller writer	Convicted burglar	Convicted car thief	Convicted smuggler	Former biker	Former stripper
Brian															
Dominic															
Gerald															
Joanne															
Marion															
Convicted burglar															
Convicted car thief															
Convicted smuggler															
Former biker															
Former stripper															
Naturalist															
Novelist															
Racehorse trainer															
Sports writer															
Thriller writer															

Clues

1. Neither Brian nor Wheeler was convicted of a criminal offense in their past life.

2. Joanne Byrd is not the naturalist and eco-campaigner.

3. Marion is a popular novelist, specializing in family sagas set in her native North Yorkshire.

4. When he was a teenager, the writer of best selling thrillers served a sentence in juvie, as institutions for young offenders were known in those days, for car theft.

5. Chester, who, while a student back in the 1970s, was given a suspended sentence for smuggling a small quantity of, um, a certain substance, is a popular writer.

6. The sports writer, whose surname is Stonehall, is not the former biker, who was, to be specific, a member of an extremely antisocial motorcycle gang called the Death Riders.

7. Gerald's surname isn't Fearn.

First name	Surname	Occupation	Secret

Stone Age Dogs

Each of these Stone Age characters decided that, for one reason or another, their family had need of a dog. There not being any pet shops around in those days, each was obliged to acquire one by bartering with a neighbor in exchange for an article he had made. From the clues given, can you work out what name each man chose for his new best friend, say why he needed it, and name the friend he obtained it from?

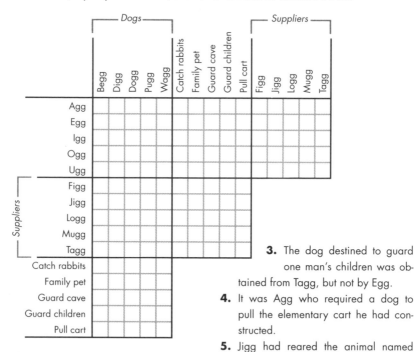

Clues

1. The dog Igg obtained by bartering with Logg was given a name beginning with the same consonant (sound-wise, that is, since there was then no alphabet) as the one intended to help catch rabbits.

2. The dog provided by Figg had a name listed just before alphabetically (in our present-day list, of course) the one acquired by Ugg.

3. The dog destined to guard one man's children was obtained from Tagg, but not by Egg.

4. It was Agg who required a dog to pull the elementary cart he had constructed.

5. Jigg had reared the animal named Pugg by its new family.

6. The dog acquired as a family pet, but not from Mugg, was named Begg by its new owner's children.

Name	Dog	Reason	Supplier

Battleships

Do you remember the old game of battleships? These puzzles are based on that idea. Your task is to find the vessels in the diagram. Some parts of boats or sea squares have already been filled in, and a number next to a row or column refers to the number of occupied squares in that row or column. The boats may be positioned horizontally or vertically, but no two boats or parts of boats are in adjacent squares—horizontally, vertically, or diagonally.

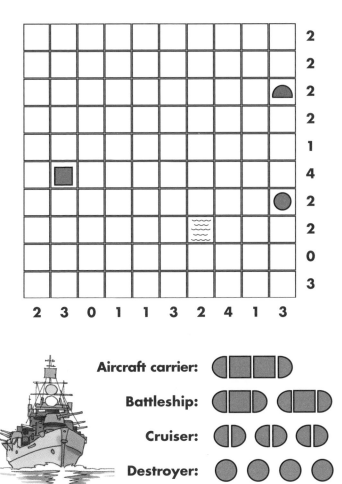

Cop Cars

The four American police cars shown below aren't what they appear to be—they're parked in the garage of Ultrafilm Studios, not ten miles from London, part of the vast fleet of vehicles assembled for their latest epic, *Mission International*. From the clues given, can you fill in the color or colors in which the car is painted, the county police force whose name appears on its front doors, and the state in which that county is supposed to be?

Clues

1. The car from the Grant County Police Department in Utah is immediately left of the all-black automobile.

2. Jordan County is in a state with a longer name than the one in which Rock County is situated.

3. The blue and white police car in position 4 is not the one from a county in Kansas.

4. The black and white police car is standing immediately right of the one bearing the name of a county police department in Florida.

5. The white car bears the name and badge of the Pallet County Police Department.

Car colors: black; black/white; blue/white; white
Police departments: Grant County; Jordan County; Pallet County; Rock County
States: Florida; Kansas; Maine; Utah

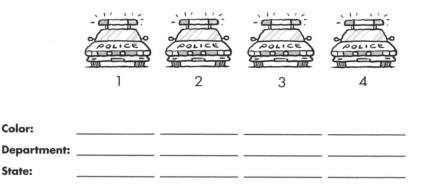

Color: _____ _____ _____ _____

Department: _____ _____ _____ _____

State: _____ _____ _____ _____

Starting tip:
Work out the color of the Grant County car.

Side-Wheelers

Surfing the Internet, I came across a Web site belonging to Bud Hunsacker from Green Bay, Wisconsin, and devoted to the side-wheeler steamers that once plied the waters of the Great Lakes, with special reference to those once commanded by his great-grandfather Capt. Reinwald Hunsacker. So, from the clues below, can you work out when Capt. Hunsacker took command of each of the listed vessels, what its eventual fate was, and on which of the lakes it met that fate?

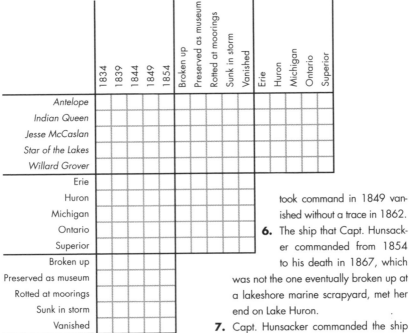

Clues

1. Reinwald Hunsacker took command of the *Willard Grover* ten years after he became captain of the ship now preserved as a museum on the banks of Lake Erie.

2. The *Antelope* was sunk in a fierce storm.

3. The *Jesse McCaslan* met her fate in the waters of Lake Superior.

4. Capt. Hunsacker took over command of the *Indian Queen* in the year 1844.

5. The ship of which Reinwald Hunsacker took command in 1849 vanished without a trace in 1862.

6. The ship that Capt. Hunsacker commanded from 1854 to his death in 1867, which was not the one eventually broken up at a lakeshore marine scrapyard, met her end on Lake Huron.

7. Capt. Hunsacker commanded the ship that was eventually left to rot at her moorings by her bankrupt owners ten years before he took over the ship that met her fate in Lake Ontario.

Steamer	Year	Fate	Lake

Gems Among the Junk

Each of five families at different addresses on Serendipity Street received one piece of welcome correspondence amid the plethora of bills and junk mail on different days last week. From the clues given, can you identify the couple who live at each address, and say which desirable item was delivered on which day?

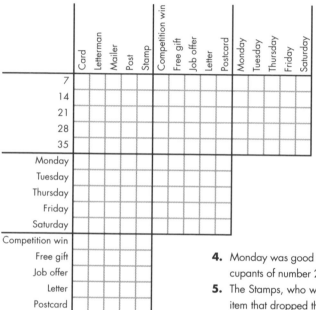

Clues

1. The Card family's house has a higher street number than the one to which a free gift from a book club was delivered the day after their own welcome item.

2. Number 35 Serendipity Street is the address of the Letterman family, who did not receive notification of a competition win.

3. The Mailers were the recipients of a postcard from their friends in Australia the day before the arrival of a job offer at another address.

4. Monday was good news day for the occupants of number 21.

5. The Stamps, who were pleased with an item that dropped through their mailbox on Friday, do not live at the nearest house on Serendipity Street to the Posts, who did not receive their welcome item on Tuesday.

6. The letter from a daughter back-packing overseas during her summer break was read by her parents at number 28.

House	Family	Item	Day

Undercover

Four FBI agents have been assigned to undercover work in different American cities, to infiltrate or keep observation on suspect groups as part of ongoing investigations. From the clues below, can you work out each agent's name, the city where he's undercover, the crime he's investigating, and the role he's taken on?

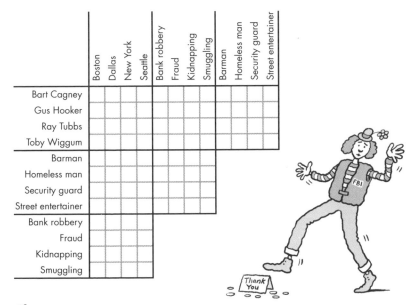

Clues

1. Agent Ray Tubbs, a native of California, has been sent to Seattle, in the northwestern United States.

2. The agent who has gone to Boston to help with an investigation into a major smuggling ring isn't the one who's had to take on the role of a street entertainer—a white-faced, mute mime-artist, to be specific—in order to watch a particular office building.

3. In New York, an agent has taken a job as a barman to infiltrate the group of criminals operating out of a posh restaurant.

4. Toby Wiggum, who isn't involved in the smuggling case, is posing as a not-too-bright and not-too-honest security guard.

5. Gus Hooker is working on the kidnapping case; the agent in Dallas isn't involved in the bank robbery investigation.

Agent	City	Crime	Role

41

Schloss Furchtbar

The ruins of Schloss Furchtbar are a major tourist attraction in Bluddengutz; most of the castle was destroyed years ago by war and the passage of time, but four towers stand almost intact, one at each corner. From the clues below can you work out the name of the tower at each corner, and say which Baron Furchtbar built it and what memento of him is still kept in it?

Clues

1. The Raven Tower, built by Gregor the Red, is on the opposite corner of the ruined Schloss to the tower that has a black marble statue of the baron who built it in its entrance hall.

2. The western tower is called the Beacon Tower; the builder, who was not Karl the Slayer, intended that the bonfire built on its uppermost storey should be lighted to summon friends in an emergency—but, alas, he had no friends.

3. In the upper room of the southern tower, visitors can see the favorite dog of the baron who built the tower—stuffed, of course, since it died in 1348.

4. The Dark Tower—so-called from its lack of windows—is the next clockwise from the Watch Tower.

5. Tibald the Devil built the eastern tower, but his armor is not on show there.

Tower	Name	Builder	Relic

At the Pick and Shovel

During the Klondyke Gold Rush, Dead-Eye Jake Costello's Pick and Shovel Saloon was the most popular drinking place in the town of Moose Hollow—mainly because it was the only one to employ saloon girls. From the clues given, can you work out each woman's real name, what she came to the Klondyke to do, how she was known at the Pick and Shovel, and what her job there was?

	Fishwife	Laundress	Midwife	Miner's wife	Ship's cook	Dixie Dinah Dunbar	Fifi La France	Gold Dust Gertie	Little Lulu	Ruby Redd	Barmaid	Blackjack dealer	Dancer	Juggler	Singer
Agatha Ramsbottom															
Effie Crabbe															
Hedwig Schwartz															
Myfanwy Griffith															
Olga Danova															
Barmaid															
Blackjack dealer															
Dancer															
Juggler															
Singer															
Dixie Dinah Dunbar															
Fifi La France															
Gold Dust Gertie															
Little Lulu															
Ruby Redd															

Clues

1. The woman who had come to the Klondyke to be a midwife, only to discover that there were very few women around, had adopted a three-word name and become the Pick and Shovel's juggler.

2. Agatha Ramsbottom, from Liverpool, was Dead-Eye Jake's barmaid.

3. Effie Crabbe wasn't known in Moose Hollow as Dixie Dinah Dunbar.

4. Myfanwy Griffith from Swansea, alias Ruby Redd, had never been a laundress and wasn't a singer.

5. Olga Danova, former wife of a Ukrainian miner, was not the woman known as Little Lulu.

6. Gold Dust Gertie, who had been a ship's cook, had a shorter original surname than the former laundress.

7. The woman known as Fifi La France was described on the payroll as a dancer.

Original name	Original job	Adopted name	Occupation

43

Jane Blonde—Licensed to Thrill

Jane Blonde (agent 0007) is the heroine of a series of films, in each of which she thwarts the plans of an evil villain bent on world domination or worse. From the clues given, can you identify the villain and his exotic female accomplice in each of the films, which are listed in the order of making, and describe his secret headquarters?

	Boris Fliptizlid	Ernst Frootkake	Julius Madman	Viktor Krakpott	Vladimir Nuttkase	Allura	Glamora Spoddie	Minnie Skurt	Prittie Thynge	Seductra	Desert hideaway	English country estate	Mountain aerie	Pacific island	Underwater city
1. *No, Doctor!*															
2. *Only for Your Ears*															
3. *You Only Live Thrice*															
4. *Live and Let Diet*															
5. *From Prussia with Gloves*															
Desert hideaway															
English country estate															
Mountain aerie															
Pacific island															
Underwater city															
Allura															
Glamora Spoddie															
Minnie Skurt															
Prittie Thynge															
Seductra															

Clues

1. The film in which Glamora Spoddie becomes jealous of Jane Blonde, because she has apparently stolen the affections of her employer, Viktor Krakpott, is the next in the series after the one where the outdoor scenes are set in a lofty mountain aerie, which is not called *Only for Your Ears*.

2. Seductra casts her spell on a remote Pacific island, allowing the director to show her charms to maximum effect in minimum swimwear, but not in *Live and Let Diet*.

3. Allura's charms are on display in *From Prussia with Gloves*, while Prittie Thynge appears in an earlier film than the one with spectacular scenes set in an underwater city, but Vladimir Nuttkase does not.

4. Ernst Frootkake operates from a hideaway in a Saharan desert oasis.

5. The villain in *Live and Let Diet* is called Boris Fliptizlid.

Film	Villain	Sidekick	Location

East Coast–West Coast

The picture below shows the seven members of the popular American folk-rock band East Coast–West Coast, three of whom are from New York, on the East Coast, and four from California, on the—well, you can guess. From the clues given, can you fill in the full name of each of the band members?

Clues

1. Bill, from the Bronx, is the only New Yorker on the upper level; he isn't standing next to Saul on the same side of the stairs.

2. The man named Pike is immediately right of Newt (it was Newton, originally) and on the same side of the stairs; both of them are Californians.

3. The man known by the surname Garth (though he was actually born Garcia), who is not Hardy, the vocalist from New York's Manhattan, is somewhere on the lower level.

4. Gary Bolt is standing on the opposite side of the staircase from Los Angeles–born drummer Joe, but on the same level.

5. There is a difference of five in the numbers indicating Mr. Baird from San Diego, California, and Mr. Maxim, who has adopted the name of a machine gun.

6. Figure 7 is the man surnamed Magee, who is not the Californian guitarist actually named Elmer, but generally (and certainly in this problem) known as Sonny.

7. No two New Yorkers are standing in adjacent positions on the same side of the stairs.

First names: Bill; Gary; Hardy; Joe; Newt; Saul; Sonny

Surnames: Alden; Baird; Bolt; Garth; Magee; Maxim; Pike

First name: _____ _____   _____

Surname: _____ _____   _____

First name: _____ _____   _____

Surname: _____ _____   _____

Starting tip: Start by positioning Pike and Newt.

Lawyers

The receptionist at the offices of high-powered law firm Billem-Quick Associates noted the arrival of five clients between 10AM and 11AM yesterday morning. From the clues below, can you work out who arrived at each of the listed times, and the name and department of the member of the company with whom he or she had an appointment?

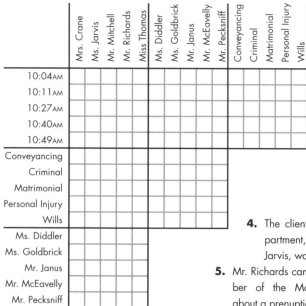

Clues

1. The client whose appointment was with Mr. Janus of the Personal Injury Department arrived after Mr. Pecksniff's client but earlier than Ms. Jarvis.

2. The client who was visiting the Conveyancing Department arrived an odd number of minutes before or after Mrs. Crane, whose appointment was with Ms. Goldbrick.

3. The client who was consulting Mr. McEavelly arrived at 10:40 AM.

4. The client visiting the Wills Department, who was not Ms. Jarvis, wasn't the last to arrive.

5. Mr. Richards came in to consult a member of the Matrimonial Department about a prenuptial agreement.

6. It was at 10:27AM that the misguided individual who was relying on a member of Billem-Quick's Criminal Law Department to organize their defense in a criminal damage case arrived.

7. Miss Thomas, who arrived at 10:04 AM, had not come to see Ms. Diddler.

Arrival	Client	Lawyer	Department

Battleships

Do you remember the old game of battleships? These puzzles are based on that idea. Your task is to find the vessels in the diagram. Some parts of boats or sea squares have already been filled in, and a number next to a row or column refers to the number of occupied squares in that row or column. The boats may be positioned horizontally or vertically, but no two boats or parts of boats are in adjacent squares—horizontally, vertically, or diagonally.

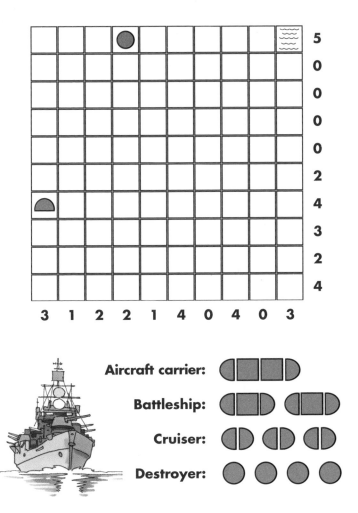

47

Pioneer to El Dorado

In the 22nd century, Earth's newly elected World Government set up the Colonization Corps, and the Corps' ship *Pioneer* was sent on its first expedition to the planet christened El Dorado, in orbit around the star Spica; but the expedition almost ended in disaster when all five of *Pioneer*'s landing-craft had problems and made forced landings miles from their selected destination on the Schmidt Plateau, named for *Pioneer*'s captain. From the clues below, can you work out what each of the landers was carrying (apart from 20 colonists), what went wrong with it, and where it landed?

	Food/lab equip.	Food/medical supp.	Labs/storage	Personnel shelters	Transport/farm equip.	Cargo shift	Computer error	Depressurization	Engine failure	Lightning strike	Duroc Plain	Lake Butterfly	Mount Silva	Onion Island	Pencil Point
Lander 1															
Lander 2															
Lander 3															
Lander 4															
Lander 5															
Duroc Plain															
Lake Butterfly															
Mount Silva															
Onion Island															
Pencil Point															
Cargo shift															
Computer error															
Depressurization															
Engine failure															
Lightning strike															

Clues

1. The lander that suffered engine failure as it began its final approach was numbered immediately below the one that ended up on the Duroc Plain, named after *Pioneer*'s First Officer, but not as low as the one carrying a mixed cargo of food and laboratory equipment.

2. The lander that ended up stranded on Onion Island (named for its shape) was numbered two lower than the one that carried the laboratory and storage shelters.

3. The lander landing at Pencil Point (a coastal feature also named for its shape) was carrying food and medical equipment.

4. Lander 2 carried the personnel shelters that were to form the pioneers' homes.

5. Lander 4, which finished up at the foot of Mount Silva (named after *Pioneer*'s astrogator), was not the one carrying the group's transport and farming equipment.

6. One lander suffered depressurization and had to make a landing near Lake Butterfly; the lander whose problems came about when it was struck by lightning was numbered immediately below the one that suffered "computer error."

7. Lander 3 had to abandon plans to touch down on the Schmidt Plateau when its badly loaded cargo shifted, ruining the vessel's stability.

Lander	Cargo	Problem	Landing place

Best-Laid Plans

Time was getting short for Betty to prepare for her vacation, but she could still do everything if she popped out in her lunch hour to finish the shopping she needed to do; she had it all planned—but unfortunately her plans didn't work out, and she ended up not buying anything! From the clues below, can you work out the order in which she visited the four shops, what she intended to buy there, and why she couldn't make the purchase?

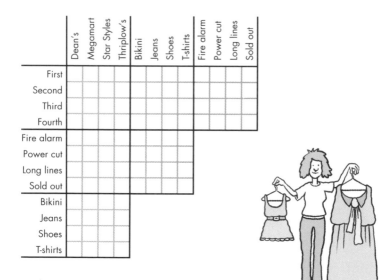

Clues

1. Betty couldn't even get into Star Styles, whose shop had been temporarily closed because somebody had accidentally triggered a fire alarm.

2. Betty had planned to visit one other shop between buying her T-shirts, which she didn't intend to purchase from Megamart, and her new jeans, which she was prevented from purchasing because a power cut had closed down all the shop's cash registers.

3. Betty meant to buy a bikini at the third shop, which traded under the name of its owner.

4. At the second shop she visited, which wasn't Dean's, Betty found they had sold out of the item she wanted in her size.

Order	Shop	Item	Problem

50

Author Tour

Well-known TV personality Celia Britty has written her autobiography, and the publisher organized a book-signing tour of bookshops around the country. From the information given below, can you work out in which bookshop and which town Miss Britty appeared each day, and the number of books that were sold and autographed?

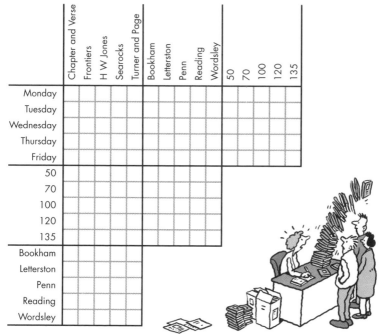

	Chapter and Verse	Frontiers	H W Jones	Searocks	Turner and Page	Bookham	Letterston	Penn	Reading	Wordsley	50	70	100	120	135
Monday															
Tuesday															
Wednesday															
Thursday															
Friday															
50											
70											
100											
120											
135											
Bookham						
Letterston						
Penn						
Reading						
Wordsley						

Clues

1. Neither the bookshop visited on Monday nor the one in Bookham had an "and" in their names, and at both Celia signed fewer books than at Chapter and Verse, where she appeared the day before the signing session at Searocks bookshop.

2. She sold more books in Reading than at Frontiers bookshop.

3. Celia was in Penn on Thursday, later in the week than the event at which she signed 70 books in Turner and Page's bookshop.

4. The fewest number of books were sold on Wednesday.

5. The most were sold at Letterston.

6. The H W Jones bookshop is in Wordsley.

Day	Bookshop	Town	Books sold

Knights Non-Errant

Our five old acquaintances, the knock-kneed knights of the Round Table, had a very bad year, even by their standards. In addition to their general pusillanimity, which was permanent, each developed a particular physical or mental condition that had them signed off the path of errantry for varying periods of time by the eminent Camelot consultant who diagnosed their problems. From the clues given, can you match each knight with his condition and length of time off duty, and say which course of treatment each was prescribed?

	Fear of forests	Hippophobia	Metal allergy	Panic attacks	Vertigo	4 months	6 months	8 months	10 months	12 months	Course of tablets	Exercise regime	Liniment	Magic spell	Psychotherapy
Sir Coward de Custarde															
Sir Poltroon à Ghaste															
Sir Sorely à Frayde															
Sir Spyneless de Feete															
Sir Timid de Shayke															
Course of tablets															
Exercise regime															
Liniment															
Magic spell															
Psychotherapy															
4 months															
6 months															
8 months															
10 months															
12 months															

Clues

1. The knight who suffered hippo-phobia was unable to ride his horse for four months before treatment, which was not the course of tablets, worked.

2. Sir Poltroon à Ghaste was sent to Merlin, who cast a magic spell designed to cure his problem, but he was still out of action two months longer than his colleague who developed an allergy to metal, being totally unable to don his armor or pick up his sword.

3. Ten months was the period for which the Round Table was denied the valuable services of Sir Timid de Shayke.

4. The toughening-up exercise regime was imposed on one knight for the full twelve months he was unable to take up his duties.

5. Liniment was not the treatment prescribed for Sir Coward de Custarde.

6. "Down in the forest something stirred..." He never did find out what it was, but one knight needed a lengthy course of psychotherapy before being able to enter any wooded area, which in those days ruled out almost the entire country.

7. It was Sir Spyneless de Feete who developed regular panic attacks, especially when confronted by ugly ogres.

Knight	Condition	Time off work	Treatment

Logi-5

Each line, across and down, is to have each of the letters A, B, C, D, and E, appearing once each. Also, every shape—shown by the thick lines—must also have each of the letters in it. Can you fill in the grid?

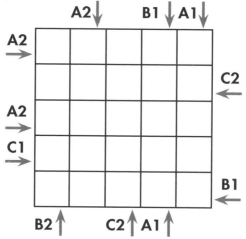

ABC

Each line, across and down, is to have each of the letters A, B, and C, and two empty squares. The letter outside the grid shows the first or second letter in the direction of the arrow. Can you fill in the grid?

Coordinated Arrests

Following an investigation lasting years, the FBI and local police forces across the USA recently carried out a series of coordinated arrests, taking into custody the (alleged) leaders of a major nationwide crime organization. From the clues below, can you work out the name of each (alleged) gangster, the name of the officer who arrested him, and in which city and location the arrest took place?

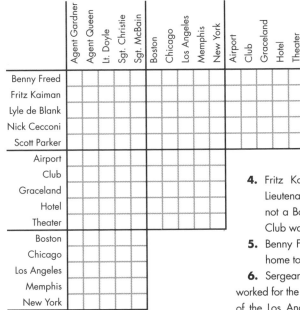

Clues

1. Nick Cecconi was arrested during the interval in a performance of *The Glass Menagerie* at Berry's Theater.

2. Scott Parker was not arrested by FBI Agent Wendell Queen; it wasn't an FBI agent who arrested the owner of the Four Aces Club in his own luxurious establishment.

3. One of the (alleged) gangsters was arrested while touring the late Elvis Presley's home, Graceland, in Memphis; he was not Lyle de Blank, who was not arrested by an FBI agent.

4. Fritz Kaiman was arrested by Lieutenant Joe Doyle, who was not a Boston cop; the Four Aces Club was not in Boston.

5. Benny Freed was arrested in his home town of Chicago.

6. Sergeant Sally-Anne Christie worked for the Organized Crime Squad of the Los Angeles Police Department; Los Angeles was not the location of either the Four Aces Club or the Howard Hotel.

7. Sergeant Kent McBain made his arrest at the international airport in the city where he works.

Gangster	Officer	City	Location

Something Special

Five ladies from Colnecaster have each just received a very special present from their husbands, in celebration of a very special event. From the clues below, can you work out each woman's full name, the special event being celebrated, and the special present she received?

	Barton	Freeman	Martin	O'Connor	Rowley	Children left home	40th birthday	Passed driving test	Silver anniversary	Tin anniversary	Balloon flight	Beauty spa	Car racing	Flying lesson	Gardening course
Alma															
Gillian															
Liz															
Nancy															
Sarah															
Balloon flight															
Beauty spa															
Car racing															
Flying lesson															
Gardening course															
Children left home															
40th birthday															
Passed driving test															
Silver anniversary															
Tin anniversary															

Clues

1. Nancy received her special gift to celebrate 5 years of happy marriage—which isn't bad, considering they've only just reached their silver anniversary—no, I'm joking; it was a silver anniversary gift, really. Liz's gift was a chance to spend a day learning to drive a racing car, finishing off with a solo lap of the Copperstone grand prix circuit.

2. Neither Sarah nor the woman who received a special tin anniversary present (that's for the tenth anniversary) received the weekend gardening course.

3. Gillian was neither the woman who, with her husband, was celebrating the last of their children leaving home, nor the one whose present was a flying lesson in a light aircraft.

4. Mrs. Martin, who received her present for (finally—after twelve tries) passing her driving test, is neither Gillian or Liz.

5. The woman who received a voucher for a weekend at a beauty spa as a 40th birthday present has a first name one letter shorter than Mrs. O'Connor's.

6. Alma Freeman's husband is an army officer; Mrs. Rowley's husband has booked her a flight in a hot-air balloon, something she's wanted to try for years.

First name	Surname	Celebration	Present

Into the Lost Valley

The picture below shows a four-man expedition from America's Harvale University exploring the Lost Valley of Verunago, in the Andes, to investigate rumors of surviving dinosaurs there. From the clues below, can you fill in every man's full name and his role in the expedition?

Clues

1. Hank, the guide—and expert rifle-shot, just in case—is somewhere above Dr. Jensen as they climb into the valley.

2. Dr. Lambros is a paleontologist—that is, an expert on extinct animals.

3. Figure C is the expedition's biologist; he isn't Randy—that is, his first name isn't Randy—and his surname isn't McCreesh.

4. Figure D is Jake.

First names: Hank; Jake; Pete; Randy
Surnames: Jensen; Kevakian, Lambros; McCreesh
Roles: biologist; guide; paleontologist; zoologist

First name: _____ _____ _____ _____

Surname: _____ _____ _____ _____

Role: _____ _____ _____ _____

Starting tip: Begin by positioning Hank.

Battleships

Do you remember the old game of battleships? These puzzles are based on that idea. Your task is to find the vessels in the diagram. Some parts of boats or sea squares have already been filled in, and a number next to a row or column refers to the number of occupied squares in that row or column. The boats may be positioned horizontally or vertically, but no two boats or parts of boats are in adjacent squares—horizontally, vertically, or diagonally.

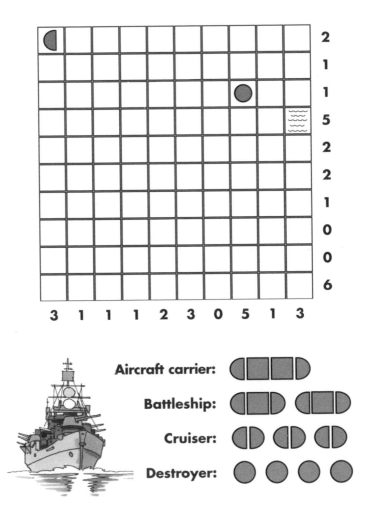

58

Cloak and Dagger

The dictator of Banania, known to his hero-worshipping citizens as El Presidente, was very upset last year when five of his secret agents abroad (that's the cloak bit) offended in various ways, and were listed for the chop (that's the dagger) by a small gang of his secret personal guards. From the clues given, can you name the agent who offended in each of the listed months (not their real names, of course), say in which country he was carrying out El Presidente's dirty work, and work out how he offended the latter?

Clues

1. One agent got very drunk at a cocktail party in Mexico and made some very insulting comments about El Presidente, which, human nature being what it is, were leaked to the media, this being the next offense after Juan's misdemeanor.

2. It was in March that Jose incurred the displeasure of El Presidente.

3. Felipe defected to the secret service of the country to which he had been sent on an espionage mission.

4. Azerbaijan was the location of the next offense after one agent embezzled the funds allotted to him for the completion of his mission abroad.

5. Hungary was where the career of one Bananian agent, who was not Roberto, was transformed from cloak to dagger in June.

6. Pedro was El Presidente's man in China.

7. Secrets were sold in August, but it was not in January that the wrath of El Presidente was aroused by one of his agents marrying a subject of the country where he was working, and so compromising his reliability.

Month	Agent	Country	Offense

Five Counties Coffee Shop

They call it the Five Counties Coffee Shop because it stands at the point in west Wyoming USA, where five counties meet; that's also the reason why you'll usually find five differently painted police cars outside, and five differently uniformed police officers drinking coffee inside. From the clues below, can you work out the names of the five officers my wife and I met there when we visited the Five Counties, which county's police force each was from, the colors of their uniforms, and the colors of their cars?

	Buzzard	Granite	King's	Linder	Pineridge	Dark blue	Dark green	Gray	Light blue	Tan	Black/pale blue	Black/white	Blue/white	Dark blue/pale blue	White/orange
Candy de Lint															
Frank Grosz															
Julie Moncada															
Nelson Pike															
Sean Tyrrel															
Black/pale blue															
Black/white															
Blue/white															
Dark blue/pale blue															
White/orange															
Dark blue															
Dark green															
Gray															
Light blue															
Tan															

Clues

1. Officer Frank Grosz's patrol car was painted in white and orange; Officer Nelson Pike's uniform was not gray.

2. Officer Candy de Lint wore a dark blue uniform; she was not from the Buzzard County Police Department.

3. The Linder County Police wear tan uniforms and white Stetson hats.

4. The cops who wear the dark green uniforms drive black cars with pale blue doors and hood and trunk panels, unlike Sean Tyrrel, who was a member of the Granite County Police Department.

5. The man from the King's County Police drove a car painted in the familiar "black and white" design.

6. The car that was painted dark blue with pale blue roof and doors did not belong to the Pineridge County Police Department.

Name	County	Uniform	Car

Travel Report

In the 30th century, reports of ion storms and other natural phenomena causing disruption to space travel are quite common, but on one particular day Terrans (inhabitants of the planet once called Earth) were surprised to be advised of four ships that had been diverted to new destinations for strictly unnatural reasons. From the clues given, can you work out the name of each ship, where it was originally going, the planet to which it's been diverted, and the reason for the change?

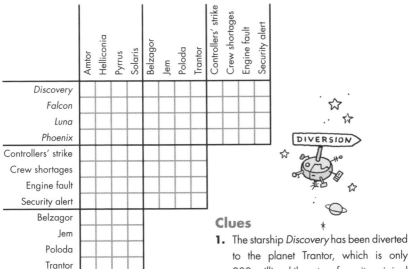

	Amtor	Helliconia	Pyrrus	Solaris	Belzagor	Jem	Poloda	Trantor	Controllers' strike	Crew shortages	Engine fault	Security alert
Discovery												
Falcon												
Luna												
Phoenix												
Controllers' strike												
Crew shortages												
Engine fault												
Security alert												
Belzagor												
Jem												
Poloda												
Trantor												

Clues

1. The starship *Discovery* has been diverted to the planet Trantor, which is only 200 million kilometers from its original destination.

2. The ship that started out to go to Amtor but is now going to land on Jem, which isn't the *Phoenix*, isn't the one that has had to be diverted due to a lightning strike of Space Traffic Controllers at its original destination.

3. A security alert on Pyrrus means that no ships are currently being allowed to land there.

4. The *Luna*, which regularly flies between Terra and Helliconia, isn't the ship that has had to divert to Belzagor because of an engine fault.

Starship	Original destination	New destination	Reason

Fish Tale

My friend Neil is one of the country's leading collectors of exotic catfish, and the huge aquarium in his living room contains examples of six of the rarest types, as shown below. From the clues below, can you fill in on the plan the name of each of the fish, and the two parts of the type's popular name?

Clues

1. Fish number 1 is called N'Chips, though it probably doesn't realize the fact.

2. Cake, who is called a "pop-eyed" catfish for the obvious reason, isn't fish 1 or fish 6.

3. The European catfish, which is not adjacent to the Australian example, is between Fillet and the red catfish, which isn't fish 6.

4. Fish 4, the Mexican type, is not called Pie—that would be silly, wouldn't it?

5. The Nile spotted catfish—which comes from Egypt and has spots—is next to the Hudson Bay catfish.

6. Fish 2 is a "long-tail" catfish, though Neil's particular one has only an average-length tail due to a run-in with an Iranian canni-bal catfish now kept in its own separate tank.

7. Finger is the Chinese catfish, though—like all Neil's fish—he's British-born.

8. The Australian catfish is immediately right of the "whistling" catfish—which, of course, doesn't whistle—it only sounds as though it's whistling.

Fish names: Cake; Fillet; Finger; N'Chips; Pie; Stick
1st part: Australian; Chinese; European; Hudson Bay; Mexican; Nile
2nd part: blue-fin; long-tail; pop-eyed; red; spotted; whistling

Starting tip:
What type of fish is fish number 1?

1   2   3   4   5   6

Fish name: _____ _____ _____ _____
1st part: _____ _____ _____ _____
2nd part: _____ _____ _____ _____

Fish name: _____ _____ _____ _____
1st part: _____ _____ _____ _____
2nd part: _____ _____ _____ _____

Down These Mean Streets

Hack writer Bob Wheel has signed a contract to write five detective novels "in the style of the late Raymond Chandler" for a straight-to-paperback publisher during next year, and he has already decided on some of the basic details—the actual writing he'll leave to the last few days before the deadline, as usual. From the clues below, can you work out the title of the book he'll provide in each of the listed months, the name of its Philip Marlowe–like (though, in a couple of cases, female) detective, and the pen name he intends to use for it?

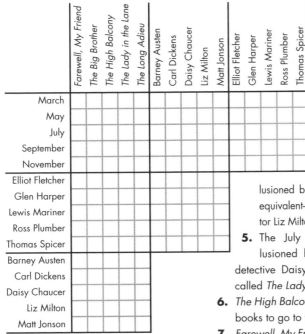

feature chivalrous though disillusioned private eye Barney Austen.

4. As Lewis Mariner, Bob is going to write about disillusioned but whatever-the-feminine-equivalent-of-chivalrous-is investigator Liz Milton.

5. The July book featuring disillusioned but—er, never mind—detective Daisy Chaucer will not be called *The Lady in the Lane*.

6. *The High Balcony* will be the first of the books to go to the publisher.

7. *Farewell, My Friend*, which will feature a detective who is disillusioned, chivalrous, and male, is not the book due to be at the publishers in November.

Clues

1. *The Big Brother* will appear as the work of Thomas Spicer.

2. *The Long Adieu*, featuring disillusioned but chivalrous private investigator Matt Jonson, should be with the publisher two months earlier than the book for which Bob will use the pen name Glen Harper.

3. The pen name Elliot Fletcher will be used for the May book, which will not

Month	Title	Detective	Pen name

Battleships

Do you remember the old game of battleships? These puzzles are based on that idea. Your task is to find the vessels in the diagram. Some parts of boats or sea squares have already been filled in, and a number next to a row or column refers to the number of occupied squares in that row or column. The boats may be positioned horizontally or vertically, but no two boats or parts of boats are in adjacent squares—horizontally, vertically, or diagonally.

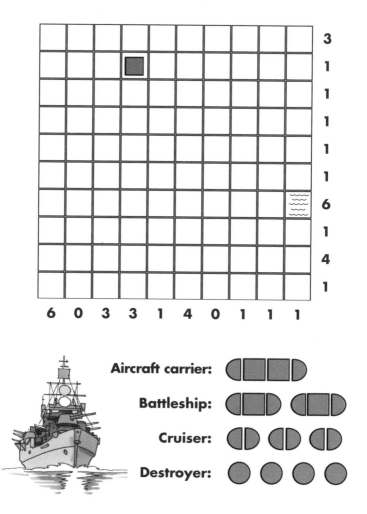

Aircraft carrier:

Battleship:

Cruiser:

Destroyer:

Sporting Writes

Over the past few weeks, four sports stars have had their first books published. From the clues, can you work out each man's full name, his sport, and what sort of book he has written?

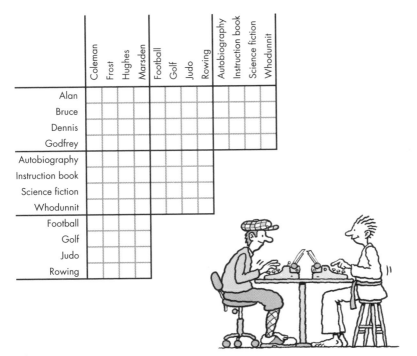

	Coleman	Frost	Hughes	Marsden	Football	Golf	Judo	Rowing	Autobiography	Instruction book	Science fiction	Whodunnit
Alan												
Bruce												
Dennis												
Godfrey												
Autobiography												
Instruction book												
Science fiction												
Whodunnit												
Football												
Golf												
Judo												
Rowing												

Clues

1. Mr. Coleman's first name is one letter longer than that of the judo star, who has written an instruction book about his sport.

2. The golfer surnamed Hughes isn't the writer of the science-fiction novel about an invasion of Earth from the ex-planet Pluto.

3. Bruce Frost was runner-up in Albion-TV's Sports Star of the Year last year.

4. Godfrey is not the author of the who-dunnit.

5. Dennis, whose book is his autobiography, has never done any rowing.

First name	Surname	Sport	Book type

The Bootique

Five of the customers who visited The Bootique shoe store during the course of a day each tried on a varying number of pairs of shoes before making a purchase. From the clues given, can you fully identify the woman who came in at each of the listed times, and work out how many pairs of shoes she tried on?

	Anna	Jane	Louise	Marie	Paula	Foot	March	Pace	Stride	Walker	3 pairs	4 pairs	5 pairs	6 pairs	7 pairs
10:00															
11:15															
12:15															
2:00															
3:45															
3 pairs											
4 pairs											
5 pairs											
6 pairs											
7 pairs											
Foot						
March						
Pace						
Stride						
Walker						

Clues

1. Marie tried on one fewer pair than Ms. Stride, who made the preceding call at The Bootique of the five featured.

2. Louise Walker was the immediate predecessor of the woman who tried on five pairs.

3. Anna sampled a modest four pairs, the last of which she found ideal in every way.

4. Jane came in to The Bootique at 11:15 that morning.

5. The surname of the 12:15 arrival was March; she did not try on the smallest number of pairs.

6. Mrs. Pace went through six pairs of shoes before finally deciding which she liked best; she was the next of the five to visit after Paula.

7. No fewer than seven pairs adorned the feet of the 2 o'clock customer before she made her purchase.

Time	First name	Surname	Pairs

The Last Deal

The picture shows a poker table in the Silver Spur Saloon in Waco, Texas, one night in August 1872, about thirty seconds before the (unjustified) accusation of cheating that ended in a gunfight between a local gambler and outlaw Billy Dayton and the death of the latter. From the clues below, can you fill in the name and occupation of the man occupying each seat, and which cards he held in his hand after that last deal?

Clues

1. Billy Dayton's hand was the next highest-scoring above that held by the man in seat B.

2. Dan Flint sat in seat A.

3. Sam Troy, who wasn't the cowhand from the Lazy Z ranch, held a flush in hearts.

4. The gambler held the winning hand—four kings.

5. The store keeper didn't occupy seat D.

Names: Billy Dayton; Dan Flint; Jake Lincoln; Sam Troy
Occupations: cowhand; gambler; outlaw; store keeper
Hands (in ascending order of value): three of a kind; straight; flush; four of a kind

Name: _____   _____
Occupation: _____ B   C   _____
Hand: _____   _____

A

D

Name: _____   _____
Occupation: _____   _____
Hand: _____   _____

Starting tip: Name the man in seat B.

Double O . . . No!

Last week Cosmic Imports (the cover company used by MI9) held interviews for the position advertised in the local job center with the words "Agent required. Would suit inquisitive type with a taste for overseas travel, adventure, and vodka martini." Five candidates were seen but none made the grade. From the clues below can you name the candidate interviewed on each day and identify the fear that each admitted to, effectively ruling himself out of the job?

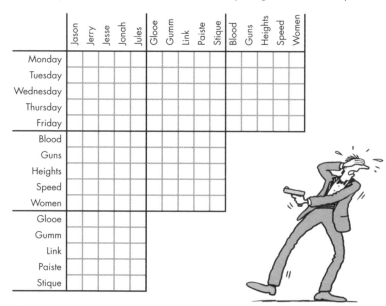

	Jason	Jerry	Jesse	Jonah	Jules	Glooe	Gumm	Link	Paiste	Stique	Blood	Guns	Heights	Speed	Women
Monday															
Tuesday															
Wednesday															
Thursday															
Friday															
Blood															
Guns															
Heights															
Speed															
Women															
Glooe															
Gumm															
Link															
Paiste															
Stique															

Clues

1. Jason's fear of guns was always going to be his downfall; he was seen later in the week than the candidate who demonstrated a fear of heights.

2. The candidate seen on Thursday admitted to a fear of blood.

3. One candidate had been practicing his opening line "The name's Gumm, Jules Gumm."

4. Mr. Glooe was the first candidate to be interviewed; Jonah was the last.

5. The interview panel thought that Mr. Link's fear of women, although not technically an obstacle to the position, would be enough of a hindrance to cause them to reject him.

Day	First name	Surname	Fear

Battleships

Do you remember the old game of battleships? These puzzles are based on that idea. Your task is to find the vessels in the diagram. Some parts of boats or sea squares have already been filled in, and a number next to a row or column refers to the number of occupied squares in that row or column. The boats may be positioned horizontally or vertically, but no two boats or parts of boats are in adjacent squares—horizontally, vertically, or diagonally.

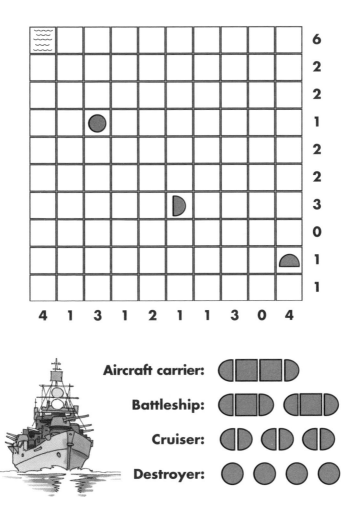

Wild West Women

Wild West Women is a comic book featuring, as you might expect, four female outlaws living in the western USA in the 1880s. They are shown in the picture below; from the clues given, can you work out each one's real first name and surname, and the nickname, totally unrelated to her real name, by which she is known?

Clues

1. Dorothy Benton was born in England, but emigrated with her family as a 4-year-old.

2. Figure 1 is the woman whose highly respectable parents named her Leah.

3. Iron Annie Stockton is holding a pistol in her hand.

4. Loco Liz is standing somewhere right of Agatha.

5. Susannah is standing left of the woman surnamed McLayne, who is not known as Texas Rose.

First names: Agatha; Dorothy; Leah; Susannah
Surnames: Benton; Delaney; McLayne; Stockton
Nicknames: Coyote Kate; Iron Annie; Loco Liz; Texas Rose

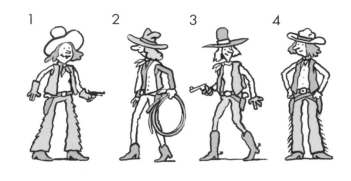

First name:	_____	_____	_____	_____
Surname:	_____	_____	_____	_____
Nick name:	_____	_____	_____	_____

Starting tip: Begin by naming figure 4.

Down Mexico Way

Lisa and her friend Vicky have just returned from a week's vacation in Mexico, where they had a wonderful time: They spent Saturday settling in and Sunday touring the local Aztec ruins, and then for the next five days each of them tried a different one of the activities offered by the hotel in the morning, and they then met for lunch and spent the afternoon sunbathing or chilling out. From the clues below, can you work out which activity each of the girls tried on each weekday morning, and which dish they chose (both making the same selection) for lunch?

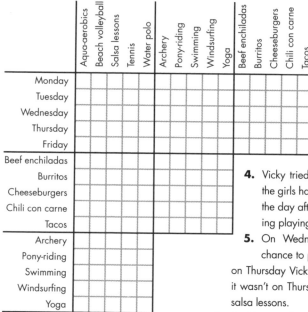

Clues

1. The morning that Lisa spent doing aqua-aerobics was the one when Vicky learned how to windsurf, which she found was hard work and spent most of her time in the water.

2. Lunch on the day that Lisa took salsa lessons was not tacos.

3. Lisa played beach volleyball on the day that the friends had traditional chili con carne for lunch.

4. Vicky tried yoga the day before the girls had beef enchiladas, but the day after Lisa spent her morning playing tennis.

5. On Wednesday, Lisa took the chance to play water polo, while on Thursday Vicky just went swimming; it wasn't on Thursday that Lisa had her salsa lessons.

6. On Monday, the girls couldn't nerve themselves to try Mexican cuisine, and settled for U.S.-style cheeseburgers at lunchtime; this wasn't the day that Vicky spent her morning on the archery range.

Day	Lisa	Vicky	Lunch

Relate

On her first day after completing her training as a marriage counsellor, Jenny was faced with a diary containing appointments with five couples. From the clues given, can you identify the pair she advised at each of the listed times, and say how long each couple had been married?

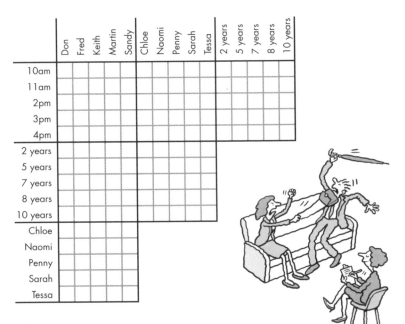

	Don	Fred	Keith	Martin	Sandy	Chloe	Naomi	Penny	Sarah	Tessa	2 years	5 years	7 years	8 years	10 years
10am															
11am															
2pm															
3pm															
4pm															
2 years															
5 years															
7 years															
8 years															
10 years															
Chloe															
Naomi															
Penny															
Sarah															
Tessa															

Clues

1. Chloe was seen later than Sandy, who had not been married as long.
2. Sarah's appointment with Jenny was at 11 o'clock in the morning.
3. Don was listed next after Naomi's husband in Jenny's appointments diary.
4. As Martin and his wife were leaving Jenny's office, Tessa and her husband, who had been married for fewer years, were coming in.
5. The first couple Jenny advised on her first day at work had been married eight years; the husband of this pair was not Keith.
6. Penny and her husband were married five years ago.
7. Fred and his wife are going through the period known in the trade as "the seven-year itch"; theirs was not the 4 PM appointment.

Time	Husband	Wife	Length

Table of Elements

Those mysterious symbols that represent the chemical elements are all based on their original Latin names, some of which are no longer in use. We have chosen eight represented by one letter and eight consisting of two, and jumbled them up into our "table of elements." From the clues given, your task is to place the correct symbol in each of the small squares forming the large one.

Clues

1. Each column and each horizontal row contains two one-letter symbols and two two-letter ones.

2. Corner square D4 contains the symbol Ca.

3. Tungsten, formerly known as Wolfram, is immediately above iron in one of the two central vertical columns.

4. The elements in C3 and B3 are both designated by the same number of letters.

5. Sulphur can be found in horizontal row D.

6. Oxygen is two squares directly below Copper, and two directly left of Iodine.

7. The single letter in B1 is later in the alphabet than the one in D1, neither being H for Hydrogen.

8. Tin is somewhere higher than Gold in one of the vertical columns.

9. The square containing Silver is higher and farther to the right than Helium, both being in direct alignment either horizontally or vertically with Nitrogen.

Elements:

C (Carbon)	N (Nitrogen)
Ag (Silver)	Fe (Iron)
H (Hydrogen)	O (Oxygen)
Au (Gold)	He (Helium)
I (Iodine)	S (Sulphur)
Ca (Calcium)	Hg (Mercury)
K (Potassium)	W (Tungsten)
Cu (Copper)	Sn (Tin)

	1	2	3	4
A				
B				
C				
D				

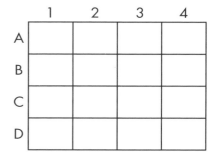

Starting tip: Begin by placing the symbol for Oxygen.

Over and Over Again

Rex Emall is a stunt driver for the movies, and his particular specialty is overturning a vehicle at high speed and having it roll over and over, usually ending with a spectacular explosion. He's not called upon to do it often—it's really dangerous, and therefore expensive for producers—but last year five films were released that featured him doing his special thing. From the clues below, can you work out the title of each movie, in which month it was released, what character Rex was doubling for, and what sort of vehicle was involved?

	February	April	July	October	November	Alien assassin	Bank robber	Crooked cop	Gangster	Private detective	Limousine	Fuel truck	Pickup truck	School bus	Sports car
Dangerous															
Face of Death															
Nightside															
The Rescue															
White Hawk															
Limousine															
Fuel truck															
Pickup truck															
School bus															
Sports car															
Alien assassin															
Bank robber															
Crooked cop															
Gangster															
Private detective															

Clues

1. In the November film, Rex crashed a Lincoln limousine, which then rolled down a railroad embankment, was hit by a freight train and exploded — though actually the crash and the explosion took place some hours apart.

2. *Dangerous* came out immediately prior to the film in which Rex took the role (briefly) of an alien assassin sent from the planet Testuga to kill an intergalactic superhero in a science-fiction fantasy that was not released in July.

3. The film in which Rex was a bank robber fleeing the scene of a failed holdup was the next released after the one for which he overturned and wrecked a fuel truck.

4. *White Hawk* came out after the movie in which Rex was a private detective — the hero's partner, in fact — but before the one in which he crashed a school bus.

5. The film in which Rex's character was a gangster involved in drug dealing, people trafficking, and other nasty stuff was not released in October.

6. *Nightside* was the next movie to be released after *Face of Death*.

7. The film released in February featured Rex as a crooked cop on the run; the vehicle in which he "died" was not the Chevrolet Corvette sports car.

Movie	Month	Character	Vehicle

Battleships

Do you remember the old game of battleships? These puzzles are based on that idea. Your task is to find the vessels in the diagram. Some parts of boats or sea squares have already been filled in, and a number next to a row or column refers to the number of occupied squares in that row or column. The boats may be positioned horizontally or vertically, but no two boats or parts of boats are in adjacent squares—horizontally, vertically, or diagonally.

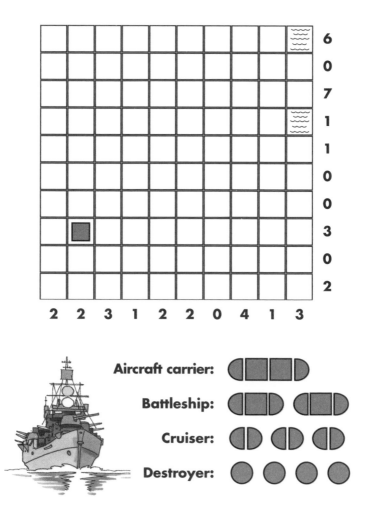

Travel Books

My friend Nadine's resolutions for the New Year include one to read more books and watch less TV, and she is beginning with four volumes about travels to different parts of the world. From the clues given, can you work out the full title of each book and the full name of its writer?

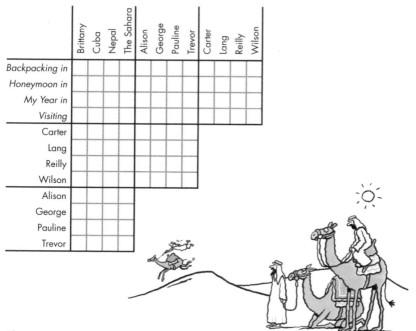

Clues

1. Pauline's book is called *Visiting* somewhere, but the missing place-name isn't Nepal, which isn't featured in the book called *My Year in* either.

2. Wilson's book is about a journey to the Sahara Desert.

3. Trevor's book doesn't even mention Cuba once, but Alison's is all about the time she spent in Brittany.

4. Ms. Reilly's book is called *Honeymoon in*.

5. George Lang's book is not *My Year in*.

First part	Second part	First name	Surname

Once Upon a Time . . .

It is bedtime in Morpheus Close, at least for the youngest members of the families. Each child has been put to bed, holding tight his or her favorite cuddly toy and listening to a bedtime story being read by a different member of the family. From the clues given, can you name the child whose bedroom is behind each window, describe his or her toy, and identify the reader in each bedroom?

Clues

1. William lives at a higher-numbered house than the child with a panda.

2. Annette, whose bedtime toy is her rabbit called Harvey, lives in the other half of the duplex from the one that is home to Gareth.

3. Mom is the story reader at no.5, while the sister is on duty at the house numbered two higher than the one where the monkey is the toy.

4. Grandma is reading a story to the child clutching the teddy bear; her listener is not Carrie, who lives at no.1 Morpheus Close.

Children: Annette; Carrie; Gareth; William
Toys: monkey; panda; rabbit; teddy bear
Story-readers: father; grandma; mother; sister

| 1 | 3 | 5 | 7 |

Child: _____ _____ _____ _____

Toy: _____ _____ _____ _____

Reader: _____ _____ _____ _____

Starting tip: Decide first who is reading to Carrie.

Color Blind

As part of his act, illusionist Dan Smart would be blindfolded and asked to identify the color of the symbols depicted on a pack of cards featuring five symbols in five different colors, selected at random by a member of the audience. However, one night, his regular assistant, who would tell him which symbol had been chosen, and ask him to name its color, was taken ill, and an ill-prepared stand-in took her place, with the result that Dan got all five answers wrong. From the clues, can you identify the symbols in the order in which they were presented to him, and say what color each actually was, and what color he thought they were?

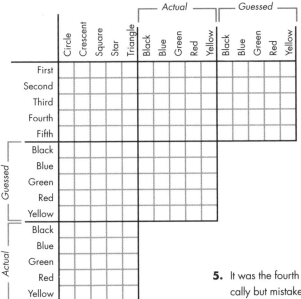

Clues

1. The yellow square was presented to Dan next after the symbol he stated to be green.

2. The actual black item was not described by the illusionist as blue.

3. The card bearing a star was the second to be put before the illusionist.

4. The circle was declared to be black, but the crescent was not the symbol wrongly asserted to be blue.

5. It was the fourth item that Dan unequivocally but mistakenly stated to be red.

6. The real color of the symbol on the third card was blue.

7. The alleged color of the triangle was the actual color of the circle, which was produced earlier.

Order	Symbol	Actual	Guessed

Logi-5

Each line, across and down, is to have each of the letters A, B, C, D, and E, appearing once each. Also, every shape—shown by the thick lines—must also have each of the letters in it. Can you fill in the grid?

Each line, across and down, is to have each of the letters A, B, and C, and two empty squares. The letter outside the grid shows the first or second letter in the direction of the arrow. Can you fill in the grid?

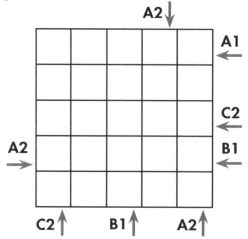

Celebrity Gallery

Sheila Snapham is a freelance photographer specializing in catching celebrity subjects on film at awkward moments. Last week she had a very successful time, having a different one of her pictures featured each day in a different paper. From the clues given, can you describe the subjects of pictures 1 to 7 (we'll save their embarrassment by not revealing names or details), and fill in the chart to say whose photo appeared in which paper on which day?

Clues

1. Sheila had a picture in the *Planet* on Thursday last week, which is indicated by a number two lower than the one in Saturday's paper.

2. The entrepreneur's photo bears a number in the gallery twice that of the one in the Sunday paper, while photo 6 did not appear on Friday.

3. An odd-numbered picture was selected by the editor of the *Graphic* for his readers.

4. Picture 3 appeared the day after the one featuring the discomfiture of a TV celebrity.

5. There is a difference of five between the numbers denoting the photo in the *Globe* and the one of the opera singer, which was published the day after the snapshot in the *Evening Herald*.

6. Picture 1, which does not depict the football player, was printed in Wednesday's paper, while photo 5 appeared the day before the one of the minor royal.

7. The *Clarion's* photo, which is number 4 on display, was seen the day after the one of the senator, which is one of the four in the bottom row.

8. The illicitly obtained snapshot of the pop star was featured by the *Morning Post*.

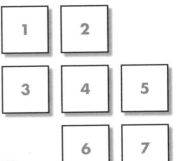

Day	No.	Subject	Newspaper
Sunday			
Monday			
Tuesday			
Wednesday			
Thursday			
Friday			
Saturday			

Subjects: senator; entrepreneur; football player; minor royal; opera singer; pop star; TV celebrity

Papers: *Clarion; Daily Chat; Evening Herald; Globe; Graphic; Morning Post; Planet*

Starting tip: Work out first the number of the picture in Sunday's paper.

Flight from Shayeia

Twenty-fifth-century criminal Nik Kapowne is anxious to get off the planet Shayeia, where the local police want to talk to him about a bank robbery, but there are only four ships on the ground at the spaceport. From the clues given, can you work out where each of them is going, what it's carrying, and why Nik would rather not travel on it?

	Beilat	New Hope	Qu'Korum	Thara	Dried vegetables	Emigrants	Frozen meat	Mining machinery	Native rebellion	Owes captain money	Swamp-fever epidemic	Wanted at destination
Anraya												
Gizink												
Lady Marie												
Rostompa												
Native rebellion												
Owes captain money												
Swamp-fever epidemic												
Wanted at destination												
Dried vegetables												
Emigrants												
Frozen meat												
Mining machinery												

Ship	Destination	Cargo	Problem

Clues

1. The ship heading for New Hope (where Nik doesn't want to go because he's already wanted there for a series of burglaries) isn't the *Lady Marie*.

2. The planet where the *Gizink* is headed is in the midst of an epidemic of swamp-fever, a disease Nik has no desire to catch; equally, Nik might find it awkward to travel on the ship carrying a cargo of frozen meat because he already owes its captain rather more than he can afford to repay.

3. The *Rostompa*, which is carrying a cargo of foodstuff, is bound for the planet Qu'Korum.

4. One ship is carrying emigrants to Beilat; the ship carrying mining machinery (and, Nik's pretty certain, a certain amount of contraband) isn't the *Anraya*.

5. The planet Thara wasn't the one in the grip of a native rebellion.

Battleships

Do you remember the old game of battleships? These puzzles are based on that idea. Your task is to find the vessels in the diagram. Some parts of boats or sea squares have already been filled in, and a number next to a row or column refers to the number of occupied squares in that row or column. The boats may be positioned horizontally or vertically, but no two boats or parts of boats are in adjacent squares—horizontally, vertically, or diagonally.

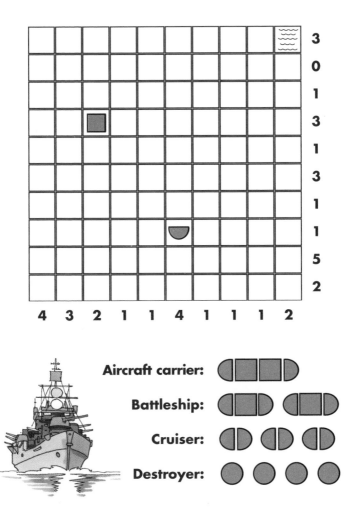

Drive-In

The picture below shows the front row of cars at the Hollywood Drive-In Cinema in Echo Rock, Nebraska, back in 1966, where the town's teenagers have gathered to watch the Elvis Presley movie *Paradise, Hawaiian Style*. From the clues below, can you fill in the make of each of the cars shown, and the names of the male and female teenagers inside?

Clues

1. The Volkswagen "beetle," which isn't car C in the picture, is standing between the Chevrolet pickup and Rocky Scott's automobile.

2. Lynn Koster is in the front passenger seat of car E, which is next to Jeff Kazan's vehicle.

3. Jo-Anne Ince is in the Oldsmobile, which is next to the car belonging to Harold Hayes but driven tonight by his son Gene.

4. The Chevrolet is neither car C nor the one in which Erica Dell and her boyfriend are sitting.

5. Teri Silva is in the car between the one in which Jo-Anne Ince is seated and the one belonging to Cliff Duvall, which isn't car B.

6. Lyle Mizner's Ford hot rod is next to the automobile in which Mindy Lee is seated with her boyfriend, who is very unhappy because Mindy is insisting on actually watching the movie.

Cars: Buick; Chevrolet; Ford; Oldsmobile; Volkswagen
Male teenagers: Cliff Duvall; Gene Hayes; Jeff Kazan; Lyle Mizner; Rocky Scott
Female teenagers: Erica Dell; Jo-Anne Ince; Lynn Koster; Mindy Lee; Teri Silva

	A	B	C	D	E

Car: _____
Male: _____
Female: _____

Starting tip: Begin by finding the position of Rocky Scott's car.

84

Sales Men

Five men have each got their eye on a particular item in a different store in the January sales. From the information given below, can you discover which store each of them will be visiting as soon as the sale opens, the item each is after, and the percentage reduction on the previous price?

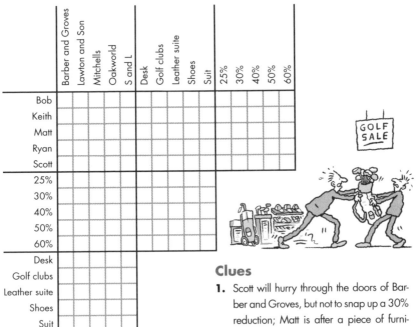

Clues

1. Scott will hurry through the doors of Barber and Groves, but not to snap up a 30% reduction; Matt is after a piece of furniture, but not in Lawton and Son's sale.

2. Bob wants to get a bargain suit, but Ryan is not after the shoes.

3. The shoes are neither the item offered with a 50% reduction nor the one sought after by Keith, who won't be waiting outside Lawton and Son.

4. The item at Mitchells is 25% off the normal price, but neither it nor the item at Lawton and Son is the set of golf clubs.

5. The desk is on offer at Oakworld.

6. The leather suite is in the sale at 60% off the list price.

Name	Store	Item	Reduction

Let's Do Lunch

Five pairs of "ladies who lunch" are enjoying fine meals at exclusive restaurants. From the details given below, can you discover who is lunching with whom, the name of the restaurant, and the name of the hunky waiter serving each?

	Flora	Gemma	Grace	Lorna	Melissa	Christoph's	Luciano's	The Riviera	The Stables	The Wisteria	Ashley	Brendan	Jason	Joel	Marco
Deborah															
Helena															
Jan															
Kate															
Lynda															
Ashley															
Brendan															
Jason															
Joel															
Marco															
Christoph's																
Luciano's																
The Riviera																
The Stables																
The Wisteria																

Dine	Companion	Restaurant	Waiter

Clues

1. Deborah's lunch companion is neither Lorna nor Flora, and Lorna is neither lunching at Luciano's nor being served by Jason.

2. Flora and her companion do not have a table at The Stables, which is not where Joel or Brendan work.

3. Brendan is serving Melissa and her friend, but not at Christoph's; Marco serves at Luciano's.

4. Helena and her lunch companion are in the capable hands of Ashley, but not at The Stables.

5. Gemma and her friend are at their regular table at the Riviera restaurant.

6. Lynda is lunching with Grace, while Jan is at The Wisteria.

The Haunted *Hammerhead*

The submarine *USS Hammerhead* served in the Pacific in World War II and is now preserved at the Florida resort of Fort Willoughby. Over the years, a number of witnesses have experienced supernatural phenomena aboard her. The clues below relate to the five most recent experiences; from them, can you work out the name and occupation of each witness, what they saw or heard, and where they saw or heard it?

	Engineer	Fund-raiser	Lawyer	Police officer	Tour guide	Heard footsteps	Heard voices	Saw officer	Saw sailors	Saw wounded sailor	After deck	Conning tower	Control room	Engine room	Torpedo room
Boyce Cramer															
Holly Jurado															
Kent Larsen															
Perry Riordan															
Velda Young															
After deck															
Conning tower															
Control room															
Engine room															
Torpedo room															
Heard footsteps															
Heard voices															
Saw officer															
Saw sailors															
Saw wounded sailor															

ghostly sailors dressed in wartime uniform, who wasn't the lawyer.

3. Velda Young saw a wounded sailor with a bandage around his head—but she could also see right through him; it wasn't in the control room that one person saw a U.S. Navy officer in his "dress white" uniform, who some researchers believe may have been the submarine's first captain.

4. The engineer who heard ghostly voices wasn't Holly Jurado, who is not a lawyer.

5. Kent Larsen is a police officer from Mobile, Alabama, who was in Fort Willoughby on vacation with his family, and so was a particularly reliable witness.

Clues

1. The lawyer had an experience on the after deck; the person who heard voices in an empty part of the submarine was not Perry Riordan, whose experience was in the torpedo room.

2. The person who heard footsteps in the engine room wasn't the tour guide who shows groups over the vessel; Holly Jurado, who isn't the former naval petty officer who now works as a fund-raiser, wasn't the one who saw a group of

Name	Occupation	Experience	Location

Battleships

Do you remember the old game of battleships? These puzzles are based on that idea. Your task is to find the vessels in the diagram. Some parts of boats or sea squares have already been filled in, and a number next to a row or column refers to the number of occupied squares in that row or column. The boats may be positioned horizontally or vertically, but no two boats or parts of boats are in adjacent squares—horizontally, vertically, or diagonally.

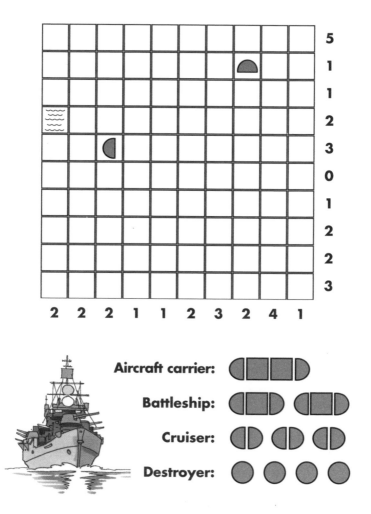

Aircraft carrier:

Battleship:

Cruiser:

Destroyer:

Medical Center

Five people visiting the new Narrowhouse Medical Center in Pottersfield were a little disturbed when they found out who would be treating them, though it all came out right in the end. From the clues below, can you work out each patient's name, what ailed them, the name of the doctor they saw, and what he prescribed for them?

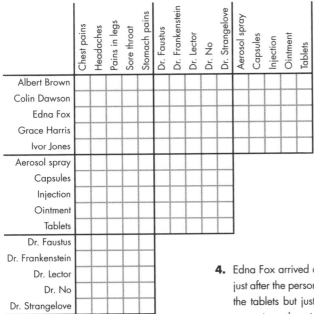

Clues

1. One man had a severe sore throat; the patient who was prescribed an ointment for his or her chest pains wasn't Albert Brown.

2. Colin Dawson, who was suffering from stomach pains, didn't see Dr. Strangelove; Dr. Faustus's patient with leg pains was not prescribed an aerosol spray.

3. The tablets were prescribed for a problem somewhere above the shoulders; the capsules were prescribed for a male patient.

4. Edna Fox arrived at the Medical Center just after the person who was prescribed the tablets but just before the one who was given the ointment; Grace Harris didn't see Dr. Frankenstein.

5. Dr. No's patient had a problem somewhere below the shoulders; Dr. Frankenstein's patient was female.

6. Dr. Strangelove's male patient wasn't suffering from headaches or a sore throat.

Patient	Problem	Doctor	Prescription

Captured!

In the old Wild West, most lawmen were limited in their authority, being confined to a single town, county, or—in the case of organizations like the Texas Rangers—state; the exception were the Federal Marshals, who could make an arrest anywhere in the United States. For instance, Federal Marshal Zeke Randall spent a year hunting down the five members of the Cates Gang after a ruthless train robbery in New Mexico. From the clues below, can you work out the full name of each gang member, and the place and town where Marshal Randall and his deputies arrested him?

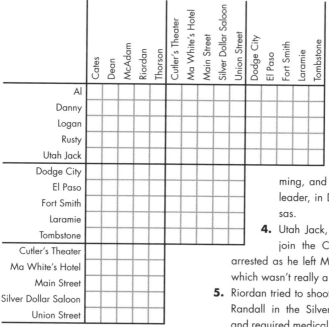

Clues

1. The robber known as Rusty, who was not the man arrested on one community's Main Street, wasn't Thorson.

2. Logan Dean, who also wasn't arrested on Main Street, was not the man Marshal Randall caught up with in El Paso, Texas, just before crossing the border into Mexico.

3. Danny was arrested in Laramie, Wyoming, and Cates, the gang leader, in Dodge City, Kansas.

4. Utah Jack, the last man to join the Cates gang, was arrested as he left Ma White's Hotel, which wasn't really a hotel at all.

5. Riordan tried to shoot it out with Zeke Randall in the Silver Dollar Saloon, and required medical treatment before being jailed.

6. The man arrested in Cutler's Theater in Tombstone, Arizona, wasn't Logan.

First name	Surname	Location	Town

Internal Valentines

Three ladies employed in the Storbury offices of Penny Corp. each received a valentine and a box of chocolates in the internal mail on the morning of February 14th, but they never realized they came from Patrick Patt, the youthful mailroom assistant who delivered them. From the clues below, can you work out each girl's full name, the design on her card, and the kind of chocolates she received?

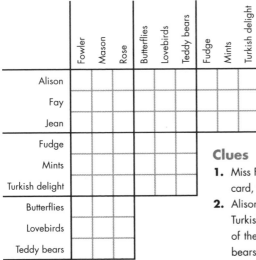

Clues

1. Miss Fowler got a box of mints with her card, which didn't have lovebirds on it.

2. Alison, who got chocolate-covered Turkish delight, wasn't the recipient of the card with the very saucy teddy bears pictured on it.

3. The card with the teddy bears went to a girl whose surname was shorter than Fay's.

4. Jean Mason had been the object of Patrick's attraction ever since they had been at school together.

First name	Surname	Design	Chocolate

Battleships

Do you remember the old game of battleships? These puzzles are based on that idea. Your task is to find the vessels in the diagram. Some parts of boats or sea squares have already been filled in, and a number next to a row or column refers to the number of occupied squares in that row or column. The boats may be positioned horizontally or vertically, but no two boats or parts of boats are in adjacent squares—horizontally, vertically, or diagonally.

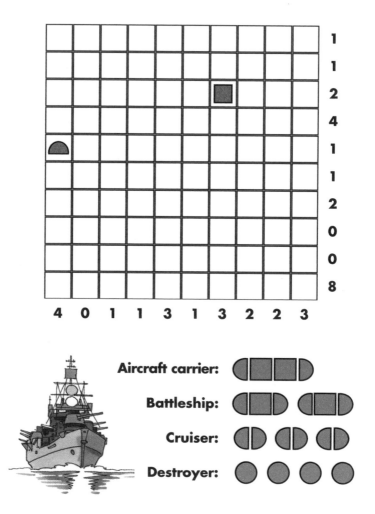

Aircraft carrier:

Battleship:

Cruiser:

Destroyer:

Jake's Treasure

Pirate captain Black-Hearted Jake buried his treasure on a small island. Then, as red herrings intended to hinder any of his rivals from digging it up before he could recover it, he painstakingly buried chests containing eight other items that happened to come to hand at suitable points scattered over the island. From the clues given, can you describe the items buried in each of the nine squares into which the map is divided, and say in what order they were interred?

Clues

1. None of the items was buried in the order corresponding with that of the square containing them, Jake's treasure being interred first in the interests of security.

2. The rusty anchor chain is buried in the square immediately below the next to last item Jake disposed of, and immediately to the right of the one containing the coconut.

3. Square 5 is where the old sea boot with a hole in the sole was carefully laid to rest; it was the third item after the one in square 4 to be concealed.

4. The fourth excavation was carried out in square 3 on the map.

5. The item in square 6 was consigned to the earth next but one before the one in square 8.

6. The rabbit's foot is in a square numbered two higher than the one containing the second item Jake buried, and is in the row above the seashells, which are not directly below it.

7. Jake placed the tin of ship's biscuits in an even-numbered square, but in an odd-numbered sequence.

8. The fish hooks and the discarded eye patch are in diagonal alignment, the latter occupying a higher-numbered square, and one of them being the seventh item Jake buried.

Items: coconut; eye patch; fish hooks; old sea boot; rabbit's foot; rusty anchor chain; seashells; ship's biscuits; treasure

Order: first; second; third; fourth; fifth; sixth; seventh; eighth; ninth

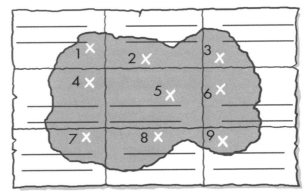

Starting tip: Start by placing the rusty anchor chain.

Learning in the Afternoon

Four young housewives from Middlehampton have all started afternoon educational courses in different subjects. From the clues given, can you work out what each one is learning, and where and when she attends her weekly lesson?

	Flying light aircraft	Juggling	Making costumes	Tai chi	Foxwell Aerodrome	Old School	Ransome Hall	St. John's Hall	Tuesday	Wednesday	Thursday	Friday
Beth Chappel												
Denise Ellis												
Fiona Gable												
Helen Ivey												
Tuesday												
Wednesday												
Thursday												
Friday												
Foxwell Aerodrome												
Old School												
Ransome Hall												
St. John's Hall												

Name	Course	Location	Day

Clues

1. The juggling lessons do not take place on Tuesdays.

2. Fiona Gable attends lessons at the Old School, used for adult education courses since it closed as a regular learning establishment more than twenty years ago.

3. One woman is learning to fly a light plane at the old Foxwell Aerodrome; her name appears in the alphabetical list immediately after that of the one who has her lessons on Thursday afternoons.

4. The woman who is doing a course at Ransome Hall has her lesson earlier in the week than does Beth Chappel, who is learning tai chi.

5. The course on making historic costumes runs on Friday afternoons, and pupils are currently learning how to create their own houppelandes—which, I expect you know, is a fifteenth-century unisex garment, close-fitting around the chest with sleeves and a very full skirt.

Battleships

Do you remember the old game of battleships? These puzzles are based on that idea. Your task is to find the vessels in the diagram. Some parts of boats or sea squares have already been filled in, and a number next to a row or column refers to the number of occupied squares in that row or column. The boats may be positioned horizontally or vertically, but no two boats or parts of boats are in adjacent squares—horizontally, vertically, or diagonally.

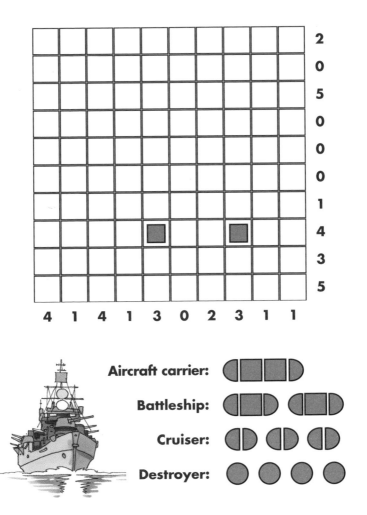

Catastrophic Games

It is some time since we visited Catastrophia, that country where everything attempted is doomed to end in disaster. Last year, for instance, the National Winter Games produced their usual quota of mishaps. From the clues given, can you fully identify the competitor who came to grief in each of the listed events (only a representative sample of the whole sorry picture), and match them with their hometowns?

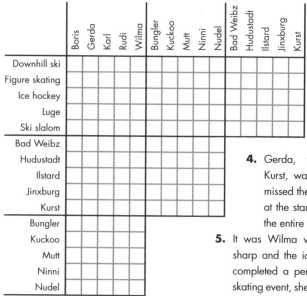

Clues

1. The man who painfully straddled the boundary marker in the ski slalom event was not the native of Ilstard.

2. Ninni, who was not from Hudustadt, was not competing in an event involving skating; Bungler's first name is not Karl.

3. Mutt was the name of the competitor who was unable to stop after reaching the finish of the downhill ski-run.

4. Gerda, whose hometown is Kurst, was not the person who missed the luge when leaping on at the start and ended up doing the entire run on their derrière.

5. It was Wilma whose skates were so sharp and the ice so thin that, having completed a perfect "0" in the figure-skating event, she promptly disappeared through the ice into the lake below.

6. Boris Nudel is not the native of Bad Weibz who almost swallowed the puck while playing ice hockey with a wide open mouth.

7. Kuckoo is the surname of the competitor from Jinxburg.

Event	First name	Surname	Hometown

A Role in the Remake

In line with current Hollywood trends, Megantic Movies are currently making five films based on old TV series—in this instance, all cop shows; and, out of the goodness of their corporate heart, they have invited the original stars of the TV shows to appear in cameo (i.e., very small) roles in the films. From the clues below, can you work out the series in which each of the listed actors appeared, the name of the character he played, and the name (or description) of his role in the movie?

	Code 10-200	Investigators	K9 Squad	Precinct 78	Tac Squad	Capt. Lon McGavin	Lt. Mike Flint	Lt. Rick Flores	Sgt. Duke Mitchell	Sgt. Jay Sherman	Capt. DiMarco	Chief Kazinski	Col. Jackson	Property sgt.	Traffic cop
Adam Burns															
Darren Earle															
Gil Horton															
Jack Kramer															
Mack Nilsson															
Capt. DiMarco															
Chief Kazinski															
Col. Jackson															
Property sgt.															
Traffic cop															
Capt. Lon McGavin															
Lt. Mike Flint															
Lt. Rick Flores															
Sgt. Duke Mitchell															
Sgt. Jay Sherman															

Clues

1. Adam Burns came to TV fame in the 1970s playing Lt. Mike Flint; Jack Kramer didn't appear on TV as Sgt. Jay Sherman or Capt. Lon McGavin.

2. Darren Earle will play the property sergeant who books in evidence in the film version of his old series, which wasn't *Tac Squad*—a Tac squad being pretty much the same thing as a SWAT team.

3. The man who played the hero of *Tac Squad* on TV—who wasn't called Capt. Lon McGavin—won't be appearing in the movie as Capt. DiMarco or a traffic cop; the man who played Lt. Rick Flores on TV will be playing Capt. DiMarco on film, but not in *Precinct 78*.

4. The original star of the military police series *Investigators* will play Col. Jackson in the film version; he's not the man who played Sgt. Sherman on TV, who won't be appearing as Chief Kazinski.

5. The hero of the TV series *K9 Squad*, about police dog handlers, was Sgt. Duke Mitchell.

6. Gil Horton appeared in the series *Code 10-200*, which took its title from a radio code meaning "police needed."

Actor	Title	TV	Film

Name That Drummer

In a television quiz game, a panel of celebrities are invited to select which one of four similar-looking guests, all seated behind a drum kit, was, in fact, the drummer in a group that reached the top of the charts some twenty-five years ago. From the clues given, can you fully identify each of the four, say what each now does, and assist the panel in deciding which one had his moment of fame?

Clues

1. The carpet fitter named Smith is not the man in position 3.

2. Terry has the insurance broker immediately to one side of him, and Kitching immediately to the other.

3. Martin, whose occupation is supermarket manager, has a higher number in the diagram than the fireman.

4. Jack, who cannot play the drums, is an immediate neighbor of the man named Chapman.

5. Dave is the contestant behind drum kit number 2.

6. The real drummer is not seated next to the contestant named Robinson.

First names: Dave; Jack; Martin; Terry
Surnames: Chapman; Kitching; Robinson; Smith
Occupations: carpet fitter; fireman; insurance broker; supermarket manager

	1	2	3	4
First name:				
Surname:				
Occupation:				

Starting tip: Begin by working out the first name to match each seat number.

Horrorscopes

Five girls working in the same office in Storbury were all delighted when their horoscopes, as given in the *Daily Lantern*, promised all manner of good things—but by the end of the day they were completely disillusioned, because not only had none of the good things come to pass, but each had had a sizeable dose of unpredicted misfortune. From the clues below, can you work out each girl's birth sign, the good thing she was promised, and the bad luck she had?

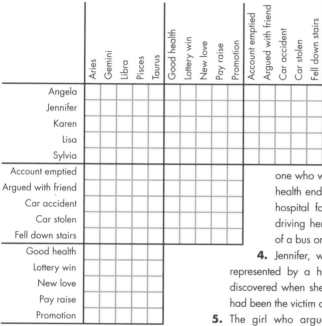

Clues

1. Karen, who isn't a Libra, read that she could expect a lottery win; not only did she not win, but she was involved in an accident which left her bruised and shaken.

2. Angela, whose birth sign is represented by two of something, wasn't the girl promised a new love; her bad luck wasn't connected with her car.

3. It was the Taurean who was told she could look forward to a pay raise; the one who was promised good health ended up going to the hospital for a checkup after driving her car into the back of a bus on her way home.

4. Jennifer, whose birth sign is represented by a horned quadruped, discovered when she left work that she had been the victim of a crime.

5. The girl who argued with her best friend hadn't been promised work-related good news in her horoscope; her birth sign wasn't Aries or Taurus.

6. Sylvia, who was born under Pisces, went home by bus.

Name	Sign	Good luck	Bad luck

Delivery Man

Dan Drury is a van driver for Middlehampton Restaurant Supplies, and today he had just five deliveries to make around the center of the town, each consisting of one food item and one beverage item. From the clues given, can you work out the name and address of the five restaurants he visited, and what two items he delivered there?

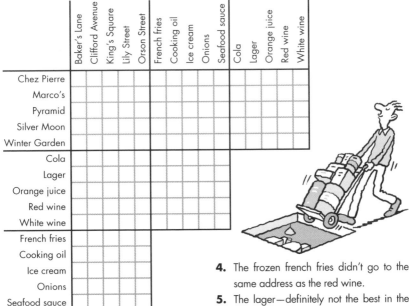

Clues

1. Dan delivered three bags of red onions to the Winter Garden, and fifty liters of orange juice to Chez Pierre, which is situated in an actual street.

2. The Silver Moon is in King's Square; Dan's delivery there did not include any ice cream or any white wine.

3. Neither the restaurant to which Dan delivered ten catering packs of seafood sauce and four crates of white wine nor the Pyramid is in Clifford Avenue.

4. The frozen french fries didn't go to the same address as the red wine.

5. The lager—definitely not the best in the world—went to the establishment in Orson Street.

6. The drums of cooking oil were actually delivered in Marton Close—no, don't worry, I haven't made a mistake; that's where you find the back door of the restaurant whose actual address is Lily Street.

Restaurant	Address	Food	Beverage

posh logic

SOLUTION KEY

1   Five-Star Problem

From clue 7, the figure in box 4 must end in a zero. It cannot be 10, since the 5 is in an odd-numbered box (clues 3 and 7), while the 20 is in box 2 (clue 5), ruling out both 20 and 40 for box 4 (clue 7). Clue 2 tells us the 15 cannot be in box 12, which rules out 30 for box 4 (clue 7). Nor is the 25 in box 12 (clue 8), ruling out 50 for box 4, which must therefore contain the number 60, with the 30 therefore in box 12 (clue 7). From numbers already placed, we can see that the sequence 15, 40, 55 (clue 2) cannot begin in any of boxes 1, 2, 3, 4, or 10. Since box 8 cannot contain the 40 (clue 1), this also rules out the 15 for box 7. Similarly, box 11 cannot contain the 55 (clue 1), ruling out the 15 for box 9. Clue 4 rules out box 6, since box 8 would then contain the 55 (clue 2), which is denied by clue 4. Since the number in box 5 ends in zero (clue 6), this leaves box 8 as the only possible starting point for the sequence, so, from clue 2, the 15 must be there, with the 40 in box 9, and the 55 in box 10. Since we know the 20 is in box 2, clue 4 now reveals that box 7 must contain the number 10. We now know the 25 is in none of boxes 2, 4, 7, 8, 9, 10, or 12, nor can it be in box 5 (clue 6), or box 11 (clue 8). Clue 8 also rules out, from numbers already placed, box 6. Nor can the 35 be in box 5 (clue 6), which rules out box 3 for the 25 (clue 8), so, by elimination, it must be in box 1, and the 35 therefore in box 3. We have now ruled out the 5 for boxes 1, 3, 7, and 9, and clue 6 rules out box 5, so, from clue 3, it must be in box 11. Now, from clue 6, the 50 must be in box 5, leaving the number in box 6 as 45.

Box 1, 25; box 2, 20; box 3, 35; box 4, 60; box 5, 50; box 6, 45; box 7, 10; box 8, 15; box 9, 40; box 10, 55; box 11, 5; box 12, 30.

2   Amateur Athletics

The woman from Loamfield didn't win the long jump or the marathon (clue 3), nor the 200 meters (clue 1), so must have won the javelin. She isn't Fiona Grey, who didn't win the long jump or marathon either (clue 3), so must have won the 200 meters, and therefore comes from Claychester (clue 1). Jane Kyle, the bank clerk, didn't win the javelin (clue 2), so, as the woman who won the long jump was a supermarket worker (clue 3), Jane Kyle must have won the marathon. She's not from Loamfield or Silton (clue 2), so she must come from Marlbourne. The packer isn't Fiona

Grey or Nina Oakes (clue 1), so must be Bridget Cook. We know that the supermarket worker who won the long jump wasn't Fiona Grey (clue 3), so she must have been Nina Oakes, and, by elimination, Fiona Grey must be a teacher. Also by elimination, Bridget Cook, the packer, must be the Loamfield resident who won the javelin, and Nina Oakes's hometown must be Silton.

Bridget Cook, packer, Loamfield, javelin.
Fiona Grey, teacher, Claychester, 200 meters.
Jane Kyle, bank clerk, Marlbourne, marathon.
Nina Oakes, supermarket worker, Silton, long jump.

3   Poker Hands

Chuck's surname is Lafayette (clue 5). Hank's is not O'Callaghan (clue 2), and, since player 3 holds a full house (clue 4), clue 2 rules him out as Cameron, in seat 4 (clue 3), so, by elimination, he must be Russell. So Cameron, who is not Jeff (clue 3), must be Billy, leaving the fourth player as Jeff O'Callaghan. Player 4 does not hold a flush (clue 3), nor does player 2, who must have a pair (clue 1), so the flush must be in the hand of player 1. So clue 2 rules out Hank as player 2. Nor can he be player 3, since player 4 is Cameron (clue 3), so he must be player 1, holding the flush. So, from clue 2, Jeff O'Callaghan must be in seat 2, and Billy Cameron holds a pair of 6s. This leaves Chuck Lafayette in seat 3, and, by elimination, Jeff, in seat 2, must hold a pair of kings.

1, Hank Russell, flush.
2, Jeff O'Callaghan, pair of kings.
3, Chuck Lafayette, full house.
4, Billy Cameron, pair of 6s.

4   The Tedd Family

The person who has been in the show for two years isn't Giles (clue 4) or Anne (clue 1), so must be Philip or Suzanne. From clue 1, each of the pairs mentioned must have been in the show for a total of seven years, so, since either Philip or Suzanne has been in it for two years, the other must have been in it for five years, and thus, from clue 4, Giles must have been in the show for three years and Anne for four years. From clue 2, Giles must be Mead, and Philip must play "Tessie." Since Giles is Mead, it can't have been Philip who has been in the cast for two years (clue 5), so it must be Suzanne, and Philip must have been in the show for five years, and, from clue 5, must be Hewitt. Ms. Lawton plays "Tommy" (clue 3), so

Giles, who also plays a male Tedd (clue 4), must play "Timothy." Therefore, from the same clue, Ms. Lawton, who plays "Tommy," who has joined the cast more recently than the person who plays "Tina" (clue 3), must have been in the show for two years, and is therefore Suzanne. So the person playing "Tina" must have been doing so for four years, and is therefore Anne, whose surname by elimination must be Kersey.

Anne Kersey, "Tina," 4 years.
Giles Mead, "Timothy," 3 years.
Philip Hewitt, "Tessie," 5 years.
Suzanne Lawton, "Tommy," 2 years.

5 Battleships

6 Unfancied Dress

The man from Tudor Road ordered the skeleton suit (clue 4) and the man from New Street must have ordered either the Dracula outfit or the one for the Wolfman (clue 3); Eddie Hill lives in Queens Road (clue 6), so Lee Moss, who ordered the zombie outfit and doesn't live in Station Road (clue 7), must live in The Croft, and thus received the Cleopatra costume (clue 5). Colin Ford can't be the man from Tudor Road who ordered the skeleton suit (clue 3), nor is his home in New Street (clue 3), so must live in Station Road. So Colin Ford from Station Road and the man from New Street must each have ordered the Dracula or Wolfman outfit (clue 3). Therefore Eddie Hill from Queens Road must have ordered the ghost outfit and received the Santa Claus suit (clue 2). We now know which costumes were received by two men; Ray Todd received the fireman outfit (clue 1), so Vic Wade, who didn't get the Wonderwoman outfit (clue 8), must have received the Tarzan outfit. By elimination, it must have been Colin Ford who got the Wonderwoman costume.

From clue 3, the man from New Street wasn't Vic Wade, who received the Tarzan outfit, so must have been Ray Todd, who got the fireman costume, leaving Vic Wade as the man from Tudor Road who ordered the skeleton suit. Finally, from clue 1, the man who ordered the Dracula outfit wasn't Ray Todd, so must have been Colin Ford, leaving Ray Todd as the man from New Street, who must have ordered the Wolfman costume.

Colin Ford, Station Road, Dracula, Wonderwoman.
Eddie Hill, Queens Road, ghost, Santa Claus.
Lee Moss, The Croft, zombie, Cleopatra.
Ray Todd, New Street, the Wolfman, fireman.
Vic Wade, Tudor Road, skeleton, Tarzan.

7 Logi-5

D	C	A	B	E
E	D	B	A	C
C	A	E	D	B
A	B	C	E	D
B	E	D	C	A

8 ABC

B			C	A
		A	B	C
C	A	B		
A	B	C		
	C		A	B

9 On the Catwalk

From clue 5, the wife lettered D cannot be married to the men in positions 1 or 4, and clue 4 tells us the wife of the man in seat 2 is in position A on the catwalk, so, by elimination, wife D must be married to husband 3. He is not Reg (clue 5), nor can he be Jim (clue 1), and Arnold's wife cannot be D either (clue 2), so husband 3 must be Tony. Therefore clue 3 places Nicole's husband in seat 4. So, from clue 5, Sally's husband must be number 2, and she is therefore wife A on the catwalk, and Reg must be Nicole's husband in seat 4. Jim cannot be number 1 (clue 1), so he must be in seat 2, and is married to Sally, leaving number 1 as Arnold. His wife is not Pauline (clue 2), so she must be Laura, which leaves Pauline as Tony's wife, lettered D on the catwalk. Clue 2 now places Laura as wife C in the parade, leaving

Nicole in position B.
1, Arnold, Laura, C.
2, Jim, Sally, A.
3, Tony, Pauline, D.
4, Reg, Nicole, B.

10 Battleships

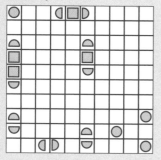

11 The (Old) Day Job

Jessica's surname is Del Rey (clue 3). Brenda isn't Wallace, who writes war novels, or Gordon (clue 1), nor McIlwain, whose first name is listed alphabetically after that of the fantasy writer (clue 2), so her surname must be Tiptree, and she was formerly a flight attendant (clue 5). She therefore does not write humorous novels, which is the genre of the former ferry boat captain (clue 3). The woman who does write the humorous novels (clue 3) isn't Penny, who writes whodunnits (clue 2), so must be Jessica Del Rey. We know that Penny, the whodunnit writer, isn't Del Rey, Tiptree, or Wallace, nor is she McIlwain (clue 2), so she must be Gordon. McIlwain isn't the fantasy writer (clue 2), so must write science fiction, leaving Brenda Tiptree as the fantasy writer. McIlwain, the science fiction writer, isn't Mike (clue 4), so must be Dave, the former teacher (clue 6), leaving Mike as Wallace, who writes war novels. He's not the former forensic scientist (clue 1), so must have been an undertaker, leaving the ex-forensic scientist as Penny Gordon, who now writes whodunnits.

Brenda Tiptree, fantasy, flight attendant.
Dave McIlwain, science fiction, teacher.
Jessica Del Rey, humorous novels, ferry boat captain.
Mike Wallace, war novels, undertaker.
Penny Gordon, whodunnits, forensic scientist.

12 Zongs

Bart D'Angelo, star of *Zong the Destroyer*, wasn't a police officer (clue 4), the body builder, who was Joe Lyle (clue 2), or the truck driver, who starred in *Zong Attacks!* (clue 3), so must have been a wrestler. The star of *Kill Zong!*, released in 1970 (clue 5), wasn't the police officer (clue 4), so he must have been the body builder, Joe Lyle. By elimination, the police officer must have appeared in *Return of Zong*. This wasn't released in 1934 (clue 1) or 1958 (clue 4), so must have come out in 1946. *Zong Attacks!*, featuring the truck driver, didn't come out in 1958 either (clue 3), so must have been released in 1934, leaving *Zong the Destroyer*, starring Bart D'Angelo, the wrestler, as the 1958 release. The truck driver was therefore Earl Gruber (clue 3), and, by elimination, the police officer who starred in 1946's *Return of Zong* must have been Randy Thorson.

Bart D'Angelo, wrestler, *Zong the Destroyer*, 1958.
Earl Gruber, truck driver, *Zong Attacks!*, 1934.
Joe Lyle, body builder, *Kill Zong!*, 1970.
Randy Thorson, police officer, *Return of Zong*, 1946.

13 Home, James!

The 10:30 journey back from location 2 (clue 3) cannot have been from the visit to Lady Manners (clue 1), so, from that clue, Lady Bountiful must have left the Manners residence at 11:30 in the morning. Clue 5 also rules out 10:30 as the time of leaving the dress-maker's, so the latter cannot be in location 2, and, from clue 5, must be in location 4. This fact tells us, from clue 1, that Lady Manners's house is in location 3, so, back with clue 5, Lady Bountiful must have left her dress-maker's at 2:30PM, and, by elimination, it must have been at 3:30 that she left location 1. We know this is not Lady Manners's house or the dress-maker's, and clue 4 tells us it is not the convent she visited on Thursday, so, by elimination, it must be where the wine merchant plies his trade, leaving the convent in location 2. We know that the dress-maker was not visited on Thursday, and clue 2 now also rules out both Wednesday and Friday for the 2:30 trip home, so the visit to the dress-maker must have been on Tuesday. So, from clue 2, the trip to the wine merchant's was on Wednesday, leaving Friday as the day of the visit to Lady Manners.

1, wine merchant, Wednesday, 3:30.

3, Lady Manners, Friday, 11:30.
2, convent, Thursday, 10:30.
4, dress-maker, Tuesday, 2:30.

14 Off the Subs' Bench

Ruth was called in during the fifth week (clue 3). Odette, in position 8, was not the first replacement to be called upon, in the second week (clue 2), and it was position 5 that had to be filled in the seventh week (clue 4). Clue 3 rules out position 8 for the fourth week's substitution, which leaves Odette as Katie's replacement in week nine (clue 5). We know the position to be filled in the seventh and ninth weeks was not 10, nor was that the position of Ruth, the fifth-week replacement (clue 3), and that clue also rules out number 10 as the position replaced in the fourth week, so it must have been filled in the second week of the run. This was not when Carianne replaced Mary-Jo (clue 6), and we know neither Ruth nor Odette were brought in that week, nor was Melissa (clue 1), so, by elimination, it must have been Jackie who joined the chorus line in the second week in position 10, so, from clue 3, the position filled in the fourth week was 7. The person replaced was Suzie (clue 7). We have now named either an original or a replacement in four weeks, so, by elimination, it must have been in week 7 that Carianne was brought in to replace Mary-Jo in position 5. By elimination, Suzie's replacement in week 4 must have been Melissa. So, from clue 1, Laura must have been replaced in the second week by Jackie. By elimination, Ruth must have taken up position 2 in the line in the fifth week, and the dancer she replaced must have been Darlene.

Second week, Laura, Jackie, number 10.
Seventh week, Mary-Jo, Carianne, number 5.
Fourth week, Suzie, Melissa, number 7.
Ninth week, Katie, Odette, number 8.
Fifth week, Darlene, Ruth, number 2.

15 Battleships

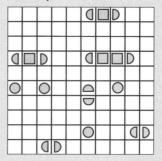

16 *Party Pieces*

Faith Long was the impressionist (clue 3) and the juggler was described as "worse than useless" (clue 6), so Guy Benton, whose act was described by Silas as "a waste of time" (clue 5) but who wasn't a ventriloquist or a singer (clue 5), must have been the magician. The singer was the third act (clue 4), so Phil Hart was not the "abominable" first performer (clue 2), nor was it Victor Bull (clue 1), so it must have been Ivor Hope who, by elimination, must be the ventriloquist. Faith Long was not described by Silas as a "no-hoper" (clue 3) or as "worse than useless," so she must have been judged to be "utterly talentless," leaving the "no-hoper" as the singer. The "utterly talentless" performer must therefore have been on fourth, with Phil Hart third and the "waste of time" magician fifth (clue 2). Therefore Phil Hart must have been the "no-hoper" and, by elimination, the "worse than useless" juggler must have been Victor Bull, who must have appeared before the judges second.

1, Ivor Hope, ventriloquist, "abominable."
2, Victor Bull, juggler, "worse than useless."
3, Phil Hart, singer, "no-hoper."
4, Faith Long, impressionist, "utterly talentless."
5, Guy Benton, magician, "waste of time."

17 Logi-5

C	B	D	A	E
D	A	E	B	C
E	D	B	C	A
B	C	A	E	D
A	E	C	D	B

18 ABC

A		C		B
	B	A	C	
C		B	A	
B	A		C	
	C		B	A

19 The Diver

Since Davy worked with Cliff Kerr in May (clue 4), from clue 1 the expedition on the *Hammerhead* for the *U-76* film can't have been in March or November; the ship in September was the *Cherokee* (clue 6), and the film in July was about the Bermuda Triangle (clue 7), so Davy must have worked on the *U-76* film in May, with director Cliff Kerr. So, from clue 1, Joe Ramsey was the director in July, for the Bermuda Triangle film. We've now matched two directors with films, and Frank Byng directed the film on sharks (clue 5), so Mel Calder's film, which wasn't about the *Waratah* (clue 2), must have been about *Queen Anne's Revenge,* leaving the director of the *Waratah* film as Zack Tryon. We know that the November film wasn't about the Bermuda Triangle or the *U-76,* nor was its subject the *Waratah* (clue 2) or the *Queen Anne's Revenge* (clue 3), so it must have been the film about sharks directed by Frank Byng. Mel Calder's film about *Queen Anne's Revenge* wasn't made in March (clue 2), so must have been made in September; so, from clue 3, the *Pearl* must have been the ship used for Frank Byng's November film. Now, by elimination, the March film must have been Zack Tryon's one about the *Waratah.* The ship used for this wasn't the *Viking* (clue 6), so must have been the *Lady Jackie,* leaving the *Viking* as the ship used for July's Bermuda Triangle film.

March, Zack Tryon, *Lady Jackie, Waratah.*
May, Cliff Kerr, *Hammerhead, U-76.*
July, Joe Ramsay, *Viking,* Bermuda Triangle.
September, Mel Calder, *Cherokee, Queen Anne's Revenge.*
November, Frank Byng, *Pearl,* sharks.

20 *Comrades in Arms*

Wilder will become an intelligence officer in the movie (clue 2), and Alvin, in the film, will win the Medal of Honor (clue 7). Glen Bergman isn't the one who in the book is killed in a plane crash but in the movie will marry a duke's daughter (clue 4), nor can he be the man who in the movie is posted to a training unit, whose surname has fewer than seven letters (clue 3), so in the film he must become a movie star. His fate in the book is not being jailed for his wife's murder (clue 5), and we know he isn't killed in a plane crash; it's Nelson who is executed by the Nazis (clue 1), and Horowitz who commits suicide (clue 6), so Glen Bergman's fate in the book must be to lose both legs. We know that Horowitz's film fate is not to become an intelligence officer or a movie star, nor to marry a duke's daughter; clue 3 rules out a posting to a training unit, so Horowitz must win the Medal of Honor in the film, and is therefore Alvin. We know that the man jailed for killing his wife in the book isn't Alvin, Glen, or Nelson, and clue 5 rules out Dean, so he must be Ray, and, by elimination, Dean must be the man who is killed in a plane crash in the book but marries a duke's daughter in the film. So his surname isn't Wilder, and we know it isn't Bergman or Horowitz, so he must be either Joad or Greco. So, from clue 5, Ray, jailed for his wife's murder in the book, must be Wilder or Bergman. We know he's not Bergman, so Ray must be Wilder, who becomes an intelligence officer in the film, and, from clue 5, Dean's surname must be Joad. Now, by elimination, Nelson must be Greco, and, while he's executed by the Nazis in the book, in the film he must get posted to a training unit.

Alvin Horowitz, suicide, awarded Medal of Honor.
Dean Joad, killed in plane crash, marries duke's daughter.
Glen Bergman, loses both legs, becomes movie star.
Nelson Greco, executed by Nazis, posted to training unit.
Ray Wilder, jailed for wife's murder, becomes int. off.

21 Battleships

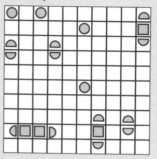

22 Buccaneers Bay

Cutlass ran onto a coral reef and *Storm* was Inigo Malice's ship (clue 3), so Ezra Grimm's ship, which caught fire and which wasn't *Dragon* (clue 1), must have been *Marauder*, sunk in 1765 (clue 2). It was in 1705 that one ship collided with a whale (clue 4), so the one punctured by the swordfish, which didn't sink in 1675 (clue 2), must have gone down in 1735. So it wasn't *Dragon* (clue 1) and must have been Inigo Malice's *Storm*, leaving *Dragon* as the ship that collided with the whale. It wasn't Orlando Ruddy's ship (clue 4), so must have been Abel Deth's, leaving Orlando Ruddy as the captain of *Cutlass*, whose end on a coral reef must, by elimination, have been in 1675.

Cutlass, **Orlando Ruddy, ran onto coral reef, 1675.**
Dragon, **Abel Deth, collision with whale, 1705.**
Marauder, **Ezra Grimm, caught fire, 1765.**
Storm, **Inigo Malice, punctured by swordfish, 1735.**

23 All Change

From clue 1, girl 3, whose ex is Andy, is not currently dating either him or Mike, while Hugo is now with Daniel's ex (clue 4), so he is not with girl 3 either. Therefore Daniel must be. So, from clue 2, Vanessa must be in position 4. Angie is girl number 2 (clue 3). So girl 3, now dating Daniel, is not Angie or Vanessa, and Tina is currently going out with Andy (clue 1), so, by elimination, it must be Delia who is now Daniel's girlfriend, and was Andy's. So, by elimination, Tina must be in position 1. Therefore her ex is not Hugo (clue 4), and must be Mike. So, from clue 3, the latter must

be Angie's current boyfriend, and, by elimination, it must be Vanessa who is now with Hugo, and was with Daniel.

1, Tina, now Andy, ex Mike.
2, Angie, now Mike, ex Hugo.
3, Delia, now Daniel, ex Andy.
4, Vanessa, now Hugo, ex Daniel.

24 No Checkered Flag

Helen Jones's car skidded off (clue 1) and the Olimpio's brakes failed (clue 3), so Mike Nash's Ivanhoe, which did not lose a wheel (clue 1), must have suffered engine failure. Ben Clay's car, which completed 24 laps, was not the Crabshaw (clue 2), so, as the Olimpio's driver was female (clue 3), Ben Clay must have been driving the Fidessa, which, by elimination, must have lost a wheel. Helen Jones's car wasn't the Olimpio (clue 1), so must have been the Crabshaw, leaving Sally Thorp as the Olimpio driver. Neither she nor Mike Nash, whose engine failed, completed only 12 laps (clue 4), so Helen Jones must have done so, and, also from clue 4, Sally Thorp must have completed 18 laps and Mike Nash 30 laps.

Ben Clay, Fidessa, lost wheel, 24 laps.
Helen Jones, Crabshaw, skidded off, 12 laps.
Mike Nash, Ivanhoe, engine failure, 30 laps.
Sally Thorp, Olimpio, brakes failed, 18 laps.

25 Versatility

The book by Bentley Wells appeared in August (clue 2). The western novel published in January was not by Royce Verne (clue 7), and Morris Doyle writes whodunnits (clue 5). Since the March title was *Beyond All Hope* (clue 4), clue 1 also rules out January for the work by Ford Christie, so, by elimination, Desmond's pen name for westerns is Austin Dickens, and this one was therefore entitled *Green Sunset* (clue 6). Clues 1 and 2 rule out the light romance, *Highland Fling*, as the November book, and we know the months in which two other titles were published. Clue 3 rules out *Dark Journey* for November, which leaves *Shooting Stars* as that month's offering. From clues 4 and 5, *Beyond All Hope*, published in March, cannot be the espionage novel, nor is *Shooting Stars*, released in November (clue 3), so, by elimination, espionage must be the theme of *Dark Journey*. So, from clue 5, Morris Doyle's whodunnit cannot have been published in March or June, and we know it did not come out in January or August, so it must be the November book, *Shooting Stars*, and, from clue 5, *Dark Journey* must have been released in August. Now, by elimination, the June book must have been *Highland Fling*, the light romance, which leaves *Beyond All Hope* as the science-fiction work. From clue 1, it must have been written under the pen name of Ford Christie, which leaves Royce Verne as the author of *Highland Fling*.

Beyond All Hope, March, sci-fi, Ford Christie.
Dark Journey, August, espionage, Bentley Wells.
Green Sunset, January, western, Austin Dickens.
Highland Fling, June, light romance, Royce Verne.
Shooting Stars, November, whodunnit, Morris Doyle.

26 Rangers

Rusty is played by Stamford (clue 2), and Brazos is Lubbock (clue 4), so Houston, who is played by Lowell and isn't Dixie (clue 6), must be Sarge. Austin is played by Ben (clue 3), so can't be Dixie (clue 6), and must be Rusty, so Ben is Stamford. By elimination, Dixie, Gary's character (clue 6), must be Beaumont. Now, from clue 4, Chester, played by Scott, who can't be Brazos Lubbock, must be Sarge Houston, and Scott is thus Lowell. By elimination, Russ must play Brazos Lubbock. Chester Sarge Houston isn't figure B (clue 4), and can't be figure D (clue 6). Figure A is Abraham (clue 5), so Chester must be figure C, and, from clue 6, Dixie Beaumont, played by Gary, must be figure D. Therefore he isn't Randall (clue 1), and we know Abraham is figure A, so Dixie Beaumont must be Will. Therefore Gary, who plays him, isn't Modesto (clue 1), and must be Flint, leaving Modesto as Russ, who's playing Brazos Lubbock. We now know the first name for three characters, so Randall must be figure B. Therefore he isn't Brazos Lubbock, and must be Rusty Austin, played by Ben Stamford, leaving figure A as Abraham Brazos Lubbock, played by Russ Modesto.

A, Abraham Brazos Lubbock, Russ Modesto.
B, Randall Rusty Austin, Ben Stamford.
C, Chester Sarge Houston, Scott Lowell.
D, Will Dixie Beaumont, Gary Flint.

27 The Jay-Birds

Since the fifth song reached position 2 (clue 6), this cannot be "Take Me with You" (clue 3), nor can it be "Something's Bust" (clue 1), or "Frolic at the Fair," featuring Jenny (clue 2), and "Don't Look" was the group's second song (clue 4), so, by elimination, their fifth offering must have

been "Cheeky Monkey." This cannot have been sung by Jackie, whose solo item reached only position 4 (clue 5), and that clue also rules out June, and we know Jenny did not sing it. Julie sang the solo part on their first release (clue 7), so, by elimination, it must have been Jill who sang "Cheeky Monkey." Therefore, from clue 2, "Frolic at the Fair" was the group's fourth release. Since we know Julie's song was the first, clue 5 now tells us Jackie, who reached number 4, cannot have sung the second, so June must have done, and Jackie must have starred on the third release. So this cannot be "Take Me with You" (clue 3), and must be "Something's Bust," leaving "Take Me with You" as the group's first offering. The song that stuck at number 10 in the charts cannot have been the second (clue 4), or the first (clue 7), so it must have been "Frolic at the Fair," their fourth release. Clue 4 now tells us "Don't Look" must have reached number 6, and "Take Me with You," therefore, number 8.

First, "Take Me With You," Julie, number 8.
Second, "Don't Look," June, number 6.
Third, "Something's Bust," Jackie, number 4.
Fourth, "Frolic at the Fair," Jenny, number 10.
Fifth, "Cheeky Monkey," Jill, number 2.

28 Battleships

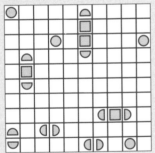

29 Heading Back East

The gambler wasn't Jake Kovac (clue 2), Frank Glaser (also clue 2), Charlie Dean, who was a trail boss (clue 6), or Rick Skelton, who was either a bank robber or a train robber (clue 3), so must have been Nate O'Farrell, who became an industrialist (clue 1). He didn't settle in Massachusetts (clue 2), Florida (clue 1), New York, where the train robber settled (clue 4), or South Carolina, where one man became a politician (clue 1), so must have moved to Pennsylvania. The Texas Ranger didn't take up politics or journalism (clue 1); it was the former bank robber who remained a bank robber (clue 5), and we know it was the gambler who became an industrialist, so the Texas Ranger must have become a hotelier. As the train robber settled in New York, the man who became a politician in South Carolina must have been Charlie Dean, the trail boss, and, by elimination, the train robber must have become a journalist. He wasn't Rick Skelton (clue 3), who must therefore, from the same clue, have been the bank robber who remained a bank robber. Jake Kovac didn't become a journalist (clue 2), so must have become a hotelier and was therefore the former Texas Ranger; he didn't settle in Massachusetts (clue 2), so in Florida. By elimination, Frank Glaser must have been the train robber who became a journalist and settled in New York, and bank robber Rick Skelton must have continued robbing banks in Massachusetts.

Charlie Dean, trail boss, politician, South Carolina.

Frank Glaser, train robber, journalist, New York.

Jake Kovac, Texas Ranger, hotelier, Florida.

Nate O'Farrell, gambler, industrialist, Pennsylvania.

Rick Skelton, bank robber, bank robber, Massachusetts.

30 Cops

The 13th Precinct covers East Hanway (clue 6). The burglar was arrested in the 7th Precinct, which doesn't cover Chinatown (clue 4), Belfry Hill (clue 3), or Dysart Park, where the mugger was arrested (clue 1), so must cover Kelvin Heights, and the burglar was therefore arrested by Wes Tanaka (clue 1). Mac McRuen is based in the 9th Precinct (clue 2), so Rose Silva, who arrested the car thief (clue 3), must be based at a precinct numbered 12 or higher, and the one covering Belfry Hill must be numbered higher still. It's not the 13th Precinct (clue 6), so it must be the 17th. The criminal arrested in Belfry Hill wasn't the gang leader (clue 2), so must have been the bank robber. Mac McRuen of the 9th Precinct didn't arrest the gang leader or the bank robber (clue 2), so he must have arrested the mugger in Dysart Park. By elimination, the 12th Precinct must cover Chinatown. Jake Lebas didn't arrest the gang leader (clue 2), so he must have arrested the bank robber, and is therefore based in the 17th Precinct, covering Belfry Hill. Finally, Gus

Hagan's not from the 12th Precinct (clue 5) so he must be the cop from the 13th Precinct who made his arrest in East Hanway, and, by elimination, he must have arrested the gang leader. This leaves Rose Silva arresting her car thief in the part of the 12th Precinct known as Chinatown.

Gus Hagan, 13th Precinct, East Hanway, gang leader.

Jake Lebas, 17th Precinct, Belfry Hill, bank robber.

Mac McRuen, 9th Precinct, Dysart Park, mugger.

Rose Silva, 12th Precinct, Chinatown, car thief.

Wes Tanaka, 7th Precinct, Kelvin Heights, burglar.

31 Help's on the Way

Steve headed for location 2 (clue 4). Since the collapse was in location 3 (clue 2), clue 1 rules out Alan as Andy's driver to location 1 (clue 5), and Bob was Lawrie's driver (clue 3), so, by elimination, it must have been Gerry who drove Andy. We know they did not attend the collapse, nor did they go to the fire (clue 6) while Joe was at the road accident (clue 5), so the domestic accident must have taken place in location 1. Therefore, from clue 1, Alan must have driven to the collapse in location 3, which leaves Bob and Lawrie heading for location 4. So their incident must have been the fire, and Joe must have been Steve's crewman at a road accident, leaving Alan's crewman at the collapse as Graham.

1, Gerry, Andy, domestic accident.

2, Steve, Joe, road accident.

3, Alan, Graham, collapse.

4, Bob, Lawrie, fire.

32 Secrets of Age

The 101-year-old puts his or her longevity down to never having smoked (clue 6). Maud used to cycle everywhere (clue 1), and the resident who never married is younger than Albert (clue 2), so 102-year-old Daisy, who doesn't attribute her long life to ballroom dancing (also clue 1), must put it down to a daily glass of sherry, and therefore must be the occupant of room 14 (clue 4). So Ernie, who is a year younger than the occupant of room 12 (clue 2), cannot be either 101 or 99. The occupant of room 3 is 99 (clue 5), so Ernie is also not 98 and must be 97. Therefore the person in room 12 must be 98 (clue 2). Ethel occupies room 10 (clue 3), so she is neither 98 nor 99, and must be the 101-year-old who puts her long life down to never having smoked. The resident who never married is not Albert (clue 2), so it must be 97-year-old Ernie and, by elimination, Albert must attribute his continuing health to ballroom dancing. So, from clue 5, Albert must be the 99-year-old in room 3 and the 98-year-old in room 12 must be inveterate cyclist Maud, leaving 97-year-old Ernie in room 4.

97, Ernie, room 4, never married.
98, Maud, room 12, cycled everywhere.
99, Albert, room 3, ballroom dancing.
101, Ethel, room 10, never smoked.
102, Daisy, room 14, daily glass of sherry.

33 Logi-5

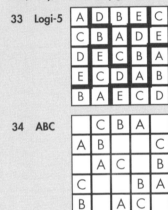

34 ABC

35 Exercise Can Be Dangerous

Hawkes's exercise was swimming (clue 1); Alan, whose exercise was judo (clue 2), can't be Ellery, who broke his or her big toe (clue 3); nor was Ellery's exercise squash (clue 3 again), so, by elimination, it must have been weight-lifting. So Ellery isn't Alice (clue 3) nor Dennis, who suffered a broken nose (clue 4), so must be Dolores. We now know which injuries were received by Dennis and Dolores, so the person who broke a collar bone must have been either Alan or Alice, and therefore so must Hawkes, who took up swimming (clue 1). Alan's exercise was judo, so Hawkes the swimmer must be Alice, and Alan must have broken his collar bone. By elimination, Alice Hawkes must have broken her ankle, and Dennis, who broke his nose, must have taken up squash. Dennis isn't Wright (clue 4), so must be Norton, leaving Wright as Alan, who took up judo and broke his collar bone.

Alan Wright, judo, broken collar bone.
Alice Hawkes, swimming, broken ankle.

Dennis Norton, squash, broken nose.
Dolores Ellery, weight-lifting, broken big toe.

36 Dark Secrets

From clue 1, both Brian and Wheeler must be either a former biker or a former stripper, so Joanne Byrd (clue 2) must have been convicted of a crime; the thriller writer convicted of car theft is male (clue 4) and it's Chester who is a convicted smuggler (clue 5), so Joanne Byrd must be a convicted burglar. We know that the convicted car thief isn't surnamed Byrd or Chester, and clue 1 rules out Wheeler; Stonehall's a sports writer (clue 6), so the thriller writer who was a car thief must be Fearn. Since Stonehall isn't the former biker (clue 6) he must be the former stripper, leaving the former biker as Wheeler. So, from clue 1, Brian must be Stonehall. Joanne Byrd isn't the naturalist (clue 2), so, as Marion is the novelist (clue 3), Joanne Byrd must be a racehorse trainer. Fearn, the thriller writer, isn't Gerald (clue 7), so must be Dominic, leaving Gerald as the naturalist. From clue 5, he can't be Chester, so must be Wheeler, leaving the convicted smuggler Chester as Marion, the novelist.

Brian Stonehall, sports writer, former stripper.
Dominic Fearn, thriller writer, convicted car thief.
Gerald Wheeler, naturalist, former biker.
Joanne Byrd, racehorse trainer, convicted burglar.
Marion Chester, novelist, convicted smuggler.

37 Stone Age Dogs

Agg needed a dog to pull a cart (clue 4), and the one supplied by Tagg was to guard the children (clue 3). Clue 1 tells us the one obtained by Igg from Logg was not to catch rabbits, and clues 1 and 6 taken together tell us this animal cannot have been Begg, who was to be a family pet, so, by elimination, it must have been intended to guard Igg's cave. We know Begg, the family pet, was not acquired from Logg or Tagg, and clue 6 rules out Mugg, while the one from Jigg was called Pugg (clue 5), so Begg must have been obtained from Figg. Clue 2 therefore reveals that it was Ugg who called his dog Digg, so, from clue 1, this animal must have been intended to catch rabbits, and the guard dog Igg got from Logg must have been called Dogg. We have now matched four reasons with either a dog's name or a supplier, so Pugg, obtained from Jigg, must have been required to pull Agg's cart. By elimination, Ugg's dog, Digg, must have been supplied by Mugg, and the children's guard dog from Tagg must have been called Wagg. Clue 3 tells us Egg did not acquire him, so Ogg must have done so, leaving Egg as the new owner of Begg.

Agg, Pugg, pull cart, Jigg.
Egg, Begg, family pet, Figg.
Igg, Dogg, guard cave, Logg.
Ogg, Wagg, guard children, Tagg.
Ugg, Digg, catch rabbits, Mugg.

38 Battleships

39 Cop Cars

The white car is from Pallet County (clue 5). The car from Grant County in Utah (clue 1) can't be the blue/white one, car 4 (clues 1 and 3); nor is it black (clue 1), so it must be black/white. Clue 1 rules this out as car 3 and car 4, and clue 4 for car 1, so it must be car 2. Therefore, from clue 1, the black car must be car 3, leaving the white one from Pallet County as car 1, and, from clue 4, Pallet County must be in Florida. The blue/white car, which isn't from Kansas (clue 3), must be from Maine, leaving the black car 3 coming from Kansas. Thus, from clue 2, the black car must be from Jordan County and the blue/white car 4 from Rock County.

1, white, Pallet County, Florida.
2, black/white, Grant County, Utah.
3, black, Jordan County, Kansas.
4, blue/white, Rock County, Maine.

40 Side-Wheelers

The ship Hunsacker took over in 1849 later vanished (clue 5). The ship he commanded from 1854 wasn't preserved as a museum on Lake Erie (clue 1), nor did it rot at its moorings (clue 7) or get broken up for scrap (clue 6), so it must have sunk in a storm, and so was the *Antelope* (clue 2), which went down in Lake Huron (clue 6). Hun-

sacker took over the *Indian Queen* in 1844 (clue 4). From clue 1, he didn't take over the *Willard Grover* in 1834 or 1839, so he must have taken over in 1849, and the *Willard Grover* therefore subsequently vanished. So, from clue 1, it must have been in 1839 that he took over the ship preserved as a museum on Lake Erie. We now know the years in which he took over three ships. As the *Jesse McCaslan* met her fate on Lake Superior (clue 3), she can't have been the ship Hunsacker took over in 1839, so he must have taken over in 1834, and, by elimination, 1839 must have been the year he took over the *Star of the Lakes*. The ship that rotted at her moorings must have been taken over in either 1834 or 1844. As the *Antelope*, his 1854 ship, sank in Lake Huron, from clue 7 it must have been the *Jesse McCaslan*, taken over in 1834, that rotted at her moorings, and the ship that met her fate in Lake Ontario must have been the *Indian Queen*, taken over in 1844. By elimination, she must have been broken up, and the vanishing of the *Willard Grover* must have taken place on Lake Michigan.

Antelope, 1854, sunk in storm, Lake Huron.
Indian Queen, 1844, broken up, Lake Ontario.
Jesse McCaslan, 1834, rotted at moorings, Lake Superior.
Star of the Lakes, 1839, preserved as museum, Lake Erie.
Willard Grover, 1849, vanished, Lake Michigan.

41 Gems Among the Junk

The letter from a back-packing daughter was delivered to number 28 (clue 6). The Lettermans at number 35 had not won a competition (clue 2), nor can their item have been the free gift (clue 1), and it was the Mailers who had a postcard from friends in Australia (clue 3), so, by elimination, the job offer must have been delivered to the Lettermans. The Stamps received good news on Friday (clue 5). Since nothing of interest was delivered on Wednesday, clue 1 rules out the Cards, and clue 3 the Mailers, as the Tuesday recipients, nor were the Posts (clue 5), so that must be the day the Lettermans received the job offer. Therefore, from clue 3, the Mailers received their item on Monday, so they live at number 21 (clue 4). We know the Cards were not lucky on Monday, Tuesday, or Friday, and clue 1 rules out Saturday, so they must have received the Thursday item, and, from clue 1, the free gift was delivered on Friday to the Stamps. Now, by elimination, the Posts must have received their item on Saturday. We now know the Stamps must live at either number 7 or number 14, so, from clue 5, the Posts cannot live at either of those numbers. We know their house is not 21 or 35, so it must be 28. From clue 1, the Cards, who must have received news of a competition win on Thursday, must live at number 14, leaving the Stamps at number 7.

7, Stamp, free gift, Friday.
14, Card, competition win, Thursday.
21, Mailer, postcard from Australia, Monday.
28, Post, letter from daughter, Saturday.
35, Letterman, job offer, Tuesday.

42   Undercover

Ray Tubbs is in Seattle (clue 1), the agent in Boston is working on the smuggling case (clue 2), and the agent in New York is posing as a barman (clue 3), so Toby Wiggum, who isn't in Boston and is posing as a security guard (clue 4), must be in Dallas. From clue 5, he isn't investigating the kidnapping, which is Gus Hooker's case, or the bank robbery, so he must be working on the fraud case. The agent working on the Boston smuggling case isn't posing as a street entertainer (clue 2), and we know that in New York an agent is posing as a barman, so the man in Boston must be posing as a homeless man. We now know that Gus Hooker isn't in Boston, Dallas, or Seattle, so he must be in New York and is therefore posing as a barman. By elimination, it must be Bart Cagney who's working on the Boston smuggling case, posing as a homeless man, and Ray Tubbs, in Seattle, must be working on the bank robbery, and, also by elimination, must be posing as a street entertainer.

Bart Cagney, Boston, smuggling, homeless man.
Gus Hooker, New York, kidnapping, barman.
Ray Tubbs, Seattle, bank robbery, street entertainer.
Toby Wiggum, Dallas, fraud, security guard.

43   Schloss Furchtbar

Raven Tower was built by Gregor the Red (clue 1), Tibald the Devil built the eastern tower (clue 5), while Beacon Tower was in the west corner, but not built by Karl the Slayer (clue 2), so must have been built by Clovis the Fox. Dark Tower is next clockwise from Watch Tower (clue 4) and so cannot be north. The south tower contains a stuffed dog (clue 3). We know Raven Tower cannot be east, as it wasn't built by Tibald the Devil,

or west, but also is opposite the tower containing the statue (clue 1) and so cannot be north. Watch Tower is therefore north, Dark Tower east, and Raven Tower south. The statue is situated in Watch Tower, which was built by Karl the Slayer. The armor is not in the east tower (clue 5), so it must be in the west, leaving the battleaxe in the east.

East, Dark Tower, Tibald the Devil, battleaxe.
North, Watch Tower, Karl the Slayer, statue.
South, Raven Tower, Gregor the Red, dog.
West, Beacon Tower, Clovis the Fox, armor.

44   At the Pick and Shovel

Fifa La France was a dancer (clue 7); the midwife who had become a juggler also adopted a three-word name (clue 1), which, as the ship's cook became Gold Dust Gertie (clue 6), must have been Dixie Dinah Dunbar. So she wasn't originally Effie Crabbe (clue 3), Myfanwy Griffith, who became Ruby Redd (clue 4), or Agatha Ramsbottom, who was a barmaid (clue 2); nor was she Olga Danova, who had been a miner's wife (clue 5), so she must have been Hedwig Schwarz. Olga Danova's name or original occupation rule out three adopted names, nor did she become Little Lulu (clue 5), so she must have become Fifi La France, the dancer. Myfanwy Griffith was not the laundress (clue 4), and, since she became Ruby Redd, she can't have been the ship's cook, so she must have been a fishwife. Her official job wasn't as a singer (clue 4), and we know Agatha Ramsbottom became the barmaid, so Myfanwy Griffith, alias Ruby Redd, must have been a blackjack dealer. Finally, from clue 5, the former ship's cook can't have been Agatha Ramsbottom, so must have been Effie Crabbe, leaving Agatha Ramsbottom as the ex-laundress. By elimination, she must have become Little Lulu and Effie Crabbe, alias Gold Dust Gertie, must have been the singer.

Agatha Ramsbottom, laundress, Little Lulu, barmaid.
Effie Crabbe, ship's cook, Gold Dust Gertie, singer.
Hedwig Schwartz, midwife, Dixie Dinah Dunbar, juggler.
Myfanwy Griffith, fishwife, Ruby Redd, blackjack dealer.
Olga Danova, miner's wife, Fifi La France, dancer.

45   Jane Blonde—Licensed to Thrill

Allura appears in the fifth film, *From Prussia with Gloves* (clue 3), and Boris Fliptizlid is the villain in the fourth, *Live and Let Diet* (clue 5). The film featuring Glamora Spoddie and Viktor Krakpott cannot be the first, *No, Doctor!* (clue 1), and, since the second film, *Only for Your Ears*, is not set in the mountain aerie (clue 1), Glamora and Viktor cannot be in the third film, *You Only Live Thrice* (clue 1), and must be in *Only for Your Ears*. Therefore, from clue 1, the mountain aerie must be the setting for *No, Doctor!*, the first film. We now know the film depicting Seductra on a Pacific island (clue 2), is not *From Prussia with Gloves*, *Only for Your Ears*, or *No, Doctor!*; nor is it *Live and Let Diet* (clue 2), so it must be *You Only Live Thrice*. We have matched four films with either a villain or a setting, so Ernst Frootkake, in his desert hideaway (clue 4), must appear in *From Prussia with Gloves* with Allura. Clue 3 tells us Vladimir Nuttkase is not the villain in the first film, *No, Doctor!*, so, by elimination, he must appear in *You Only Live Thrice*. Therefore, from clue 3, it must be *Only for Your Ears* that is set in the underwater city, and Prittie Thynge must be in *No, Doctor!* By elimination, her employer must be Julius Madman. Also by elimination, Minnie Skurt must be in *Live and Let Diet*, and Boris's headquarters in that film must be an English country estate.

1 *No, Doctor!*, Julius Madman, Prittie Thynge, mountain aerie.

2 *Only for Your Ears*, Viktor Krakpott, Glamora Spoddie, underwater city.

3 *You Only Live Thrice*, Vladimir Nuttkase, Seductra, Pacific island.

4 *Live and Let Diet*, Boris Fliptizlid, Minnie Skurt, English estate.

5 *From Prussia with Gloves*, Ernst Frootkake, Allura, desert hideaway.

46 East Coast–West Coast

Bill is the only New Yorker on the upper level (clue 1), so two of the three New Yorkers in the band (intro) must be on the lower level. Therefore Newt and Pike, who are Californians standing side by side (clue 2), must be on the upper level, and Newt must be either figure 4 or figure 6, with Pike as either figure 5 or figure 7. But figure 7 is Magee (clue 6), so Pike must be figure 5 and Newt figure 4. From clue 5, Maxim and Baird must be figures 1 and 6, which means that Gary Bolt (clue 4) can't be any of the musicians on the upper level. So he and Joe are both on the lower level (clue 4). We already know that there are two New Yorkers on the lower level. They are not in adjacent positions (clue 7), so Joe from California

(clue 4) can't be figure 3. Therefore, from clue 4, Gary Bolt is figure 3, and Joe is either figure 1 or figure 2. The other musician on the lower level must be from New York, so he must be Hardy (clue 3). Also from clue 3, Joe must be Garth. We know that figure 1 is either Maxim or Baird, so Joe Garth must be figure 2, leaving Hardy as figure 1. As a New Yorker, Hardy can't be Baird (clue 5), so must be Maxim, and Baird must be figure 6. The remaining figures on the upper level are Bill, Saul, and Sonny. Bill and Saul are not standing next to each other (clue 1), so Sonny can't be Pike, figure 5; clue 6 rules him out as figure 7, so Sonny must be figure 6, Baird. Bill can't be Pike, since they're not from the same coast (clues 1 and 2), so figure 5 must be Saul Pike, and figure 7 must be Bill Magee. By elimination, figure 4, Newt, must be surnamed Alden.

1, Hardy Maxim.
2, Joe Garth.
3, Gary Bolt.
4, Newt Alden.
5, Saul Pike.
6, Sonny Baird.
7, Bill Magee.

47 Lawyers

Mr. McEavelly's client arrived at 10:40AM (clue 3), and Ms. Goldbrick's client was Mrs. Crane (clue 2); Miss Thomas, who arrived at 10:04AM, wasn't there to see Ms. Diddler (clue 7), nor can she have been the client of Mr. Janus of Personal Injury (clue 1), so she must have come to see Mr. Pecksniff. Mr. Janus's client wasn't Ms. Jarvis (clue 1), and we know he or she wasn't Miss Thomas or Mrs. Crane; Mr. Richards saw someone from Matrimonial (clue 5), not Personal Injury, so Mr. Janus's client must have been Mr. Mitchell. We now know that Mrs. Crane didn't arrive to see Ms. Goldbrick at 10:04AM or 10:40AM, so it must have been an odd number of minutes after 10. Therefore the person visiting Conveyancing can't have arrived at 10:49 (clue 2), and nor did the client visiting Wills (clue 4); the Criminal client arrived at 10:27AM (clue 6), so, as Mr. Mitchell can't have arrived to see Mr. Janus at 10:49AM (clue 1), by elimination that must have been the arrival time of the client for Matrimonial, Mr. Richards. The client's name or time rule out four lawyers, so the one from Matrimonial must have been Ms. Diddler. Also by elimination, Mr. McEavelly's client must have been Ms. Jarvis. So, from clue 1, Mr. Mitchell, who visited Mr. Janus of Personal Injury, who can't, from the department involved, have arrived at 10:27AM, must have arrived at 10:11AM. The client visiting Wills wasn't Ms. Jarvis (clue 4), so must have been Miss Thomas, who visited Mr. Pecksniff, leaving the visitor for Conveyancing as Ms. Jarvis, who arrived to see Mr. McEavelly at 10:40AM.

10:04AM, Miss Thomas, Mr. Pecksniff, Wills.
10:11AM, Mr. Mitchell, Mr. Janus, Personal Injury.
10:27AM, Mrs. Crane, Ms. Goldbrick, Criminal.
10:40AM, Ms. Jarvis, Mr. McEavelly, Conveyancing.
10:49AM, Mr. Richards, Ms. Diddler, Matrimonial.

48 Battleships

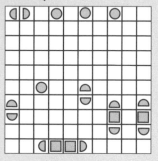

49 *Pioneer* to El Dorado

Lander 2 was carrying personnel shelters (clue 4), and the lander carrying food/medical equipment landed at Pencil Point (clue 3). The lander carrying food/laboratory equipment can't have been Lander 4 or Lander 5 (clue 1), so Lander 4, which came down at Mount Silva, which wasn't carrying transport/farming equipment (clue 5), must have been carrying the labs/storage shelters. Therefore, from clue 2, the lander that came down on Onion Island must have been Lander 2, with the personnel shelters. The lander carrying food/lab equipment didn't land on the Duroc Plain (clue 1), so the one carrying transport/farming equipment must have done so, and the one with the food/lab equipment must have come down near Lake Butterfly, and thus suffered depressurization (clue 6). It was Lander 3 whose cargo shifted (clue 7). We know that the lander with the food/lab equipment that depressurized wasn't Lander 2 or Lander 3, and clue 1 rules it out as Lander 4 or Lander 5, so it must have

been Lander 1. Lander 5 can't have suffered engine failure (clue 1) or a lightning strike (clue 6), so it must have had a computer failure. So, from clue 6, the lightning must have struck Lander 4, carrying labs/storage shelters, and brought it down at Mount Silva. Now, by elimination, the engine failure must have affected Lander 2, carrying the personnel shelters, which came down on Onion Island, so, from clue 1, the lander carrying the transport/farming equipment that came down on Duroc Plain must have been Lander 3, whose cargo shifted. This leaves Lander 5, whose computer failed, as the one carrying food/medical equipment that came down at Pencil Point.

Lander 1, food/laboratory equipment, depressurization, Lake Butterfly.
Lander 2, personal shelters, engine failure, Onion Island.
Lander 3, transport/farming equipment, cargo shift, Duroc Plain.
Lander 4, laboratories/storage shelters, lightning strike, Mount Silva.
Lander 5, food/medical equipment, computer error, Pencil Point.

50 Best-Laid Plans

Betty planned to buy a bikini at the third shop (clue 3). The shop where she planned to buy the jeans, where they had a power cut, couldn't have been visited first or second (clue 2), so must have been the fourth, and, from clue 2, she must have planned to get her T-shirts at the second shop, which was sold out (clue 4). By elimination, she must have meant to buy shoes at the first shop. Star Styles, which was closed because of a fire alarm (clue 1), wasn't where Betty planned to get her bikini (clue 3), so she must have meant to get that from the shop where she couldn't make her purchase because of long lines, and Star Styles must have been the first shop, where she meant to get the shoes. Her planned purchase from Megamart wasn't the T-shirts (clue 2) or the bikini (clue 3), so must have been the jeans, and Megamart was therefore the fourth shop and had a power cut. The second shop, where she meant to buy the T-shirts, wasn't Dean's (clue 4), so must have been Thriplow's, leaving Dean's as the third shop visited, where she meant to buy the bikini.

First, Star Styles, shoes, fire alarm.
Second, Thriplow's, T-shirts, sold out.
Third, Dean's, bikini, long lines.
Fourth, Megamart, jeans, power cut.

51 Author Tour

Fifty books were sold on Wednesday (clue 4) and the Monday bookshop didn't have an "and" in its name (clue 1), so the Turner and Page's bookshop, where 70 books were signed earlier in the week than the Thursday event in Penn (clue 3), must have been on Tuesday. It was not in Penn or Letterston, where 135 book were sold (clue 5), nor was it in H W Jones's in Wordsley (clue 6), or Bookham (clue 1), so Turner and Page's bookshop must be in Reading. In Letterston 135 books were sold and autographed, but not on Monday (clue 1), so it must have been Friday. Therefore Frontiers must have been the bookshop where 50 copies were sold on Wednesday (clue 2). It is not in Wordsley, where H W Jones's shop is located, so it must be Bookham. By elimination, Jones's bookshop must have been the one in Wordsley visited on Monday. We now know that Chapter and Verse must have been visited on Thursday and Searocks on Friday (clue 1). Since H W Jones in Wordsley sold fewer books than Chapter and Verse (clue 1), the former quantity must have been 100 and the latter 120.

Monday, H W Jones, Wordsley, 100.
Tuesday, Turner and Page, Reading, 70.
Wednesday, Frontiers, Bookham, 50.
Thursday, Chapter and Verse, Penn, 120.
Friday, Searocks, Letterston, 135.

52 Knights Non-Errant

Sir Timid was off duty for 10 months (clue 3). Sir Poltroon was not the knight with hippophobia, who was off for 4 months (clues 1 and 2), and the same two clues rule him out for 6 months. Since he was sent for one of Merlin's magic spells (clue 2), he was not out of action for 12 months, the length of time given for the exercise regime (clue 4), so, by elimination, he must have been non-errant for 8 months, and the 6-month absence from duty was therefore caused by metal allergy (clue 2). We now know Sir Poltroon's problem was not hippophobia or metal allergy, and his treatment rules him out as the knight with a fear of forests, who was given psychotherapy (clue 6), and it was Sir Spyneless who developed panic attacks (clue 7), so Sir Poltroon must have suffered from vertigo. We have matched four problems with either a length of time or a treatment, so, by elimination, the 12-month exercise regime must have been prescribed for the panic attacks of Sir Spyneless, leaving Sir Timid's problem as the fear of forests, and his treatment therefore as psychotherapy. The course of tablets was not given for the 4-month bout of hippophobia, so liniment must have been the recommended treatment. Therefore the sufferer was not Sir Coward (clue 5), and must have been Sir Sorely, leaving Sir Coward suffering metal allergy for 6 months, and his treatment, by elimination, as the course of tablets.

Sir Coward de Custarde, metal allergy, 6 months, course of tablets.
Sir Poltroon à Ghaste, vertigo, 8 months, magic spell.
Sir Sorely à Frayde, hippophobia, 4 months, liniment.
Sir Spyneless de Feete, panic attacks, 12 months, exercise regime.
Sir Timid de Shayke, fear of forests, 10 months, psychotherapy.

53 Logi-5

B	D	E	C	A
A	E	C	B	D
E	C	D	A	B
C	B	A	D	E
D	A	B	E	C

54 ABC

C		A	B	
	B		C	A
B	A			C
		C	A	B
A	C	B		

55 Coordinated Arrests

Sgt. McBain made the arrest at the airport (clue 7) and Sgt. Christie is based in Los Angeles, which is not the location of the club or the hotel (clue 6), so the man arrested in the club, who was not arrested by an FBI agent (clue 2), must have been arrested by Lt. Doyle, and was therefore Fritz Kaiman (clue 4). We know that the club wasn't in Los Angeles, nor was it in Boston (clue 4); Benny Freed was arrested in Chicago (clue 5), and Graceland was the arrest location in Memphis (clue 3), so Fritz Kaiman must have been arrested in New York. We know that the man arrested in Memphis, in Graceland, wasn't Fritz Kaiman or Benny Freed, nor was he Lyle de Blank (clue 3) or Nick Cecconi, who was arrested in the theater (clue 1), so he must have been Scott Parker. The arresting officer wasn't Agent Queen (clue 2), so must have been Agent Gardner. Sgt. Christie didn't make her arrest at the hotel (clue 6), so at the theater, and her prisoner was therefore Nick Cecconi. Since Lyle de Blank wasn't arrested by an FBI agent (clue 2), he must have been Sgt. McBain's prisoner. By elimination, the city at whose airport Sgt. McBain made his arrest must have been Boston; also by elimination, Benny Freed's arrest in Chicago must have been carried out by Agent Queen, and must have taken place in the hotel.

Benny Freed, Agent Queen, Chicago, hotel.
Fritz Kaiman, Lt. Doyle, New York, club.
Lyle de Blank, Sgt. McBain, Boston, airport.
Nick Cecconi, Sgt. Christie, Los Angeles, theater.
Scott Parker, Agent Gardner, Memphis, Grace-land.

56 Something Special

The first name of the woman celebrating her 40th birthday who received the beauty spa weekend must contain 3 or 4 letters (clue 5): Liz was given car racing lessons (clue 1), so the 40th birthday must have been that of Alma, whose surname is Freeman (clue 6). Mrs. Martin, who had passed her driving test, isn't Gillian or Liz (clue 4), nor Nancy, who was celebrating her silver anniversary (clue 1): We know she isn't Alma, so she must be Sarah. Gillian wasn't celebrating her children leaving home (clue 3), so must have been celebrating her tin anniversary, and it must have been Liz who was celebrating her children leaving home. Gillian wasn't given a flying lesson (clue 3) or a gardening course (clue 2), so must have received the balloon flight, and is therefore Mrs. Rowley (clue 6). From clue 5, Mrs. O'Connor must have a five-letter name, so she must be Nancy, leaving Liz as Mrs. Barton. Finally, Sarah Martin didn't get the gardening course (clue 2), so must have been given a flying lesson for finally passing her driving test, and Nancy O'Connor must have received the gardening course.

Alma Freeman, 40th birthday, beauty spa weekend.
Gillian Rowley, tin anniversary, balloon flight.
Liz Barton, children left home, car racing lessons.
Nancy O'Connor, silver anniversary, gardening course.
Sarah Martin, passing driving test, flying lesson.

57 Into the Lost Valley

Figure C is the biologist (clue 3), and figure D is Jake (clue 4), so, from clue 1, Hank, the guide, must be figure B and Jensen must be figure A. We know that Lambros, the paleontologist (clue 2), isn't figure A, B, or C, so he must be figure D, Jake. Thus, by elimination, figure A, Jensen, must be the zoologist. Randy isn't figure C, the biologist (clue 3), so he must be figure A, the zoologist, leaving the biologist as Pete. His surname isn't McCreesh (clue 3), so it must be Kevakian, leaving McCreesh as Hank the guide, figure B.

A, Randy Jensen, zoologist.
B, Hank McCreesh, guide.
C, Pete Kevakian, biologist.
D, Jake Lambros, paleontologist.

58 Battleships

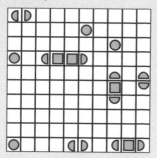

59 Cloak and Dagger

Jose offended in March (clue 2). The agent who offended in June in Hungary was not Roberto (clue 5), while Pedro was posted to China (clue 6). Since the secrets were sold in August (clue 7), clue 1 rules out Juan as the June offender, so it must have been Felipe who slipped up in that month by defecting (clue 3). The marriage to a native did not take place in January (clue 7), and we have ruled out that month for the sale of secrets and the defection. Clue 1 rules out the insulting of El Presidente in Mexico as the first offense, so the funds must have been embezzled in January. Therefore, from clue 4, Jose was in Azerbaijan in March. We now know the insulting of El Presidente by his man in Mexico did not happen in January, March, June, or August, so it must have taken place in November, and, from clue 1, Juan must have offended in August by selling secrets. By elimination, this must have been in France.

Also by elimination, Pedro must have been in China in January, so he must have embezzled the funds, the man who uttered the November insults must have been Roberto, and Jose must have married a girl from Azerbaijan in March.

January, Pedro, China, embezzled funds.
March, Jose, Azerbaijan, married native.
June, Felipe, Hungary, defected.
August, Juan, France, sold secrets.
November, Roberto, Mexico, insulted El Presidente.

60 Five Counties Coffee Shop

Sean Tyrrel was from Granite County (clue 4) and Frank Grosz's car was white/orange (clue 1), so the King's County cop, who was also male and whose car was black/white (clue 5), must have been Nelson Pike. We know that Candy de Lint wasn't from Granite County or King's County, nor was she from Buzzard County (clue 2), and, as her uniform was dark blue (clue 2), she can't have been the Linder County cop, whose uniform was tan (clue 3), so she must have been from Pineridge County. Therefore her car wasn't dark blue/pale blue (clue 6), so, as the black/pale blue car was driven by the cop in the dark green uniform (clue 4), Candy de Lint's must have been blue/white. Since Sean Tyrrel from Granite County didn't drive the black/pale blue car (clue 4), his must have been dark blue/pale blue, and, by elimination, the black/pale blue car must have been Julie Moncada's, and her uniform was therefore dark green. So she can't have been the Linder County officer in the tan uniform, and must have been from Buzzard County, and the Linder County cop in tan must have been Frank Grosz, who had the white/orange car. Finally, Nelson Pike's uniform wasn't gray (clue 1), so it must have been light blue, leaving the gray uniform worn by Sean Tyrrel of Granite County, whose car was dark blue/pale blue.

Candy de Lint, Pineridge County, dark blue, blue/white.
Frank Grosz, Linder County, tan, white/orange.
Julie Moncada, Buzzard County, dark green, black/pale blue.
Nelson Pike, King's County, light blue, black/white.
Sean Tyrrel, Granite County, gray, dark blue/pale blue.

61 Travel Report

Discovery is diverting to Trantor (clue 1) and *Luna* was going to Helliconia (clue 4), so the ship originally bound for Amtor that is diverting to Jem, which isn't *Phoenix* (clue 2), must be the *Falcon*. *Luna* isn't the ship diverted to Belzagor because of an engine fault (clue 4), so it must be diverting to Poloda, and, by elimination, the ship going to Belzagor must be *Phoenix*. From its problem, it can't be the ship that set out for Pyrrus, which has been diverted because of a security alert (clue 3), and we've identified the ships that set out for Amtor and Helliconia, so *Phoenix* must have meant to go to Solaris. By elimination, the ship diverted from Pyrrus must be *Discovery*, now headed for Trantor. *Falcon*, diverted from Amtor to Jem, isn't affected by the controllers' strike (clue 2), so must have problems due to crew shortage, and the controllers' strike must be the reason *Luna*'s diverting from Helliconia to Poloda.

Discovery, Pyrrus, Trantor, security alert.
Falcon, Amtor, Jem, crew shortages.
Luna, Helliconia, Poloda, controllers' strike.
Phoenix, Solaris, Belzagor, engine fault.

62 Fish Tale

Fish 2 is the long-tail (clue 6), so, from clue 5, the Hudson Bay fish, which is next to the Nile spotted catfish, can't be fish 1, N'Chips (clue 1); nor can the European (clue 3) or the Australian (clue 8), while the Mexican is fish 4 (clue 4) and the Chinese fish is called Finger (clue 7), so, by elimination, fish 1, N'Chips, must be the Nile spotted catfish. Thus, from clue 5, the Hudson Bay catfish must be the long-tail, fish 2. We now know that the European catfish isn't fish 1, 2, or 4, nor can it be fish 6 (clue 3), so it must be either fish 3 or fish 5. So the red catfish, which isn't fish 6 (clue 3), and which we know isn't fish 2, must be fish 4, the Mexican (clue 3). It isn't called Fillet (clue 3) or Pie (clue 4); we know it isn't N'Chips or Finger, and Cake is the pop-eyed catfish (clue 2), so, by elimination, fish 4, the Mexican red, must be called Stick. The Australian catfish is immediately right of the whistling one (clue 8), which rules out fish 1, 2, 3, 4, and 5, so the Australian must be fish 6 and the whistling catfish fish 5 (clue 8). So the European isn't fish 6 (clue 3) and must be fish 3, which places the Chinese catfish, by elimination, as fish 5, the whistling catfish, and, from clue 3, Fillet must be fish 2, the Hudson Bay long-tail. The Australian fish 6 can't be Cake, the pop-eyed catfish (clue 2), so Cake must be fish 3, the European, leaving the Australian fish 6 as the blue-fin,

which must by elimination be called Pie.
1, N'Chips, Nile spotted.
2, Fillet, Hudson Bay long-tail.
3, Cake, European pop-eyed.
4, Stick, Mexican red.
5, Finger, Chinese whistling.
6, Pie, Australian blue-fin.

63 Down These Mean Streets

The Long Adieu will feature Matt Jonson (clue 2), and *The High Balcony* is due in March (clue 6), so the July book featuring Daisy Chaucer, which won't be *The Lady in the Lane* (clue 5) or *Farewell, My Friend* (clue 7), must be going to be *The Big Brother*, to be published under the pen name Thomas Spicer (clue 1). Now, from clue 2, *The Long Adieu*, featuring Matt Jonson, can't be due in May or November; we know the title of the March book and the detective for the July one, so *The Long Adieu* must be due in September. Therefore the pen name to be used in November must be Glen Harper (clue 2). We now know the titles due in three months, so the November book, which isn't *Farewell, My Friend* (clue 7), it must be *The Lady in the Lane*, and *Farewell, My Friend* must be due in May, and therefore will appear as by Elliot Fletcher (clue 3). Its detective won't be Barney Austen (clue 3) or Liz Milton (clue 7), so it must be going to be Carl Dickens. We have now matched a detective or pen name to four months, so the book featuring Liz Milton and under the pen name Lewis Mariner (clue 4), must be the one due in March, *The High Balcony*. By elimination, Barney Austen will be the detective in November's *The Lady in the Lane*, and September's *The Long Adieu*, featuring Matt Jonson, will appear as by Ross Plumber.

March, *The High Balcony*, Liz Milton, Lewis Mariner.
May, *Farewell, My Friend*, Carl Dickens, Elliot Fletcher.
July, *The Big Brother*, Daisy Chaucer, Thomas Spicer.
September, *The Long Adieu*, Matt Jonson, Ross Plumber.
November, *The Lady in the Lane*, Barney Austen, Glen Harper.

64 Battleships

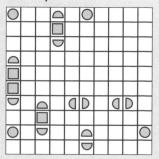

65 Sporting Writes

Since Frost is Bruce (clue 3), the judo star who has written an instruction book can't be Alan or Godfrey (clue 1), and Dennis's book is an autobiography (clue 5), so Bruce Frost must be the judo star who has written the instruction book. So, from clue 1, Coleman must be Dennis, author of the autobiography. Hughes, the golfer, didn't write the science-fiction novel (clue 2), so his book must have been a whodunnit, and, by elimination, Marsden must have written the science fiction. Hughes isn't Godfrey (clue 4), so he must be Alan, leaving Godfrey as Marsden. Dennis Coleman's sport isn't rowing (clue 5), so must be football, leaving rowing as Godfrey Marsden's sport.

Alan Hughes, golf, whodunnit.
Bruce Frost, judo, instruction book.
Dennis Coleman, football, autobiography.
Godfrey Marsden, rowing, science fiction.

66 The Bootique

Mrs. Pace tried on six pairs (clue 6), and the 2 o'clock customer tried on seven (clue 7). Since Jane came in at 11:15 (clue 4), clues 2 and 5 rule out the number of pairs tried on by the 12:15 customer named March as three or five, so, by elimination, she must have tried on four, and is therefore Anna (clue 3). Clue 1 now rules out Marie for a 10 o'clock or 2 'clock arrival, and we know she did not come in at 11:15 or 12:15, so, by elimination, she must have been the 3:45 customer. So, from clue 1, Ms. Stride was the 2 o'clock arrival who tried on seven pairs. So, from clue 1, Marie must have tried on six after coming in at 3:45, and is therefore Mrs. Pace. Clue 6 now tells us Paula made the 2 o'clock visit, and is Ms. Stride. By elimination, Louise Walker must have arrived at 10 o'clock, and Jane's surname must be Foot. From clue 2, the latter must have tried on five pairs, leaving three as the number tried by Louise.

10:00, Louise Walker, 3 pairs.
11:15, Jane Foot, 5 pairs.
12:15, Anna March, 4 pairs.
2:00, Paula Stride, 7 pairs.
3:45, Marie Pace, 6 pairs.

67   The Last Deal

Dan Flint sat in seat A (clue 2). Billy Dayton, the outlaw (intro), wasn't in seat B, since he held the hand ranking immediately above player B's (clue 1). Nor was the man in seat B Sam Troy, who had the flush (3), because it was the gambler, not the outlaw, who held the four kings, the hand ranked next above the flush (clue 4). Therefore seat B must have been Jake Lincoln's. The gambler can't have been Jake Lincoln (clues 1 and 4) or Sam Troy (clues 3 and 4), so he must have been Dan Flint. Sam Troy wasn't the cowhand (clue 3), so must have been the store keeper, leaving Jake Lincoln as the cowhand. So, from clue 1, his hand must have been three of a kind, and Billy Dayton the outlaw must have held the straight. Finally, from clue 5, the man in seat D can't have been Sam Troy, so must have been Billy Dayton, leaving Sam Troy, the store keeper, with the flush, in seat C.

A, Dan Flint, gambler, four of a kind.
B, Jake Lincoln, cowhand, three of a kind.
C, Sam Troy, store keeper, flush.
D, Billy Dayton, outlaw, straight.

68   Double O . . . No!

Jason has a fear of guns (clue 1) and the candidate with a fear of blood was seen on Thursday (clue 2), so Jonah's fear, identified by the panel on Friday (clue 4), which wasn't heights (clue 1) or speed (clue 6), must be women, and he must be Mr. Link (clue 5). The Monday candidate, Mr. Glooe (clue 4), doesn't have a fear of speed (clue 6) nor was that candidate Jason with his fear of guns (clue 1), so he must have demonstrated a fear of heights. His first name isn't Jesse (clue

6) and Jules is Gumm (clue 3), so it must have been Jerry. Jesse isn't Mr. Paiste (clue 6), so he must be Stique, leaving Jason as Mr. Paiste. Jesse Stique isn't afraid of speed (clue 6), so he must be afraid of blood and have been seen on Thursday. So, from clue 6, the candidate with a fear of speed must have been the one interviewed on Wednesday who, by elimination, must have been Jules Gumm, leaving Jason Paiste as the Tuesday candidate.

Monday, Jerry Glooe, heights.
Tuesday, Jason Paiste, guns.
Wednesday, Jules Gumm, speed.
Thursday, Jesse Stique, blood.
Friday, Jonah Link, women.

69   Battleships

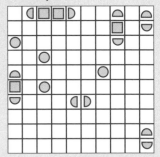

70   *Wild West Women*

Figure 1 is Leah (clue 2). Figure 4 can't be Agatha (clue 4) or Susannah (clue 5), so must be Dorothy Benton (clue 1). Figure 2 isn't Iron Annie Stockton (clue 3), and we know her surname isn't Benton; clue 5 rules out McLayne, who is immediately right of Susannah, so figure 2 must be Delaney. Now, from clue 5, Susannah can't be figure 3, so she must be Delaney, figure 2, and figure 3 must be Agatha. So Dorothy Benton must be Loco Liz (clue 4), and, from clue 5, Agatha must be McLayne, leaving Leah as Stockton, nicknamed Iron Annie. Agatha McLayne isn't nicknamed Texas Rose (clue 5), so her nickname must be Coyote Kate, leaving Texas Rose as Susannah Delaney, figure 2.

1, Leah Stockton, Iron Annie.
2, Susannah Delaney, Texas Rose.
3, Agatha McLayne, Coyote Kate.
4, Dorothy Benton, Loco Liz.

71 Down Mexico Way

On the day that Lisa did aqua-aerobics, Vicky went windsurfing (clue 1), and on Wednesday Lisa played water polo (clue 5), so Thursday, when Vicky went swimming and Lisa didn't take salsa lessons (clue 5) or play tennis (clue 4), must have been the day Lisa played beach volleyball and the two girls had chili con carne for lunch (clue 3). The beef enchiladas weren't eaten on Monday or Tuesday (clue 4), and we know the Thursday menu; since Vicky went swimming on Thursday the beef enchiladas can't have been eaten on Friday (clue 4), so must have been lunch on Wednesday, when Lisa played water polo. Therefore Lisa must have played tennis on Monday and Vicky must have done yoga on Tuesday (clue 4). By elimination, on Tuesday Lisa must have taken salsa lessons, and it must have been on Friday that Lisa did aqua-aerobics and Vicky went windsurfing. On Monday, when Lisa played tennis, Vicky didn't do archery (clue 6), so she must have gone pony-riding before they had their lunch of cheeseburgers (clue 6). By elimination, Vicky must have done her archery on Wednesday. Finally, Tuesday's lunch wasn't tacos (clue 2), so the girls must have had tacos on Friday, leaving Tuesday's lunch as burritos.

Monday, tennis, pony-riding, cheeseburgers.
Tuesday, salsa lessons, yoga, burritos.
Wednesday, water polo, archery, beef enchiladas.
Thursday, beach volleyball, swimming, chili con carne.
Friday, aqua-aerobics, windsurfing, tacos.

72 Relate

The first couple, seen at 10AM, have been married for 8 years (clue 5), so the woman in question is not Penny, married for 5 (clue 6), nor can she be Chloe (clue 1), or Tessa (clue 4), while Sarah's appointment was at 11AM (clue 2), so, by elimination, Naomi must have been the wife in the first couple Jenny advised. So, from clue 3, Don must be Sarah's husband, seen at 11AM. Naomi's husband, seen at 10AM, is not Keith (clue 5), or Fred, who has been married 7 years (clue 7), and, since we know the wife seen at 11AM was Sarah, clue 4 rules out the 10AM appointment for Martin. We know Naomi is not married to Don, so her husband must be Sandy. So, from clue 1, Chloe must have been married 10 years. We have now matched four women with a husband or a length of marriage, so, by elimination, Fred's

wife of 7 years must be Tessa. Also by elimination, Don and Sarah must have been married for just 2 years. From clue 4, Fred and Tessa must have been seen at either 3PM or 4PM, but clue 7 rules out 4PM, so they must have had the 3 o'clock appointment. So Martin and his wife must have been seen at 2 o'clock (clue 4). That clue also tells us they have been married more than 7 years, but we have named the pair married for 8, so they must have been together 10, and Martin's wife is therefore Chloe. By elimination, Penny's husband must be Keith, and their appointment must have been at 4PM.

10AM, Sandy and Naomi, 8 years.
11AM, Don and Sarah, 2 years.
2PM, Martin and Chloe, 10 years.
3PM, Fred and Tessa, 7 years.
4PM, Keith and Penny, 5 years.

73 Table of Elements

From clue 6, O for Oxygen must be in one of squares C1, C2, D1, or D2. Since D4 contains Ca for Calcium (clue 2), clue 6 rules out D2 for the O. Nor, since a single letter occupies B1 (clue 7), can O be in D1 (clue 6), and, since both B1 and D1 contain single-letter symbols (clue 7), clue 1 rules out a single O for C1, so, by elimination, O for Oxygen must be in C2, and, from clue 6, Cu for Copper must be in A2, and I for Iodine in C4. Clue 1 now tells us that C1 and C3 must both contain two-letter symbols, therefore, from clue 4, so must B3. Clue 3 rules out columns 1 and 4 for Tungsten and Iron, and, with elements already placed, it also excludes column 2, so they must be in column 3. We have seen that B3 and C3 both contain two-letter symbols, so W for Tungsten, which cannot be in D3 (clue 3), must be in A3, and Fe for Iron therefore in B3. S for Sulphur, which is in row D (clue 5), is now the last in alphabetical order of the single-letter symbols to be placed, so, from clue 7, it cannot be in D1. If it were in D2, D1 and D2 would both contain single-letter symbols, so, from clue 1, D3 and D4 would both contain two-letter ones. But we already know B3 and C3 both contain two letters, so, again from clue 1, D3 cannot. Therefore, S for Sulphur, which we know is not in D4, must be in D3. We have placed at least one two-letter symbol in columns 2, 3, and 4, so, from clues 1 and 8, Sn and Au must be in column 1. We know single letters are in B1 and D1, so, from clue 8, Sn for Tin must be in A1, and Au for Gold in C1. We know square C3 is not in alignment with N for Nitrogen in any direction, so neither Silver nor Helium can be there (clue 9). Row A already has two two-letter symbols, as has column 1, so clue 9 also rules out A4 and B2 for the Ag symbol, as well as B1, D1, and D2, so it must be in B4. We have seen that Helium cannot be in C3, and we know it is not in D1 (clue 7). Clue 9 now rules it out for row B, so, by elimination, it must be in D2, and clue 9 places N for Nitrogen in B2. From clue 1, the missing symbol in C3 must be the remaining two-letter one, Hg for Mercury. Clue 7 finally reveals that H for Hydrogen must be in A4, with K for Potassium in B1 and C for Carbon in D1.

Sn	Cu	W	H
K	N	Fe	Ag
Au	O	Hg	I
C	He	S	Ca

74 Over and Over Again

As the film with the crooked cop came out in February (clue 7) and the one with the limousine crash in November (clue 1), from clue 4 *White Hawk* must have come out in July, the film with the private detective in April, and the one with the school bus crash in October. The film with the alien assassin wasn't released in July (clue 2), and we know it didn't come out in February or April, so it must have come out in October or November. But we know *Dangerous* wasn't released in July, so, from clue 2, the alien assassin must have wrecked the limousine in the November release, and *Dangerous* must have come out in October and featured the school bus crash. So this wasn't the film with the gangster (clue 5), and, by elimination, must have featured the bank robber, leaving the gangster as the character in *White Hawk*, the July release. Now, from clue 6, *Face of Death* must be the February release with the crooked cop, and *Nightside* must be the April release with the private detective, leaving the film with the alien assassin as *The Rescue*. From clue 3, it must be the gangster in *White Hawk* who crashes the fuel truck. Finally, from clue 7, the vehicle crashed by the crooked cop in *Face of Death*, which isn't a sports car, must be a pickup truck, leaving the sports car as the vehicle crashed by the private detective in *Nightside*.

Dangerous, October, bank robber, school bus.
Face of Death, February, crooked cop, pickup truck.
Nightside, April, private detective, sports car.
The Rescue, November, alien assassin, limousine.
White Hawk, July, gangster, fuel truck.

75 Battleships

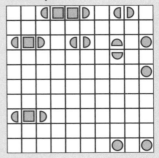

76 Travel Books

Honeymoon in is by a woman surnamed Reilly (clue 4), but not Pauline, whose book is *Visiting* (clue 1), so it must be by Alison, and is therefore about Brittany (clue 3). George Lang's book isn't *My Year in* (clue 5), so it must be *Backpacking in*, and *My Year in* must be Trevor's book. Nepal doesn't feature in Pauline's or Trevor's book (clue 1), so George Lang's book must be *Backpacking in Nepal*. Trevor's book isn't about Cuba (clue 3), so it must be *My Year in the Sahara*, and his surname is therefore Wilson (clue 2). Pauline's book must be *Visiting Cuba*, and her surname must be Carter.

Backpacking in Nepal, George Lang.
Honeymoon in Brittany, Alison Reilly.
My Year in the Sahara, Trevor Wilson.
Visiting Cuba, Pauline Carter.

77 Once Upon a Time . . .

Carrie, at number 1, is not being read to by her grandma, whose grandchild has the teddy bear (clue 4), nor can her sister be on duty there (clue 3), while the same clue tells us that the mother is reading at number 5, so it must be Carrie's father who is reading to her. Since she lives at number 1, clue 2 rules out number 3 for both Annette and Gareth, so William must live there. So, from clue 1, the panda must be Carrie's. Since the reader at number 5 is the mother, clue 5 rules out the monkey as William's toy, and we know his companion is not the panda. Annette owns the rabbit (clue 2), so William must have the teddy bear, and his grandma must be reading to him. By elimination, the monkey must belong to Gareth, so clue 3 places him at number 5, leaving Annette at number 7, and, from clue 3, her sister must be

reading her bedtime story.
1, Carrie, panda, father.
3, William, teddy bear, grandma.
5, Gareth, monkey, mother.
7, Annette, rabbit, sister.

78   Color Blind

The yellow square cannot have been on the first card presented (clue 1), while the second bore a star (clue 3), and the real color of the third card was blue (clue 6). Since the fourth was wrongly stated to be red (clue 5), clue 1 rules out the yellow square for the fifth card, so it must have been on the fourth, and was therefore stated to be red. So, from clue 1, the third item, though blue, was asserted to be green. We now know the actual black symbol was not wrongly claimed to be blue or red, and obviously Dan did not correctly identify it as black. Nor did he say it was blue (clue 2), so he must have thought it was yellow. Since the circle was claimed to be black (clue 4), it was not presented third, and we know it was not the second or fourth item. Nor can it have been the fifth (clue 7), so, by elimination, it must have been the first. So its actual color cannot have been black, blue, or yellow, and must have been red or green. So the triangle must have been claimed to be green or red (clue 7), but we know it was the square that was said to be red, so the triangle must have been wrongly identified as green, and was therefore presented third. From clue 7, the actual color of the circle was therefore green. By elimination, the fifth symbol must have been the crescent. Also by elimination, the red item must have been stated to be blue. This was not the crescent (clue 4), so the latter must have been black, and guessed to be yellow, leaving the star as the symbol really red, but asserted to be blue.
First, circle, green, black.
Second, star, red, blue.
Third, triangle, blue, green.
Fourth, square, yellow, red.
Fifth, crescent, black, yellow.

79   Logi-5

B	E	A	D	C
E	A	D	C	B
D	C	B	E	A
A	D	C	B	E
C	B	E	A	D

80   ABC

B	C	A		
	A		B	C
	B	C		A
C			A	B
A		B	C	

81   Celebrity Gallery

The picture in Sunday's paper must be one of 1, 2, or 3 (clue 2). Picture 1 appeared on Wednesday (clue 6), and clue 4 rules out Sunday for picture 3, so it must be number 2 that was seen by the readers of the Sunday paper. So, from clue 2, the entrepreneur is the subject of picture 4, which was in the *Clarion* (clue 7). From their titles, none of the *Daily Chat*, the *Morning Post,* or the *Evening Herald* can be the Sunday paper, while the *Planet* featured Sheila's work on Thursday (clue 1). The Graphic printed an odd-numbered photo (clue 3), and clue 7 rules out Sunday for the *Clarion*, so, by elimination, the Sunday photo must have been in the *Globe.* From clue 5, therefore, the opera singer is the subject of picture 7. Clue 1 rules out photos 6 and 7 for the *Planet*, and we know it did not print 1, 2, or 4. Since picture 5 was not printed on Saturday (clue 6), clue 1 also rules out picture 3 for the *Planet*, which must therefore have featured picture 5. So, from clue 1, picture 7, of the opera singer, appeared in Saturday's paper, and, from clue 6, the minor royal was seen on Friday. Clue 5 now tells us the *Evening Herald* printed Sheila's photo on Friday. So this was not picture 4, in the *Clarion*, and we know it was none of pictures 1, 2, 5, or 7. Nor was it photo 6 (clue 2), so it must have been number 3, and clue 4 tells us picture 5 was of the TV celebrity. The senator's photo is in the bottom row, and we have identified the subjects of photos 4, 5, and 7, so the senator's photo must be number 6, and clue 7 therefore tells us photo 4, in the *Clarion*, was not printed on Monday, so, by elimination, that must have been the Tuesday photo, and, from clue 7, the senator's picture 6 must have been seen on Monday. This cannot have been in the *Graphic* (clue 3), while the *Morning Post* had the pop star's picture (clue 8), so the Monday photo must have been in the *Daily Chat.* Now, the football player, who is not in photo 1 (clue 6), must be in picture 2 in Sunday's *Globe*, leaving the pop star in picture 1, so the Wednesday paper must have been the *Morning Post* (clue 8), leaving the *Graphic* as the paper which ran Sheila's picture of the opera singer on Saturday.

Sunday, 2, football player, *Globe*.
Monday, 6, senator, *Daily Chat*.
Tuesday, 4, entrepreneur, *Clarion*.
Wednesday, 1, pop star, *Morning Post*.
Thursday, 5, TV celebrity, *Planet*.
Friday, 3, minor royal, *Evening Herald*.
Saturday, 7, opera singer, *Graphic*.

82   Flight from Shayeia

The *Rostompa* is going to Qu'Korum (clue 3); the *Gizink* is going to the planet suffering a swamp-fever epidemic (clue 2), while Nik is wanted in New Hope (clue 1). As the *Lady Marie* isn't going to New Hope (clue 1), it must be the *Anraya*. The *Anraya* isn't carrying frozen meat, as Nik does not owe that captain money (clue 2); nor is it carrying emigrants as it is not going to Beilat (clue 4); nor is it carrying mining machinery (clue 4), so it must be carrying dried vegetables. The *Rostompa* is carrying foodstuff, so must be loaded with frozen meat and it is to this captain Nik owes the money. Thara is not the planet with the rebellious natives (clue 5), so instead is experiencing an epidemic of swamp-fever. The *Gizink* is therefore going to Thara and can only be carrying mining equipment, as the emigrants traveling to Beilat must be on the *Lady Marie*. Let's hope the rebellion is over before they arrive in their new home.

Anraya, New Hope, dried vegetables, wanted at destination.
Gizink, Thara, mining machinery, swamp-fever epidemic.
Lady Marie, Beilat, emigrants, native rebellion.
Rostompa, Qu'Korum, frozen meat, owes captain money.

83   Battleships

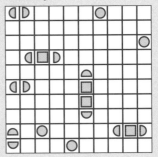

84   Drive-In

The Volkswagen is between the Chevrolet and Rocky Scott's car (clue 1). It isn't car C (clue 1), so must be either car B or car D, and either the Chevrolet or Rocky Scott's car is car A or car E, and the other is car C. The Chevrolet isn't car C (clue 4), which must thus be Rocky Scott's car, and the Chevrolet must be car A or car E. The Oldsmobile in which Jo-Anne Ince is seated isn't Gene Hayes's car (clue 3), Cliff Duvall's (clue 5), or Lyle Mizner's, which is the Ford (clue 6). Since the Oldsmobile is next but one to Cliff Duvall's car, which isn't car B (clue 5), it can't be car D, which is Jeff Kazan's (clue 2), so must be Rocky Scott's car C. Gene Hayes's car is next to the Oldsmobile (clue 3), but isn't car D (clue 2), so must be car B. Lyle Mizner's Ford and Cliff Duvall's car must each, by elimination, be either car A or car E, so the Buick, like the Volkswagen, must be either car B or car D. Lynn Koster is the girl in car E (clue 2), so the one in car A, who can't be Teri Silva (clue 5) or Mindy Lee, who is in the car next to Lyle Mizner's Ford (clue 6), which we know isn't car D, must be Erica Dell. Therefore Mindy Lee is in car B with Gene Hayes, and, by elimination, Teri Silva must be in car D with Jeff Kazan. We know that the Chevrolet isn't car A, so it must be car E, in which Lynn Koster is seated, and which, by elimination, must be Cliff Duvall's. So, from clue 1, the Volkswagen must be car D, containing Jeff Kazan and Teri Silva, and, by elimination, the Buick must be car B, containing Gene Hayes and Mindy Lee.

A, Ford, Lyle Mizner, Erica Dell.
B, Buick, Gene Hayes, Mindy Lee.
C, Oldsmobile, Rocky Scott, Jo-Anne Ince.
D, Volkswagen, Jeff Kazan, Teri Silva.
E, Chevrolet, Cliff Duvall, Lynn Koster.

85 Sales Men

Bob is after the suit (clue 2) and Matt has his eye on an item of furniture (clue 1), so the shoes, which are not the sale item sought by Keith (clue 3) or Ryan (clue 2), must be the target of Scott and they must be on offer at Barber and Groves (clue 1). The saving is not 50% (clue 3), 30% (clue 1), 60%, which is the leather suite (clue 6), or 25%, which is the offer on the item at Mitchells (clue 4), so the shoes must be 40% off. The golf clubs are not in the sale at Mitchells or at Lawton and Son (clue 4), nor is it Oakworld, where the desk is on offer (clue 5), so it must be S and L. The leather suite is 60% off, so the Mitchells item at 25% off is therefore the suit that Bob wants. By elimination, the leather suite must be in Lawton and Son's sale. It is not Matt's chosen buy (clue 1), so he must want the desk. Keith will not be hurrying to Lawton and Son's sale (clue 3), so it must be S and L, and he must be after the golf clubs, and as they are not in the sale at 50% off, the reduction must be 30%. By elimination, Lawton and Son must be offering the item wanted by Ryan, and Matt must want a new desk at 50% off.

Bob, Mitchells, suit, 25%.
Keith, S and L, golf clubs, 30%.
Matt, Oakworld, desk, 50%.
Ryan, Lawton and Son, leather suite, 60%.
Scott, Barber and Groves, shoes, 40%.

86 Let's Do Lunch

Marco is a waiter at Luciano's Restaurant (clue 3), so the waiter at The Stables who isn't Joel nor Brendan (clue 2) or Ashley, who is serving Helena and her companion (clue 4), must be Jason. Melissa and her friend are being served by Brendan (clue 3), so they are not lunching at Luciano's or The Stables, nor are they at The Riviera, where Gemma is lunching (clue 5), or Christoph's (clue 3), so it must be The Wisteria, and Melissa must be lunching with Jan (clue 6). Lynda and Grace are lunching together (clue 6), so Deborah, who is not lunching with Flora or Lorna (clue 1), must be with Gemma at The Riviera, where, by elimination, their attendant must be Joel. This leaves Helena lunching at Christoph's. Lorna is not at The Stables being served by Jason, nor at Luciano's (clue 1), so she must be with Helena at Christoph's. Flora and her friend are not lunching at The Stables (clue 2), so that pairing must be Lynda and Grace, and Flora must be with Kate, at Luciano's, being served by Marco.

Deborah and Gemma, The Riviera, Joel.
Helena and Lorna, Christoph's, Ashley.
Jan and Melissa, The Wisteria, Brendan.
Kate and Flora, Luciano's, Marco.
Lynda and Grace, The Stables, Jason.

87 The Haunted *Hammerhead*

Holly Jurado isn't the fund-raiser (clue 2), the engineer who heard voices or the lawyer (clue 4), or the police officer, who is Kent Larsen (clue 5), so must be the tour guide. Thus she didn't hear footsteps in the engine room (clue 2), nor did she see the sailors (clue 2 again); Velda Young saw the wounded sailor (clue 3), and we know the engineer heard voices, so Holly Jurado must have seen the officer. Therefore her experience wasn't in the control room (clue 3), nor on the after deck, where the lawyer had his or her experience (clue 1), or the torpedo room, where Perry Riordan's experience took place (clue 1 again); we know it wasn't in the engine room, so it must have been in the conning tower. The lawyer didn't see the sailors (clue 2), and since he or she had an encounter on the after deck, can't have heard the footsteps; we know the engineer heard the voices and tour guide Holly Jurado saw the officer, so the lawyer must have seen the wounded sailor, and is therefore Velda Young (clue 3). We now know the locations for three experiences, so, since the engineer who heard voices didn't do so in the torpedo room (clue 1), he or she must have done so in the control room, and Perry Riordan, who had his experience in the torpedo room, must have seen the sailors. By elimination, the engineer who heard voices in the control room must have been Boyce Cramer. Finally, Kent Larsen, the police officer, must have heard footsteps in the engine room, leaving Perry Riordan, who saw the sailors in the torpedo room, as the fund-raiser.

Boyce Cramer, engineer, heard voices, control room.
Holly Jurado, tour guide, saw officer, conning tower.
Kent Larsen, police officer, heard footsteps, engine room.
Perry Riordan, fund-raiser, saw sailors, torpedo room.
Velda Young, lawyer, saw wounded sailor, after deck.

88 Battleships

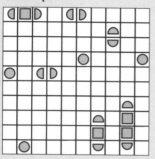

89 Medical Center

Dr. Frankenstein's patient was female (clue 5), but wasn't Grace Harris (clue 4), so must have been Edna Fox. Colin Dawson, who had stomach pains, wasn't seen by Dr. Strangelove (clue 2), and Dr. Faustus's patient had leg pains (clue 2 again), so Dr. Strangelove's patient, who was male and didn't have headaches or a sore throat (clue 6), must have had chest pains, and so was prescribed an ointment (clue 1). He wasn't Albert Brown (clue 1), and we know he wasn't Colin Dawson, so he must have been Ivor Jones. Dr. No's patient didn't have headaches or a sore throat (clue 5), and we know who treated the patients with chest pains and pains in the legs, so Dr. No's patient must have had stomach pains, and was therefore Colin Dawson. Edna Fox, Dr. Frankenstein's patient, can't have been the person with a sore throat, who was male (clue 1), and her doctor's name rules out pains in the legs, so she must have had headaches. By elimination, the man with the sore throat must have seen Dr. Lector, and must have been Albert Brown, leaving Dr. Faustus's patient with leg pains as Grace Harris. The tablets were prescribed for a problem above the shoulders (clue 3), but not to Edna Fox, who had headaches (clue 4), so must have been for Albert Brown with the sore throat. The capsules went to a male patient (clue 3), so, by elimination, must have gone to Colin Dawson, who had stomach pains. Finally, Dr. Faustus didn't prescribe an aerosol spray for Grace Harris (clue 2), so he must have given her an injection, and the aerosol spray must have been prescribed for Edna Fox by Dr. Frankenstein.

Albert Brown, sore throat, Dr. Lector, tablets.
Colin Dawson, stomach pains, Dr. No, capsules.
Edna Fox, headaches, Dr. Frankenstein, aerosol spray.
Grace Harris, pains in legs, Dr. Faustus, injection.
Ivor Jones, chest pains, Dr. Strangelove, ointment.

90 Captured!

Utah Jack was arrested in Ma White's Hotel (clue 4). Logan Dean (clue 2) wasn't arrested in Cutler's Theater in Tombstone (clue 6), or on Main Street (clue 2), and Riordan was arrested in the Silver Dollar Saloon (clue 5), so Logan Dean must have been arrested on Union Street. This wasn't in El Paso (clue 2). Cates was arrested in Dodge City (clue 3) and Danny in Laramie (clue 3 again), so Logan Dean must have been arrested in Fort Smith. Cates wasn't Utah Jack (clue 4), who was arrested at Ma White's Hotel, so he must have been arrested on Main Street. Danny, who was arrested in Laramie, can't have been arrested on Main Street or at Cutler's Theater, so he must have been arrested in the Silver Dollar Saloon, and was therefore Riordan. By elimination, Ma White's, where Utah Jack was arrested, must have been in El Paso. Rusty can't have been Cates, arrested on Main Street (clue 1), so he must have been arrested in Cutler's Theater, Tombstone, leaving Cates, arrested on Main Street, Dodge City, as Al. Rusty's surname wasn't Thorson (clue 1), so must have been McAdam, leaving Thorson as Utah Jack.

Al Cates, Main Street, Dodge City.
Danny Riordan, Silver Dollar Saloon, Laramie.
Logan Dean, Union Street, Fort Smith.
Rusty McAdam, Cutler's Theater, Tombstone.
Utah Jack Thorson, Ma White's Hotel, El Paso.

91 Internal Valentines

Jean's surname is Mason (clue 4), so Fay, who can't be Rose (clue 3), must be Fowler, and thus received the mints (clue 1); by elimination, Alison, who got the Turkish delight (clue 2), must be Rose. Also by elimination, Jean Mason must have received fudge. Fay Fowler's card didn't have lovebirds on it (clue 1), nor teddy bears (clue 3), so must have had butterflies on it. The teddy bears card didn't go to Alison Rose either (clue 2), so must have gone to Jean Mason, and, by elimination, Alison Rose's card must have been decorated with lovebirds.

Alison Rose, lovebirds, Turkish delight.
Fay Fowler, butterflies, mints.
Jean Mason, teddy bears, fudge.

92 Battleships

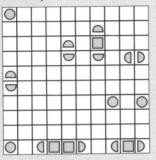

93 Jake's Treasure

The old sea boot is in square 5 (clue 3); clue 2 therefore rules out squares 1, 2, 3, 4, 6, and 7 for the rusty anchor chain. Since square 3 contains the fourth item Jake buried (clue 4), and the eighth item cannot be in square 8 (clue 1), clue 2 also rules out square 9 for the anchor chain, which must therefore be buried in square 8. So clue 2 tells us the coconut must be in square 7, and the eighth item buried must be the sea boot in square 5. Therefore, from clue 5, the item in square 4 was buried fifth. The rabbit's foot is not buried in any of squares 5, 7, or 8, and clue 6 rules out 1, 2, 6, and 9. Also, the second item cannot be in square 2 (clue 1), which rules out square 4 for the rabbit's foot (clue 6), so, by elimination, the latter must be the item buried fourth in square 3, and, from clue 6, the second item must be in square 1. Clue 6 also places the seashells in square 4. Square 1 cannot contain the treasure, buried first (clue 1), or the ship's biscuits (clue 7), so it must contain either the fish hooks or the eye patch. Clue 8 tells us it must be where the fish hooks are buried, with the eye patch therefore in square 9; from that clue, this must have been buried seventh. Clues 1 and 6 rule out sixth or ninth for the item in square 6, which must therefore have been buried first or third. So square 8 must contain an item buried either third or fifth (clue 5). But we know the fifth item is in square 4, so the third must be the rusty anchor chain in square 8, and, from clue 5, Jake's treasure, buried first, must be in square 6. Clue 7 places the ship's biscuits in square 2, and tells us they were not put there sixth, so they must have been ninth, leaving the coconut in square 7 as the sixth item Jake buried.

1, fish hooks, second.

2, ship's biscuits, ninth.
3, rabbit's foot, fourth.
4, seashells, fifth.
5, old sea boot, eighth.
6, treasure, first.
7, coconut, sixth.
8, rusty anchor chain, third.
9, eye patch, seventh.

94 Learning in the Afternoon

Beth Chappel isn't doing her tai chi lessons at Ransome Hall (clue 4), the Old School, where Fiona Gable has lessons (clue 2), or Foxwell Aerodrome, where the flying lessons are being given (clue 3), so the tai chi must be at St. John's Hall. The course on making historical costumes that meets on Friday (clue 5), isn't held at Ransome Hall (clue 4), so must be at the Old School, and the woman learning to make the costumes is thus Fiona Gable (clue 2). By elimination, the course taught at Ransome Hall must be juggling. The juggling lessons aren't on Tuesday (clue 1) or Thursday (clue 4), so must be on Wednesday. The flying lessons at Foxwell Aerodrome aren't on Thursday either (clue 3), so they must be on Tuesday, leaving Beth Chappel's tai chi lessons as the Thursday ones. Thus it's Denise Ellis who is learning to fly (clue 3), and, by elimination, the juggling student must be Helen Ivey.

Beth Chappel, tai chi, St. John's Hall, Thursday.

Denise Ellis, flying light aircraft, Foxwell Aerodrome, Tuesday.

Fiona Gable, making historical costumes, Old School, Friday.

Helen Ivey, juggling, Ransome Hall, Wednesday.

95 Battleships

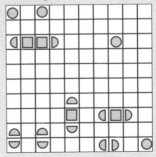

96 Catastrophic Games

Gerda, from Kurst, was not taking part in the luge (clue 4), nor was she in the ski slalom event (clue 1). The ice hockey player was from Bad Weibz (clue 6), and it was Wilma who cut a perfect "0" in the figure skating (clue 5), so, by elimination, Gerda must have competed in the downhill ski event, and is therefore Mutt (clue 3). The ice hockey player from Bad Weibz is not Boris Nudel (clue 6), and we know his or her surname is not Mutt. Kuckoo is from Jinxburg (clue 7), and Ninni was not a skater (clue 2), so the ice hockey player must be Bungler. This is not Karl (clue 2), and we know it is not Gerda, Boris, or Wilma, so it must be Rudi. Ninni cannot be Wilma, the figure skater (clue 2), so he must be Karl, leaving Wilma's surname as Kuckoo, so she is from Jinxburg. Clue 2 tells us Karl Ninni is not from Hudustadt, so he must be a native of Ilstard, leaving Boris Nudel's hometown as Hudustadt. So, from clue 1, the ill-fated slalom skier must be Boris, leaving Karl, from Ilstard, as the man who missed the luge.

Downhill ski, Gerda Mutt, Kurst.
Figure skating, Wilma Kuckoo, Jinxburg.
Ice hockey, Rudi Bungler, Bad Weibz.
Luge, Karl Ninni, Ilstard.
Ski slalom, Boris Nudel, Hudustadt.

97 A Role in the Remake

The actor from *Investigators* will play Col. Jackson in the movie (clue 4), so the one from *Tac Squad*, who won't be playing Capt. DiMarco or the traffic cop (clue 3), and who isn't Darren Earle, who will play the property sergeant (clue 2), must be going to play Chief Kazinski. The man who is to play Capt. DiMarco played Lt. Rick Flores on TV (clue 3): we know he's not in *Investigators* or *Tac Squad*, nor is he in *Precinct 78* (clue 3) or *K9 Squad*, which had Sgt. Duke Mitchell as its TV hero (clue 5), so Lt. Rick Flores must have been the hero of *Code 10-200*, played by Gil Horton (clue 6). Adam Burns played Lt. Mike Flint on TV (clue 1), so Jack Kramer, who didn't play Sgt. Jay Sherman or Capt. Lon McGavin (clue 1), must have played Sgt. Duke Mitchell in *K9 Squad*. By elimination, he must be playing a traffic cop in the movie, and Darren Earle must be in *Precinct 78*. Sgt. Jay Sherman wasn't the hero of *Investigators* or *Tac Squad* (clue 4), so must have been in *Precinct 78*, and played by Darren Earle, who is the property sergeant in the film. The hero of *Tac Squad* wasn't Capt. Lon McGavin (clue 3), so

must have been Lt. Mike Flint, played by Adam Burns. By elimination, Mack Nilsson must have played Capt. Lon McGavin, and he must be the actor who was in *Investigators* and will play Col. Jackson in the film.

Adam Burns, *Tac Squad*, Lt. Mike Flint, Chief Kazinski.
Darren Earle, *Precinct 78*, Sgt. Jay Sherman, property sergeant.
Gil Horton, *Code 10-200*, Lt. Rick Flores, Capt. DiMarco.
Jack Kramer, *K9 Squad*, Sgt. Duke Mitchell, traffic cop.
Mack Nilsson, *Investigators*, Capt. Lon McGavin, Col. Jackson.

98 Name That Drummer

Dave is number 2 (clue 5), so, from clue 2, Terry, who cannot be 1 or 4, must be number 3. Nor is number 1 Martin, the supermarket manager (clue 3), so he must be number 4, leaving number 1 as Jack. So, from clue 4, Chapman must be number 2, Dave. Since we know number 4, Martin, is not an insurance broker, clue 2 tells us he must be Kitching, and the insurance broker must be Dave Chapman, number 2. Smith, the carpet fitter, is not number 3, Terry (clue 1), so he must be number 1, Jack, which leaves Terry's surname as Robinson, and his occupation as fireman. Clue 6 therefore rules out the real drummer as Dave or Martin, nor is he Jack (clue 4), so he must be number 3, Terry Robinson, the fireman.

1, Jack Smith, carpet fitter.
2, Dave Chapman, insurance broker.
3, Terry Robinson, fireman (former drummer).
4, Martin Kitching, supermarket manager.

99 Horrorscopes

Sylvia's sign is Pisces (clue 6), so Angela's sign, also represented by two of something (clue 2) must be Gemini. Her horoscope didn't forecast a new love (clue 2), a lottery win (clue 1), or a pay raise (clue 3); since she didn't have a car accident (clue 2), she can't have been told she'd have good health (clue 3), so must have been expecting a promotion. The girl born under Taurus was told she'd get a pay raise (clue 3), so the one told she'd have good health who had a car accident (clue 3) can't have been born under Taurus, Gemini, or Pisces (clue 6); she wasn't Karen (clue 1), or Jennifer (clue 4), and the signs rule out Angela and Sylvia, so she must have been Lisa. We now know either the name or the sign to go with four forecasts, so Sylvia, born under Pisces, must have been told she'd find a new love. By elimination, the Taurean expecting a pay raise must have been Jennifer. The girl who was told to expect a lottery win wasn't born under Libra (clue 1), so her sign must have been Aries, leaving Libra as the sign of Lisa, who was told she'd have good health instead. Karen had an accident (clue 1), which we know wasn't the car accident, so she must have fallen down stairs. The girl who argued with her best friend wasn't Angela, born under Gemini, who was expecting a promotion, or Jennifer, born under Taurus, who was expecting a pay raise (clue 5), so must have been Sylvia, born under Pisces. Finally, Angela didn't have her car stolen (clue 2), so she must have found that her bank account had been emptied, leaving Jennifer, the Taurean, expecting a pay raise as the one whose car was stolen.

Angela, Gemini, promotion, bank account emptied.
Jennifer, Taurus, pay raise, car stolen.
Karen, Aries, lottery win, fell down stairs.
Lisa, Libra, good health, car accident.
Sylvia, Pisces, new love, argued with best friend.

100 Delivery Man

The cooking oil went to the restaurant in Lily Street (clue 6), the onions went to the Winter Garden (clue 1), and the seafood sauce and the white wine went to the same address (clue 3), so the Silver Moon in King's Square, which didn't receive the ice cream or the white wine (clue 2), must have received the french fries. The beverage delivered there wasn't the red wine (clue 4), the lager, which went to the restaurant in Orson Street (clue 5), or the orange juice, which went to Chez Pierre (clue 1), and we know it wasn't white wine, so it must have been cola. The seafood sauce and the white wine weren't delivered to the restaurant in Clifford Avenue (clue 3), so must have gone to the one in Baker's Lane. We know that the restaurant in Orson Street received the lager, so Chez Pierre, which received the orange juice and is also in a street (clue 1), must be in Lily Street, and therefore also received the cooking oil. The seafood sauce and white wine didn't go to Pyramid (clue 3), so the restaurant in Baker's Lane that received them must be Marco's, leaving Pyramid as the restaurant that received the ice cream. Pyramid's not in Clifford Avenue (clue 3), so must be in Orson Street, leaving the Winter Garden, which received the onions, in Clifford Avenue, and their beverage delivery as red wine.

Chez Pierre, Lily Street, cooking oil, orange juice.
Marco's, Baker's Lane, seafood sauce, white wine.
Pyramid, Orson Street, ice cream, lager.
Silver Moon, King's Square, french fries, cola.
Winter Garden, Clifford Avenue, onions, red wine.

FREE PUZZLE SOCIETY MEMBERSHIP—

ACCESS TO THOUSANDS OF PUZZLES!

The Puzzle Society would like to thank you for your purchase by offering a free 90-day subscription to our online puzzle club. With this membership, you will have exclusive, unlimited access to 70+ updated puzzles added each week and 8,000+ archived puzzles.

To take advantage of this special membership offer, visit **PuzzleSociety.com/play/ posh** and start playing today!

puzzlesociety.com

TWO MOONS

TWO MOONS

EMILY RODDA

A DIVISION OF EDC PUBLISHING

First American Edition 2016
Kane Miller, A Division of EDC Publishing

For information contact:
Kane Miller, A Division of EDC Publishing
PO Box 470663
Tulsa, OK 74147-0663
www.kanemiller.com
www.edcpub.com
www.usbornebooksandmore.com

Library of Congress Control Number: 2015954194

Printed and bound in the United States of America

1 2 3 4 5 6 7 8 9 10

ISBN: 978-1-61067-526-0

CONTENTS

1 - The Finalists

Beneath the morning sun, the Silver Sea was gleaming as if it had been newly polished. Sea serpents coiled in the waves of the north, hunting flying fish that skimmed over the surface like slivers of rainbow light. Giant turtles paddled lazily in the warmer waters of the south, where seabirds circled the enchanted Isle of Tier.

Within the ring of glittering black sand, the trees of the island were deep, lush green. Orchids with petals like pale, speckled flesh clustered at the trees' roots, clung to their rough trunks, trailed from their forked branches.

The orchids' scent was faint now, but as the day warmed it would grow stronger and richer, rising to wreathe the island in a haze of dizzying sweetness. By then the wisest birds would have risen higher, or broken the spell of the place and flown away. Those that lingered in the vapor would be overcome and would fall from the sky. The island would welcome them. No matter how often it fed, it was always hungry.

The being who called himself the King of Tier sat in the jeweled splendor of his cavern, clutching the ancient Staff that was the source of his power. It came to him that he had not stirred for a long time—he could not tell how long. The hand that gripped the Staff was as stiff as if it were carved out of wood. He willed the fingers to move, to flex, and at last they did. The wraiths that clustered about him sighed, pressing closer.

Larsett, they whispered. *Master of the Staff. Larsett ...* They never tired of the words. They loved the warmth that flowed from the Staff whenever they breathed the Master's name. In the gray chill of their half-life, that warmth was their only comfort.

But the whispering was fainter than usual. The King slowly pondered this, and then remembered. The wraiths were fewer than before. He had sent some of them away, to spy for him in a place he could not go— would never see again. He had sensed the beginning of a train of events that boded ill. He had ordered the wraiths to seek out the girl who had been in his thoughts.

Yes. The King began to relax. Then, with a tiny start, he recalled that the wraiths had in fact returned not long before—only hours before, perhaps. They had found the girl, and the news they had brought of her had troubled him. What was more, they had learned who she was, and were excited by the knowledge. He had not expected that. It had displeased him. Angrily, without thinking, he had sent them back to learn more.

Slowly it occurred to him that perhaps he should not have done that. Perhaps, indeed, it had been a mistake to send the wraiths to find the girl in the first place. The thought was strange. The King of Tier had grown unused to the idea that he could be in error.

He caused a crystal bowl to fill with sugared dates. He was not hungry, but he ate. He knew that if he did not eat he would waste away and die like the pirate Bar-Enoch, who had perished with the Staff that could grant eternal life in his hand.

As the King tasted sugar on his tongue, it came to him like a dream that once he had had another life. Once he had sailed the Silver Sea in a great ship with white sails. Once he had felt wind and spray on his face, and talked and laughed with other men. Once he had counted the years and feared growing old.

That was before the magic Staff became his. That was before he fled with it to Tier, the haunted place of its creation, felt the wraiths twining about him in welcome, and stepped out of time. How long ago?

Not so long, surely, he thought. But long enough, it seemed, for a fierce, eager, dark-haired child to become a young woman and tear herself away from the bonds of home. Time had not stood still for her— for Britta of Del.

Old memories were rising from the depths of

his mind, bringing with them disturbing feelings. Dazzled by dreams of glory, he had not thought of the future when he had taken the Staff for his own. He had thought only of the present when he had betrayed his trust, sacrificed his crew, abandoned his ship. He had feared nothing.

He had brought the fabled Hungry Isle back to life. He had rejoiced as it began to prowl the Silver Sea again, hiding itself when concealment was useful, preying on everything that fell in its way. Tier was his kingdom, and in it he was all-powerful. It was for others to fear him, not the other way round.

And so it had been—until now. The Rosalyn Trust contest—the contest to become Apprentice and heir to Mab, the Trader Rosalyn ... he had forgotten all about it, as he had forgotten so many things. Yet— another dank shred of memory drifted to the surface of his clouded mind—there had been a time when he had thought it very important.

He could still taste the rage he had felt when he learned that by the will of the first Trader Rosalyn, the contest was open only to girls. Yes. He had resented that bitterly, once upon a time. And now ...

Memories of the flickering pictures the absent wraiths had brought to the cavern rose before his eyes. Little Britta, grown up. Britta of Del, buttoned tightly into a demure white shirt and dull blue skirt, her rippling hair bound in a tight knot at the nape of her neck.

4

She looked so different that at first glance he might not have known her, but her dark eyes snapped with a light that was all too familiar. Britta had been tamed only on the surface. Her spirit still burned as brightly as ever. Her fierce longing to become the sea-going trader she was born to be had not lessened with the years.

She was still the same Britta. Daring enough to seize her only chance to fulfill her dream. Strong enough to conceal from Mab and everyone else that she was the daughter of a man they hated and despised. Clever and determined enough to be one of the four finalists who were now setting sail with Mab on a trading voyage, competing for the glittering prize.

Your daughter, Larsett! the wraiths twining about him murmured lovingly. *Bone of your bone, flesh of your flesh. Child of the Staff …*

The King felt a twinge of panic. He had been careless. They had shared his visions. The thought filled him with nausea.

"Be still!" he ordered, the last traces of sugar turning bitter in his mouth. "My daughter is no business of yours! Get back! Give me air!"

The wraiths moaned and retreated, but only a little.

He tried to calm himself. The absent wraiths would return when they learned where the girl's ship was to go. Perhaps what they told him would relieve him of the cloud that brooded over him, robbing him of peace. The *Star of Deltora* might carry Britta far from the Silver Sea.

And if it did not? Given the chance, would Britta try to seek him out? Would she somehow find a way...?

The King of Tier felt the Staff quiver. Its tip was buried deep in the island's heart, but still it trembled. Or was the trembling his?

He caused a cup to fill to the brim with wine, and drank deeply. He tried to shut his ears to the yearning whispers of the wraiths.

Larsett's daughter. Child of the Staff. Britta. Britta. Britta ...

*

At that very moment, far across the waves, Britta's heart was singing as the *Star of Deltora* surged from the safety of Del harbor into the open sea. Soon, very soon now, she would know where the ship was bound. She would know the three ports where she and the other contest finalists were to match wits and trading skills.

A twelve-week voyage had been planned—three glorious months of freedom! There would be no news of home in all that time, for messenger birds did not fly over the sea, but Britta found that this did not trouble her at all.

The fears and shocks that had racked her as she strove to become a finalist in the Rosalyn competition seemed strangely distant now. Images of the people she had left behind—her hurt, angry mother, her tearful sister, old Captain Gripp, who had started it all by entering her in the contest—even Jantsy, waving his red scarf from the shore—were no longer sharp and compelling. It was as if she had folded them and put them away at the back of her mind, like sheets stored with lavender in a carved wooden chest.

Her rivals, standing beside her now at the ship's rail, seemed far more real to her. Jewel of Broome, Sky of Rithmere, Vashti, the Del trader's daughter—all so different, but all, Britta was sure, feeling the same elation as she was, and the same powerful hunger to win.

It would have been easy to feel a kind of affection for them at this moment. Easy ... except that one of them was more enemy than rival. One of them had struck her down and locked her in a cellar to try to stop her winning a place on the *Star of Deltora*.

Trader Mab, like everyone else, seemed to assume that the attack had been a coincidence. She thought that Britta had taken a foolish risk, wandering alone in the Del harbor backstreets after dark. It had not seemed to occur to her that one of the other finalists in the contest could have been the culprit.

But Britta was certain that her instinct was right. She had not been robbed, or even badly hurt. Someone had just wanted her out of the way. She glanced sideways at her companions, wondering which one was more ruthless than she seemed.

Vashti was the obvious choice. Her wide blue

eyes and sweet smile did not fool Britta for an instant. Still, it was hard to imagine the kittenish Vashti actually hitting someone. Sly trickery was more her style.

Sky? Perhaps. With her lean, olive-skinned face, her shabby trousers and tunic and her long hair jingling with tiny ornaments, Sky seemed cool, and scornful of pretense. But there was a reckless twist to her mouth, and her dark eyes were veiled so that it was impossible to guess what she was thinking.

And then there was Jewel, towering over them all, her shaved head stained with swirling red patterns, a hunting knife at her belt and a pouch of spears hanging from one shoulder. Jewel came from a wild, rough part of Deltora. She would not hesitate to use force to get something she badly needed. And yet ... Jewel seemed to be the sort of person who preferred a fair fight to winning by stealth.

Seemed. Britta shook her head. That was the problem. How could she guess which of the other finalists was her enemy? One of them was skilled at deceiving. One of them was not what she seemed.

Any more than *I* am what I seem, she reminded herself grimly. I would not be here now if anyone knew who my father was.

The bright sun seemed to dim. Shadows flickered before her eyes. Britta frowned. This had happened a few times lately, especially when she was feeling some strong emotion. She told herself that it was the result of nerves stretched to the limit by the events of the past two days. It would pass. She blinked, and the shadows vanished.

She heard soft footfalls and saw that Mab was approaching, with Healer Kay, sturdy and watchful, close behind her. Britta held her breath. Were she, Jewel, Sky and Vashti about to learn where they were to go?

Blue-painted eyelids drooping, crest of dyed red hair a shocking contrast to her drawn, wrinkled face, Mab cleared her throat to command attention.

"Bosun Crow will take you below to stow your belongings, Finalists," she said in a flat voice. "As I have already said, two of you must share a cabin. Settle that matter between yourselves now, will you?"

She withdrew a little with Kay, who instantly began muttering to her, no doubt urging her to go below herself, and rest.

"Jewel has already offered to share," Sky said, blandly ignoring Jewel's scowl, "so I suggest the rest of us draw for it."

Britta felt a sharp stab of panic. The thought of sharing a cabin with someone she could not trust was unbearable! Jewel was the person she suspected least of attacking her in Del, but it was impossible to be sure.

Frantically she tried to think of an excuse to avoid taking part in the draw. She could think of nothing. She had not told anyone of her suspicions of her fellow candidates. If she suddenly tried to insist that her safety depended on having a cabin to herself, no one would believe her.

From somewhere Sky had produced three pieces of straw—two long, one short. She put her hands behind her back, then brought one hand to the front again, three even lengths of straw poking from her closed fist. Britta felt a prickle of suspicion. There had been something about the smoothness of the action that made her think Sky had done the same thing many times before.

"Short straw shares with Jewel," Sky said, holding out her fist.

Vashti smiled sweetly at Britta. "After you!" she purred. She made it sound as if she was being polite, but Britta knew better. Vashti also suspected that Sky was playing some sort of trick.

Britta hesitated, feeling trapped. It seemed impossible to accuse Sky of cheating—impossible to insist that Vashti must choose first.

"Anything wrong?" Sky murmured, raising an eyebrow.

Britta pulled out the middle straw. Without surprise she saw that it was short. She looked up resentfully. Sky shrugged and opened her hand to display the two long straws lying on her palm.

There was nothing to be said, though Britta was positive that she had been duped. It did not make her feel any better when she glanced at Mab and saw the old trader turning away, hiding a smile.

So Mab, while pretending to have no interest in

the matter of the cabins, had actually been keeping a sharp eye on the dealings between Sky, Vashti and Britta. And the result had amused her.

No doubt, Britta thought bitterly, the voyage was going to be a series of similar tests. If so, she had just lost the first round. She could only hope that she had not lost her chance of reaching their first port in safety, as well.

2 - The Three Ports

Crow, a hulking, glowering man who looked more like a pirate than a Rosalyn fleet bosun, was waiting by the narrow stairway that led down to the lower deck. Jewel was already standing beside him, intent on being the first to choose a cabin. Shouldering her bundle, Britta went to join them, forcing a smile in response to Jewel's broad grin. Jewel might be exactly what she seemed, and it was not her fault that Britta had drawn the short straw.

"Bad luck, little nodnap," Jewel muttered, using the annoying nickname she had given Britta on their first meeting. "Still, I confess I am relieved. Sky might not have been so bad—she talks little enough, at least—but she is a strange fish. And if I had been forced to share with Vashti I might have been driven to murder by the time the voyage ended."

With Sky close behind them and Vashti for once

12

trailing at the rear, they followed Crow below. He gestured at the three cabin doors lining the narrow passage at the bottom of the steps. "Take your pick," he grunted. "They've all got two bunks."

He looked down at his hands, pretending to pick at a ragged fingernail, but not before Britta had caught his smirk.

So this is another test, she thought. We are expected to bargain with one another for the best cabin, and no one cares if Jewel and I end up crammed together like pickles in a jar.

She squeezed past Jewel and moved quickly to the third door. "We will take this one," she called back over her shoulder, throwing the door open.

She was amused to see Crow's sparse eyebrows shoot up in surprise. With even greater pleasure she caught a glimpse of Vashti glaring from the foot of the steps. So, Vashti had been told that the third cabin in line was by far the largest. That was why she had come down last. Vashti had hoped that Jewel, Britta and Sky would waste time looking into the first two cabins while she slipped along behind them to claim the spacious one for herself.

But thanks to the model of the *Star of Deltora* in Captain Gripp's sitting room, Britta knew as much about the ship as Vashti's parents did. Perhaps she knew more, in fact, since almost certainly they had never seen the cargo and food storage holds, or the places where the crew ate and slept.

Second round to me, Vashti, she thought, surveying her prize through the open door. As she had hoped, the third cabin was just as it was in the model— over twice the size of its neighbors, and fitted with a small table and two seats as well as upper and lower bunks. Over the table was a mirror that reflected bright morning light streaming in through the porthole.

"Good work, little nodnap!" cried Jewel, looking over Britta's head, then glancing into the dim, cramped space that Sky had claimed next door. "How in the nine seas did you know?"

"I just had a feeling," Britta said vaguely, moving into the cabin. She had decided to keep the story of Gripp's model to herself. Her knowledge of the ship had been an advantage once and might be so again— especially if no one else suspected it.

"Sheets and pillows!" Jewel crowed, slinging her bundle onto the neatly made lower bunk. "By the stars, this is luxury! In Broome we sleep in hammocks at sea. Do you mind taking the upper bunk, Britta? I like to be near the door, and in any case I fear that my weight might test that flimsy little ladder too far."

"I do not mind at all," Britta said truthfully. She knew that she would feel more private in the top bunk—and safer, too, if Jewel did not trust the ladder.

As they set about stowing their belongings in the drawers below the bottom bunk, it suddenly occurred to her that she might actually be safer sharing with Jewel than she would be in a cabin alone. An enemy

14

would think twice before creeping into a cabin where Jewel was sleeping. And if Jewel herself were the enemy, *she* would think twice before doing Britta harm in the night, for she would be the obvious suspect.

Watching her companion out of the corner of her eye, Britta was relieved to see her sliding her pouch of spears and the knife from her belt into the narrow gap between the wall and the back of the drawer.

"I promised Mab I would not go armed on the ship," Jewel said, without looking round.

Britta jumped. Did the woman of Broome have eyes in the back of her head?

"My weapons will be out of the way here," Jewel went on calmly. "Please tell no one where they are. And do not touch them yourself."

"I have no wish to touch them," Britta snapped.

"I meant no insult," Jewel said, pushing the drawer shut and sitting back on her heels. "It is just—" She broke off, lifting her head alertly.

"What is it?" Britta demanded.

"We are changing course," Jewel said, springing to her feet. "Can you not feel it?"

She turned and left the cabin. Britta hurried after her along the passage and up to the main deck.

Sky was already there, leaning on the rail. She looked tense and pale and did not speak or even turn her head when Jewel and Britta joined her.

Small, choppy waves were splashing against the *Star*'s sides as she turned slowly away from the sun.

15

Flying fish were leaping in the spray like arrows of rainbow light. Looking across the gently heaving deck as the ship straightened, Britta saw the coast of Deltora, a lumpy line far to her right. Her heart turned over.

After a few minutes, Vashti emerged from below and strolled to the group by the rail. She was clearly trying to appear perfectly calm, but her cheeks were flushed, as if she had been running.

"So we are heading west," she said brightly. "It is the Silver Sea for us, it seems."

The Silver Sea ... The Silver Sea ... Whispers filled Britta's mind, hissing like foam on a sandy shore.

"You do not look happy, Jewel," Vashti cooed. "Are you afraid of the Hungry Isle?"

Jewel made no answer.

"There is no need to be, I assure you," Vashti persisted, with an irritating little laugh. "These days, every sighting of the Hungry Isle is reported to the Traders' Hall in Del. Its course is plotted, so our traders and their captains can predict where it is likely to be at any given time, and can keep well clear of it. It is an excellent system. Perhaps, when you return to Broome, you can tell your people about it."

"They know of it already," Jewel growled, driven into speech. "I do not fear the Hungry Isle. I am simply disappointed because I was hoping for the east, and the Sea of Serpents. I know the islands there. The Silver Sea is a different matter."

"A good trader is at home in any port," Vashti

said. She yawned and turned to look over the rail. "But of course," she added softly, "a poor savage from nowhere could not be expected to understand that."

She squeaked as Jewel reached her in a single stride and seized her by the throat.

"Watch your tongue, trader's daughter, or you will lose it!" Jewel snarled.

"Jewel!" Britta cried in fright, but Jewel took no notice. Towering over the cowering Vashti, she was no longer a genial giant but a wild, terrifying figure.

"What is this?" a voice barked. "Jewel of Broome, stand back this instant!"

Her face creased with anger, Mab shouldered her way between Britta and Sky and faced Jewel.

"Stand back!" Mab ordered again.

Jewel's smoldering eyes held the old trader's furious gaze for a long moment, then her hand dropped from Vashti's throat and she turned away.

"I will not have brawling on this vessel," Mab said coldly. "Another incident like that, Jewel, and you will be put off at the next port. Is that understood?"

Jewel pressed her lips together, and nodded. Behind her, Vashti made a great play of rubbing her neck, wincing as if it hurt her.

"Vashti began it!" Britta found herself exclaiming. "Vashti insulted—"

"I am not interested in childish excuses!" snapped Mab. "Self-control is the first rule for a good trader. The trader who forgets herself in a foreign port may well find herself in serious trouble—not to mention disgracing her ship and her fleet! I will thank you to remember that, Britta!"

Britta bit her lip, cursing herself for opening her mouth. Now she had become the target of Mab's anger while Jewel, who was perfectly capable of speaking for herself, had wisely kept silent.

"Very well," said Mab curtly. "As you know, we will be visiting three ports on this voyage. Now we are at sea, it is time for you to know what these ports will be so that you can begin making your trading plans."

She smiled faintly as the four finalists became very still. She knew very well that they had all been waiting impatiently for this moment.

"As I daresay you have noticed, Captain Hara has set our course due west. All three of our chosen destinations are in the Silver Sea. Our first stop will be Maris."

Maris! Britta's heart gave a great thud of relief. She had read a great deal about Maris and heard even more, for it had been one of Captain Gripp's favorite ports. Quickly she glanced under her eyelashes at the other finalists.

Jewel was shrugging, as if the news was not as bad as it might have been. Plainly she knew something of Maris, even if it was far from her home.

Sky had bent her head and her long hair had swung forward, hiding her face, but Britta could see that her left hand was gripping the rail so hard that

18

the knuckles were white. It seemed that Sky was either very disappointed or very excited.

Vashti was looking smug. Well, of course! A Del trader's daughter would know everything there was to know about Maris. No doubt Vashti's parents had been there often—she might even have visited it herself, as part of her training.

Not for the first time, Britta wondered if Vashti had been destined to become Mab's Apprentice from the first. Perhaps Britta, Sky and Jewel—three outsiders, after all—had been chosen just for show. Perhaps their only purpose was to make it seem that a real contest was being held according to the rules of the Rosalyn Trust.

"Our second destination," Mab went on briskly, "is the island of Two Moons."

Britta's throat closed. She swallowed hard, trying not to show her shocked dismay. Two Moons was the last port her father was known to have visited on his last, ill-fated voyage.

She clenched her fists. Of all the islands in the Silver Sea, why had Two Moons been chosen for the trial? Was she never to escape her father's shadow? Was she never to be allowed to forget him?

"Two Moons!" Jewel cried, her broad face lighting up. "Why, that is where the sorcerer Tier was born—and where sunrise pearls are found!"

Vashti tittered, covering her mouth with her hand. Sky had still not raised her head.

"You are on this voyage to trade, Jewel, not go chasing rainbows!" Mab snapped. "You will have ten gold coins to spend. That sum would not buy you a glance at a true sunrise pearl. The imitations you will see are merely worthless pink beads."

By the time Jewel finished protesting that she was perfectly aware of that, Britta had managed to pull herself together. She had forced herself to breathe again. She had made her hands relax.

"Our third port," Mab droned, with the air of finishing off a tiresome duty, "will be Illica."

Maris. Two Moons. Illica ...

The air around Britta seemed to shift, as if a freak breeze was eddying around her, then rushing past her and away. For an instant she thought she was going to faint, but the dizziness passed quickly. The next moment she felt lighter and happier than she had for days—as if a heavy cloak had been lifted from her shoulders.

She could not think why. It was certainly not because Mab had announced that the third port would be Illica. All Britta knew about Illica was that it was far away, the most distant island in the Silver Sea.

Healer Kay had moved forward and touched Mab's arm. The old trader turned to her with a scowl.

"Illica?" Jewel muttered in dismay. "I have never heard of it! Have you, Britta? Sky?"

Sky did not answer. Her head was still bent. Her hand still gripped the ship's rail. Even for Sky, Britta thought, the behavior was strange.

Vashti wrinkled her pretty nose. "There is not very much good trading in Illica," she said in an undertone. "I cannot think why it was chosen—especially in this season."

"Really?" Britta asked innocently, her eye on Mab, who seemed to be finishing her conversation with Kay.

Vashti looked superior, and nodded. "Illica is unbearably hot in summer, and the people there are very odd and ignorant. My parents never bother with it these days. It is too far to go for too little gain, my father says."

"Opinions differ!" snapped Trader Mab. As Britta had hoped, she had turned round in time to overhear.

Vashti blushed in confusion, and Britta silently rejoiced to see the perfect finalist caught out for once. She met Jewel's amused eyes, and winked.

"The four of you are free to consult the books in the reading room for more information on the three ports," Mab said. "Books must not be taken from the room, but read at the table provided. After use, they must be returned to the place where they were found. That is all."

She nodded, turned, and stalked off with the healer, who seemed at last to have persuaded her to go to her cabin and rest. Vashti, still very pink in the face, moved away from her companions and pretended to be studying the horizon.

Jewel glanced slyly at Sky. "By the stars, I am hungry!" she announced. "Do you know what I long for? A thick slab of oily white fish on bread fried in pig rat dripping!"

She grinned as Sky abruptly bent over the rail and was violently sick.

"The open sea is different from the River Broad in Rithmere, it seems," Jewel said cheerfully to Britta. "Ah—there is nothing worse than seasickness! If only I had known how Sky was feeling, I would never have mentioned oily food in front of her."

Her grin broadened. "Still, looking on the bright side, at least one of us will not be wanting the best books just now."

With that, she vanished down the stairway to the lower deck, plainly in search of the reading room.

And Britta was left to follow, leaving Sky to her misery and thinking ruefully that Jewel too, it seemed, had to be watched.

3 - The Reading Room

Flitting low over wastes of foam-capped water, visible only to the great sea-going birds soaring above them, the wraiths that had been following Britta returned to the Isle of Tier. They sensed at once that their news was not pleasing. It was only by a great effort of will, in fact, that the King of the island managed to hide from them the fear that stabbed him like a blade as they whispered the names "Maris," "Two Moons" and … "Illica."

The ports are chance only, he told himself, as the wraiths milled anxiously about the cavern walls. They mean nothing!

He summoned up ragged memories. He forced his clouded mind to follow old paths.

Maris and Two Moons were popular trading ports—ideal places for young traders to test their wits against the best. Illica was … a port like no other—a port where only the most cunning of traders would do well.

Mab and the Rosalyn Trust committee had set the Star's course for those reasons. Britta could have had no say in the choice of destinations. So what did it matter where she landed? She would surely be too intent on trying to win the contest to think of anything else.

Britta! the returned wraiths whispered, images of the girl's face shimmering among them. *Larsett's daughter! Child of the Staff! She shines like a star. She warms us ...*

The being on the throne writhed to hear them. He longed to order silence, but instinct told him to tread warily. For the second time, he wondered if it had been a mistake to send the wraiths to find out what he wanted to know. He had not considered that, away from him, they might begin to bond with another who had a tie with their treasure—a tie of name and blood.

Uneasily he shifted on his golden throne. He had not realized that the mystic power of the Staff would stretch so far. He had failed to respect the strength of the sorcerer Tier's magic.

As he had at the beginning. The thought swam into his mind and circled like a foul, stinging thing, oozing venom. He beat it down. It was too late for regrets. Far too late.

We cannot protect her, we can only watch, but despite her enemies she prospers, the wraiths who had returned were whispering to those who had stayed. *Fate is drawing her closer to Tier. Soon the Staff will call her, and she will be with us.*

With us ... with us ... The hissing echoes filled the cavern. Slim shadows swarmed forward, twining around the throne, pressing themselves to the Staff.

"No!" the King cried aloud, his control breaking. "Leave me in peace! Get back!"

Too late, he saw his error. In a breath, the wraiths so recently returned had vanished. Not sorrowfully this time, but gladly, they were following the order they had chosen to hear. They had left him. They were going back—to Britta.

Britta knew exactly where to find the *Star*'s reading room. Playing with Captain Gripp's model of the ship in her childhood, she had always been fascinated by the small space lined with shelves of tiny books, tucked away on the cabin deck. So she was already sitting at the long table, with a heavy volume in front of her, when Jewel threw open the reading room door.

"Are you a magician, or just lucky, Britta?" Jewel exclaimed. "I have been searching for this place since I last saw you!"

Britta shrugged. "I found it quite easily," she said, with perfect truth. "But I am not having the same luck in finding something useful to read."

She gestured at the shelves to the right of the

door. "That is the Silver Sea section. There are books about every island I can think of—except Two Moons and Illica, which were the ones I really wanted."

She saw Jewel eyeing the book she was reading, and shook her head. "This one has short notes on all the islands—maps too—but if the section on Maris is any guide, it will not be very helpful."

Frowning, Jewel turned and began scanning the shelves. Britta went back to *The Islands of the Silver Sea*, and began reading the paragraph beneath the map headed "Two Moons."

TWO MOONS is a wealthy island, though little food can be grown there, most of its land being sour swamp. It is a thriving trading port, and it is a common saying that "gold is king in Two Moons." The many stores offer a great array of goods from all over the Silver Sea and beyond, but the island is most famous for its rare pink pearls. "Sunrise pearls," as they are known, are found only in the Two Moons swamplands and are highly prized ...

Britta scanned the rest of the text, and sighed. Like the note on Maris, it had told her nothing she did not know already. She turned to the page headed "Illica," glumly telling herself that since she knew nothing at all about the third port, this section would at least provide facts that were new to her.

The map showed a small, round island almost completely ringed by cliffs and underwater rocks. The note below it was very short.

ILLICA is the most remote trading island in the Silver Sea, and is the home of three clans known as "The Collectors." The towerlike castles of these clans are museums of precious objects gathered over the centuries and added to by each new generation. Collectors rarely travel, so welcome foreign traders offering unusual, high-quality goods.

Britta closed the book with the strong feeling that she did not like the sound of Illica. She hated to admit that Vashti was right, but it seemed an odd place for Mab to have chosen as their last stop.

She decided to focus on Maris and Two Moons. There was nothing in the rules of the contest that said she had to trade in all three ports.

In Maris she would use the ten gold coins provided by the Rosalyn Trust to buy goods that were prized in Two Moons. Then, in Two Moons, if all went well, she would trade her Maris purchases for a rare item that would fetch a very high price in Del.

Of course, her rivals were no doubt planning to do the same. It sounded as if Vashti had no intention of trading in Illica, and it was unlikely that Jewel and Sky would risk it either, since information about Illica was so scarce.

Well, Britta told herself, I will just have to think more cleverly than they do—and work harder. She vowed to scour her memory for everything Captain Gripp had ever told her about Maris and Two Moons. She would also search every book on the Silver Sea shelf and note down even the tiniest facts about the two ports. And she would use her secret weapon—her old treasure, *A Trader's Life*.

She had brought the tattered book with her not because she thought it would be useful, but because she feared her mother would burn it if she found it. Now she felt that it was more likely to be of help to her than anything she could find in the reading room.

She yawned. "I think I will have a nap," she said. "I had very little sleep last night. Do you want me to leave this book on the table for you?"

Jewel, absorbed in the bookshelves, barely nodded as Britta slipped away.

Alone in the cabin, Britta pulled *A Trader's Life* from the drawer beneath the lower bunk. She climbed the ladder to her own bunk, flipped to the page she wanted, and stretched out to read:

My first visit to Maris was a great surprise to me, despite all I had read and heard.

For example, I knew that Maris had no harbor, but

faced the open sea, and naturally this worried me. Rough seas, I reasoned, could be disastrous to our schedule, or even prevent our reaching the town at all.

The late Trader Wix, whose assistant I was on this voyage, tried to put my mind at rest. He told me that the weather was always fair for trading ships in Maris. This, he said, was because the Maris leader, who is known as "The Keeper," can control the winds and the tides by the power of a magic Crystal.

Being young and raw at the time, I found this hard to believe, but of course I was soon to discover that it was the simple truth ...

Britta read on, reminding herself of all the other things Trader Sven had found surprising in Maris. She smiled over his dealings with the strange, chilly Maris people, and paid more attention than ever to his shrewd advice on good trading in the town. Her confidence rose. *A Trader's Life* was old-fashioned, she knew, but she doubted that much had altered in Maris since Sven's time. The Maris people did not seem to welcome change.

She read that fine fabric woven from the wool of inland beasts called "bukshah" was sometimes on sale in Maris, and would always trade well in cold climates. She read that the Maris people also sold high-quality silk, dried fish, good cheeses, hoopberry wine, tricks, toys and "the best honey in the Silver Sea." Not to mention beautiful objects made of glass and silver, and precious jewelry inlaid with the tiny, rare blue shells called *odi*.

Sven also mentioned the pickled eggs of a creature called the Kirrian worm, but Britta remembered Captain Gripp telling her that no one but a Maris would eat Kirrian worm eggs, and put them out of her mind.

At length, the familiar words began to blur before her eyes and her need for sleep overcame her. She woke with a start some time later, without knowing what had disturbed her. Her skin was prickling. The cabin seemed wreathed in whispering shadows. The light, happy feeling that had come to her that morning had vanished, and once again a dark cloud seemed to be weighing her down, like the lingering memory of a bad dream.

This is what comes of sleeping in the daytime, Britta told herself irritably. She pushed her book into hiding under her pillow and took herself out on deck, to try to clear her head.

And, softly murmuring her name, the returned wraiths followed her, unseen.

★

Before too long, the *Star of Deltora* had passed from the Ocean of the South into the Silver Sea, and soon the west coast of Deltora was just a faint smudge on the horizon. Huge, glittering sea serpents began following the ship, and transparent, eellike fish the crew called "bird banes" became common sights, shooting up from the waves and snatching unwary seabirds out of the air.

On the third day, Sky reappeared on deck, thinner and more silent than ever, but no longer ghastly pale. Her seasickness seemed to have left her. Vashti was the only one to mention it, asking Sky often how she felt, and warning in sympathetic tones that there was bound to be rougher weather later in the voyage.

For Britta, life on board the *Star* fell into a routine of sleeping, waking, eating dull food, taking exercise on deck, working on her trading plan and gathering what scraps of information she could from the books in the reading room. Mab was rarely seen except at meals. Vashti took every chance she could get to needle her companions, her blue eyes wide, her sweet smile never wavering. The weather remained favorable. The days slipped by like beads on a necklace, every day just like the last, as the first week gave way to the second.

And then, the evening before their expected arrival in Maris, something happened. Britta was alone in the reading room, about to pack up for the day. The gong announcing dinner had already sounded, and it did not do to be late. She tried to return the book she had been reading to the top shelf, and found that it would not slide easily into place. Something was blocking it. Sighing in irritation, Britta took a chair from beside the table and stood on it, groping in the back of the shelf.

Sure enough, there was a small, thick volume

lying there, wedged into the corner nearest the door. No doubt it had at first been standing upright, hidden behind the other books, but now it had fallen flat.

Britta drew it out. It looked very old. It was covered in dusty blue-green velvet, slightly rubbed but still beautifully decorated in faded gold. Its title was *Cladda's Mysteries of the Silver Sea*.

Britta's heart began to beat very fast, she was not sure why. Her fingers trembled as she turned to the Contents page. *The Isle of the Four Sisters*, she read, *The Heart of Gold ... The Crystal of Maris ... The Sunrise Pearls of Two Moons ... Tier—the "Hungry Isle" ...*

Her eyes blurred. Quickly she snapped the book shut, and as she did the edge of a flimsy slip of paper that had been pressed between the back cover and the last page slid into view. Britta pulled the paper out. It was a trader's receipt.

Two Moons Treasure House

Received from: *Dare Larsett, Trader of Del*
8 Gold Coins

In trade for: *1 copy of Cladda's Mysteries of the Silver Sea (slightly worn)*

Mull

The reading room door slammed open, crashing against the edge of the chair Britta was standing on and nearly making her lose her balance. She grabbed the top of the bookshelf for support.

"Ho, Britta!" Jewel bawled, leaning through the doorway. "Are you not coming to—?" She broke off, seeing the room apparently empty.

"I am here!" Britta said, hastily stuffing the receipt into her pocket and pushing the *Mysteries* book out of sight behind the others on the top shelf.

She jumped down from the chair, emerged from behind the door and hastily joined Jewel, who laughed at her all the way to the dining room.

All through dinner, Britta thought of the book. She longed to retrieve it, but knew that if she wanted to read it in private she would have to wait until Jewel, Sky and Vashti were asleep.

With difficulty, she made herself keep away from the reading room all evening. The hours passed more slowly than any she could remember since the voyage began. In a fever of impatience she strolled on the deck, sat at the writing table in the cabin and chatted with Jewel as they prepared for bed.

But at last all was dark, and the only sounds were the soft creaking of the ship and the lapping of the water against the hull. Lying in her bunk, her cloak in a bundle beside her, Britta waited. Her mind wandered. She drowsed. Then she stirred, sat up and pulled the cloak around her shoulders.

The curtains had been drawn over the porthole as usual, and the cabin was very dark. Slowly, feeling her way, Britta climbed down the ladder, stole past Jewel's bunk and let herself out into the passage. After that, it was only moments before she was turning the knob of the reading room door.

Silently closing the door behind her, she felt for the chair she had used to reach the top bookshelf. It was just where she had left it. Gingerly she crawled up on the seat, and stood. She felt the spines of the books packed together on the top shelf. She lifted the first three away, and felt with her other hand for the book she had hidden in the corner behind them.

Her groping fingers touched nothing but bare, dusty shelf. *Cladda's Mysteries of the Silver Sea* was gone.

4 - Maris

Britta spent a feverish ten minutes feeling behind all the books on the Silver Sea shelf before giving up the search. Someone had found *Cladda's Mysteries* and taken it. She cursed herself for leaving the chair behind the door. It had made someone curious. She might as well have left a blazing arrow pointing to the top shelf!

But who was the culprit—Vashti, Sky or Jewel? She knew they had all spent some time in the reading room that evening while she was pacing the deck, waiting for the hours to pass. One of them had the book—the book that must contain very valuable information, since her father had been willing to pay so much for it.

Crossly she crept back to the cabin and climbed into her bunk. Lying there, listening to the creaking of the ship and Jewel's even breathing, she slowly began to feel better. What did the book matter, after all? From what she had read on the Contents page, it lived up to its name. It dealt with mysterious legends, not with facts a trader needed to know.

She had her trading plan. Tomorrow she would begin to carry it out. The book would have been a distraction, and it was just as well that it had gone. The thief, whoever she was, was welcome to it. And may it bring her ill fortune, Britta thought grimly. She turned over, and willed herself to sleep.

*

The next day, just before noon, a thin, dark line became visible across the vast expanse of shining water.

"Maris!" caroled Jewel. "May the stars favor us, little nodnap!"

"Indeed!" Britta agreed fervently, and at that moment she really did wish Jewel good fortune—as long as her own luck was even better.

Sky, leaning lazily on the rail nearby, said nothing. The breeze tossed her waist-length hair, fluttered the bright scarf knotted at her throat and tugged at the fabric of her loose tunic and trousers. Otherwise, nothing about her moved except two of her fingers absently playing with one of the little ornaments tied to the braids that dangled on either side of her face.

If Sky felt nervous or excited at the sight of their first trading port, she was hiding it well. And Vashti had not even bothered to come on deck.

Two hours later, they were so close to Maris that across the choppy waves they could see pebbled streets and low, rounded buildings behind the long strip of beach. Slim figures in hooded cloaks of blue, green and silver stood in small groups on the sand. A few raised their arms to the approaching ship, but most simply watched.

"Not exactly a warm welcome," Jewel commented.

Vashti, who had made her appearance only moments before, smiled sweetly. "You would not know, Jewel, of course," she purred, "but experienced traders do not expect warmth from the Maris folk. They are not like us. It takes a long time to get to know them."

She sighed and gave a little yawn, as if to show that for her this arrival was a routine matter. "We will drop anchor in line with that offshore island," she trilled on, pointing to a small, thickly forested hump of land jutting from the water not far from shore. "Then we will be rowed to the beach in the landing boat. That is how it is always done here."

None of the other finalists answered. Sky was staring in fascination at the little island. Jewel was frowning towards the town. And Britta—Britta was struggling to remain expressionless as a strange feeling crept over her, growing stronger by the moment.

Shadows had begun flickering before her eyes again. Her skin was warming and tingling. It was as if invisible bodies were pressing closely around her, as if invisible fingers were brushing her hands, her face, her neck. She shivered, and heard Vashti give a tinkling laugh.

"Poor Britta is very nervous," Vashti cooed to Sky, loudly enough for Britta to hear. "She is shaking in her boots! I am not surprised. The Maris are cunning, and expert traders. She will need more than luck to do well here."

Do not react, Britta ordered herself fiercely. You should be used to Vashti's needling by now. She gripped the rail, pretending she had not heard, and found with relief that her irritation had broken her strange mood. Her vision had abruptly cleared, and the close, prickling feeling had gone. Vashti had done her a favor without knowing it.

"It seems you are nervous too, Sky of Rithmere," Vashti went on smoothly. "Why do you stare so at the little island? There is no trading to be done there."

"The island interests me," Britta heard Sky answer shortly. "I would like to see it more closely."

There was the tiniest pause, then:

"Well, why not?" Vashti murmured, lowering her voice so that Britta had to strain to make out the words. "We will be in Maris for three whole days. You could easily slip away for a time without being noticed. The island is not far from shore, and you claim to be able to swim like a fish."

"Indeed," Sky said thoughtfully. "It is a tempting idea."

Britta stiffened. "Sky, no!" she exclaimed, swinging round impulsively. "The little island is forbidden to all but the Keeper of Maris, and if you set foot on it the Keeper will know. He feels everything that happens in these waters. Vashti is trying to get you into trouble!"

Vashti's eyes flashed with baffled anger, then she gave her silvery laugh again. "Oh, Britta, how stern and serious you are!" she cried. "Do you not know a joke when you hear it?"

"Yes," said Britta evenly. "And you were not joking."

"Of course I was!" Vashti retorted. "And I should tell you, Britta, for your own good, that *ladies* do not eavesdrop on private conversations!"

She tossed her head and flounced away to stand by the rail on the other side of the ship.

"Thank you for your concern," Sky drawled, turning to stare at Britta, "but my ignorance is not so great as you and Vashti plainly think it is. I know perfectly well that to set foot on that island would end my promising career before it has begun."

Britta felt her face grow hot. "But I thought—"

"It suited me to let Vashti think I was taken in," Sky said. "At the very least, she would have been confused when I came to no harm. But that little plan has come to nothing, thanks to you."

"Oh!" By now Britta's cheeks were burning. She felt angry and foolish in equal measure. "I am sorry," she said, with all the dignity she could muster. "I was only trying to help."

She thought for an instant that Sky's dark eyes had softened, but then it was as if a shutter had fallen over the lean face, leaving it blank and expressionless.

"I can look after myself," Sky muttered, looking away. "Keep your nose out of my affairs in future!"

"Do not worry!" Britta snapped. "From now on, I would rather jump overboard than lift a finger to help … "

The words died in her throat as she heard shouts ringing out around her, and suddenly became aware that something very strange was happening.

The brisk wind had ceased as abruptly as if a door had slammed, shutting it out. The choppy sea had smoothed and calmed till not a single white fleck marred its surface, and nothing stirred in the depths below.

With no wind or tide to drive her, the *Star of Deltora* slowed and finally could move no more. In minutes she was floating motionless on what looked like a vast sheet of blue-green glass, her sails sagging on her masts like limp white curtains.

It was utterly still. Even the seabirds had fallen silent. The only sounds were the creaking of the ship's timbers and the shocked curses of the crew.

"Sorcery!" Jewel hissed, backing away from the rail.

Britta swallowed. The creeping, prickling feeling

that had oppressed her before had returned. She shook her head, determined not to give way to it.

"The Keeper has halted us," she managed to say. "He does not want us to come any closer."

"But why?" Jewel exclaimed. "Vashti said it was usual for ships to drop anchor in line with the offshore island, and that is still quite a way ahead!"

Stiffly Britta turned her head and looked towards the shore. Waves no longer crashed and foamed on the long strip of sand, which was now completely deserted. Blue, green and silver glinted in the spaces between the buildings of the town beyond. The colors were massed together as if the streets were crowded with people standing perfectly still, shoulder to shoulder, waiting.

"Something is wrong," she said.

She knew it was true. She knew it by the empty beach, by the stillness of the people in the town. She knew it by the frightened curses of the crew, who had plainly never seen a ship stopped in this way before. And she knew it by the sight of Mab, who was standing rigidly at the prow with Captain Hara, her hands on her hips, her red hair flaming in the sunlight, her whole body radiating anger.

"*Wrong?* But what in the nine seas could be wrong?" Jewel demanded.

"I think we are about to find out," Sky murmured. She was gazing at the limpid stretch of sea between the *Star of Deltora* and the shore.

Britta followed Sky's eyes, and her stomach

41

turned over. A small boat was approaching, gliding smoothly over the glassy water. The craft's white hull looked as frail as a shell. No sail hung from the slender mast, and there were no oars in sight. Yet the boat moved—moved steadily towards the *Star of Deltora*—leaving no ripples behind to show its path. In it stood a slim figure wearing a tightly hooded blue cloak made of some shining fabric Britta did not recognize.

Sky began to edge towards Mab and Captain Hara. Britta and Jewel quickly followed. Hara glanced at them and frowned, but the old trader did not turn. Either she did not hear their approach or she did not care what they did. She waited in silence as the Maris craft drew closer, never taking her eyes from the strange being standing so upright by the mast.

Only when the craft stopped a little way from the ship did her mellow voice ring out, loud in the unnatural silence.

"Greetings, Perlain of the clan Pandellis! What is the meaning of this?"

Craning her neck around Sky, Britta caught her breath as she saw the Maris man clearly. Beneath his cloak he was clothed from head to foot in tight garments of shining blue. His skin was glistening blue gray, his eyes were pale, flat and empty of expression. The fingers that grasped the mast were webbed.

"Greetings, Mab, the Trader Rosalyn," the being replied, with a slight bow. "Greetings, Captain Hara! The people of Maris regret the inconvenience, but sadly we cannot welcome you to our shores at present. We must ask you to leave us."

"*Leave?*" roared Captain Hara. "What madness is—?"

He broke off as Mab laid a warning hand on his sleeve.

"There has always been goodwill between Maris and the Rosalyn fleet, Perlain," Mab said calmly. "For centuries our friendship has profited us both. I would be sorry to think that the situation had changed."

"It has not changed," the Maris man said, with equal calm. "But on this occasion we regret that we cannot accept your visit. That is our right, as I am sure you will agree."

"Of course," Mab replied. "But as I am sure *you* will agree, Perlain, our long friendship gives *us* the right to ask for an explanation."

Perlain hesitated. His webbed hand tightened briefly on the mast.

"Is there plague in the town?" Captain Hara asked suddenly. "By the heavens, if that is so—"

"There is no plague in Maris," Perlain broke in. And something about the way he said it sent a shiver down Britta's spine. Surely there had been a very slight emphasis on the last word. *There is no plague in* Maris. In *Maris*.

Mab had not missed the hint. Her whole body stiffened. "Do I gather that the Keeper feels the seeds of plague aboard the *Star of Deltora*?" she asked quietly.

"If so, he is mistaken. We have sailed directly from Del. If plague were aboard it would have shown itself by now, and there has been no sign of it."

Again the Maris man hesitated. Britta heard Jewel curse under her breath, felt her own heart beating fast and hard.

"This is no time to be discreet, Perlain," Mab persisted, her voice hardening. "Maris was chosen as the first port of call on a voyage that is of great importance to the Rosalyn fleet. The Keeper has insulted us by halting our ship and refusing to offer welcome. If you wish our friendship to remain unbroken, you must tell me why."

"And if you fear the truth will cause panic aboard this vessel, you can put that out of your mind, man of Maris," Hara growled. "Any member of my crew who attempts to land without permission will die at my hand—I give you my oath on that."

Perlain bent his head briefly and then looked up, straight at Mab. His long, lipless mouth opened.

"I will be plain, since you wish it," he said. "The Keeper senses a fearful presence on your ship, Trader Rosalyn. Someone aboard is wreathed in shadows. The evil may be illness of the body or mind. It may be ... something worse. But whatever it is, the odor of death is at its heart, and we do not want it here."

5 - The Warning

Captain Hara made a sudden movement, quickly controlled. Mab did not look at him. Nor did she glance behind her at Britta, Jewel and Sky, who had all gasped. She kept her eyes on the Maris man's face. Her back was very straight, her shoulders squared.

"With the greatest respect, I assure you that the Keeper is mistaken," she said evenly. "If there was a soul aboard the *Star of Deltora* who could or would harm your people, Captain Hara and I would know it. I ask you to trust our judgment and allow us to land."

Perlain hesitated. His eyes closed. Plainly he was listening to something no one else could hear. Then his eyes opened, and slowly he spoke.

"I am sorry, but there is nothing to be done. The Keeper cannot tell what the dread presence on your vessel is, or who is harboring it, but he knows it exists.

He feels it, by the power of the Crystal. Any other ship containing such a shadow would have been destroyed the moment it entered Maris waters. The bonds of long friendship alone have spared the *Star of Deltora* ... for now."

The threat was unmistakable. Perlain closed his lips and waited.

"I see," Mab said, her voice as firm and steady as ever. "Then we have no choice but to sail on to our next port, as soon as the Keeper sees fit to release us. We ask only that you fill our empty water barrels before we depart, for the usual fee."

"New barrels are being filled at this moment," Perlain said, glancing over his shoulder towards the town. "They will be sent to you very soon, and are offered with our compliments."

Without waiting for an answer, he gave another slight bow. "Thank you for your understanding, Trader Rosalyn. I bid you farewell and wish you fair winds. I hope to see you again, at a better time."

"I hope the same," said Mab, and watched without a tremor as the shell-like craft turned and began silently gliding back towards the shore.

Hara snorted. "New barrels, indeed!" he muttered wrathfully. "With their compliments! That would be the first time those slippery scoundrels have ever given us anything free!"

"They want nothing from this ship to touch the shore," Mab said. "They fear infection ... in any form."

She swung round and fixed Britta, Sky and Jewel with eyes as hard as stone. "Vashti!" she called sharply, without turning her head. "Come here, if you please! I have something to say, and I do not wish to have to repeat myself."

Vashti emerged from behind some empty water barrels on the other side of the ship and crossed the deck, smoothing her hair. Her face was red, she was breathing hard, and her eyes were shining with angry tears.

"I cannot believe we are forbidden to trade at our first port because of some—some foolish imagining of the Keeper!" she burst out. "How do the Maris dare to refuse entry to a Rosalyn ship on such grounds?"

"This is their territory," Mab said coldly. "They have a perfect right to refuse our visit—on any grounds."

"But—" Vashti clenched her fists. For once she was finding it difficult to control herself. "My trading plan—"

"Will have to be altered," Mab cut in. "A good trader is flexible, Vashti! Now, listen to me, all of you! If I had known what Perlain had to say to me, I would have ordered you all out of earshot. As it is, you overheard our conversation. That cannot be undone, but it is vital that you do not chatter of what you know. You must keep it to yourselves."

She paused, pressing her lips together as if it was too much of an effort to go on. Her face was gaunt. Her skin seemed stretched too tightly over her bones, and was gray beneath the rouge that stained her cheeks. Captain Hara moved a little closer to her and slid his hand under her elbow, but she twitched impatiently away from him, lifted her chin and went on.

"I need not tell you, I am sure, that there is no danger on this vessel. You are all rational beings and must see that any evil aboard would have shown itself by now. But sailors as a breed are superstitious, and because the men on this voyage are all new to the *Star of Deltora*, they are more likely to be unsettled by wild tales than our regular crew would be. The men are to know only what Captain Hara sees fit to tell them. Is that understood?"

She scanned the faces of the four standing before her, and went on only after receiving four nods.

"Good," she said, in a slightly milder voice. "It will be hard enough as it is for Hara to explain why we are not landing. The men have been looking forward to shore leave in Maris."

"They have indeed," Hara muttered. "And I must tell you that I do not like our chances of keeping this business quiet, Mab. It would be a miracle if at least some of what Perlain said was not overheard, and word will soon spread. You know what ships are."

He scowled, gesturing at the shore. "And look there! That alone will set tongues wagging. What better sign could the Keeper give that this ship is not to be touched by Maris hands?"

Britta looked at the beach and her stomach tightened. Perlain's boat was drawn up on the sand. Beside it, cloaked figures were rolling barrels into the still water. The barrels already afloat were drifting steadily towards the ship in a long, straight line. The sight was eerie.

Hara scrubbed at his beard in frustration. "It will be tedious work, retrieving those barrels from the sea. We will be stranded here for some time yet. But that is my affair. You have done your part, Mab. Go below and rest while you can."

"Do not fuss, Hara, curse you!" Mab barked. "I get enough of that from Kay!"

Hara said nothing, and after a moment the old woman sighed and shook her head. "I daresay you are right," she said grudgingly. "I will do as you say."

Scowling, she turned back to the watching finalists. "You people can go below as well. You will be in the way here, and you all have work to do. You must make new plans based on a first trade at Two Moons."

In silence the four tramped to the stern and crowded down the little staircase to the lower deck. Vashti stormed into her cabin and slammed the door. Hands in pockets, Sky sauntered on along the passage, no doubt making for the reading room. Left alone, Jewel and Britta glanced at each other, then without a word moved into their cabin and sat down with the little writing table between them.

"So," Jewel said quietly, "we load the Maris

water and sail on. Hara tries to make the crew believe some fairy tale, we keep silent, and no one says a word about the most important question."

"What question?" Britta felt so flat, and at the same time so uneasy, that she was finding it hard to think clearly. All her plans had been overturned. Her mind had been focused on Maris, on trading well in Maris, and now Maris had been denied her.

Jewel gave a snort of laughter that carried no trace of humor. "Wake up, little nodnap! The question of what the Keeper sensed! A fearful presence aboard this ship—a presence with death at its heart!"

"Mab does not believe in it," Britta said. But as she spoke, she shivered, for in her heart she knew her words were not true. Mab, and Hara too, had been shaken by Perlain's message. Their iron control had not been able to disguise the fact that they were feeling far more than simple anger at being turned away from Maris. That meant that they *did* believe the Keeper's claim—in part, at least—though they were pretending otherwise to avoid panic on the ship.

"It is dangerous to ignore such a warning," Jewel muttered. "If there is evil aboard, we should seek it out and destroy it." Sweat was beading her brow. Her right hand was pressed to her shining metal armband as if it were a talisman.

The dim walls of the cabin seemed to press in on Britta, press in on her till she could hardly breathe. Fearful whispers echoed in her mind. For an instant she was certain that she was feeling what the Keeper of Maris had felt, and dread brushed her with icy fingers.

With a great effort, she calmed herself. Do not be absurd, she told herself sternly. You are safe in your own cabin! You are imagining things, like a child who fears monsters under the bed!

"We have been at sea for almost a fortnight," she said aloud, struggling to keep her voice steady. "Whatever the Keeper senses, it has not harmed us yet."

"It may be waiting its time," Jewel answered soberly. "If it is here it is here for a reason, and that reason cannot be good. We are trapped in this cursed ship with something we cannot see, Britta. And it is a long way to Two Moons."

The moment the last water barrel had been hauled on board, a strong wind filled the *Star*'s sails and sped her away from Maris. None of the finalists appeared on deck to catch a last glimpse of the forbidden shore. Nor did Mab or Healer Kay. The crew worked sullenly, without looking back. Only Captain Hara stood watching the thin line of land fade into the distance. His bearded face was troubled, but he shared his thoughts with no one.

★

That night, Britta could not sleep. Her mind was filled with memories of what had happened in Maris, of the things that Jewel had said. She kept thinking, too, of her ruined trading plan. There would be no silk, wine or cheese to trade in Two Moons now. All her work since leaving Del was wasted.

At last she decided she could lie in her bunk no longer. She crawled onto the ladder and climbed down. Jewel was a dark, silent shape in the lower bunk. Taking care to make no sound, Britta threw her cloak over her nightgown, let herself out of the cabin and padded barefoot to the reading room. There, at least, she thought, she could light a lantern and find a book that would lull her to sleep.

She had shut the reading room door behind her, and was feeling her way towards the wall where the lantern always hung, when she heard a small sound in the passage outside.

Terror seized her. The Maris man's words echoed in her mind.

Someone aboard is wreathed in shadows. The evil may be illness of the body or mind. It may be ... something worse ...

Britta clenched her teeth, balled her hands into fists. It was ridiculous to fear a sound on the *Star of Deltora* at night! It was absurd to think that danger roamed this beautiful ship!

And yet as she heard the sound of the reading room doorknob turning, she did not hesitate. In a single movement she wrapped her cloak around her and crouched down behind the table.

She heard the door creak open. She heard

someone step, soft footed, into the dark room. She heard a soft, sliding sound and a tiny thud. And then the door was closing again, and she knew she was alone once more.

Britta let out her breath and drew fresh air into her lungs. Shakily she stood up, feeling ashamed of herself. There had been nothing at all to fear. The intruder had been simply returning a book to the shelves—returning it by night because it was forbidden to remove volumes from the reading room, and whoever it was had broken the rules.

Hard on the heels of that thought came another.

Taking her time, Britta lit the lantern. Quietly she moved a chair to the shelves beside the door. She climbed onto the seat of the chair, took the first three books from the top shelf, and groped in the space behind them.

Her fingers touched something soft, square and thick. She drew it out.

The gold decorations winked at her in the lantern light. The title shone against the blue-green velvet. *Cladda's Mysteries of the Silver Sea.*

6 - Undercurrents

Her heart beating hard, Britta climbed from the chair and sat down at the table. She held the book loosely between her hands, then let it fall open. And there before her lay the pages that she was sure the person who had taken the book had read many times. She stared at the chapter heading at the top of the left-hand page.

THE SUNRISE PEARLS OF TWO MOONS

So, despite what Mab had said, someone had been reading about sunrise pearls! Was it Jewel, or Sky? It must have been one of them. Vashti was not tall enough to reach the top shelf without standing on a chair.

Well, whoever it was plainly thought that the chapter was worth studying—and in secret, too. It would be as well to know why. Eagerly, Britta began to read.

☀ Sunrise pearls, rare pink pearls of great beauty, are one of the many mysteries of the Two Moons swamplands. They are harvested only by the swamp dwellers, whose territory is forbidden to outsiders.

☀ The pearls' exact location is a closely guarded secret. This writer has heard rumors that they are to be found in patches of a dangerous type of swamp mud, pale in color and with the ability to drag a fully grown man down to his death in less than a minute. If this tale is true, it explains why the pearls are so rare, for harvesting them must be perilous. Even the common swamp mud is treacherous.

☀ Many swamp dwellers believe that sunrise pearls are a legacy of the fabled turtle man Tier, who worked magic in the Two Moons swamplands before being set upon by fearful neighbors and cast into the sea. According to legend, Tier survived his ordeal and at last used mud from his native land to create from bare rock the isle that bears his name. He then transformed a handful of sand into a wondrous Staff which gave his island the power to move and feed. (see *Tier—the "Hungry Isle"*)

Britta caught her breath. The lantern light flickered crazily. Shadows danced across the pages of the book. She shut her eyes, scolding herself for her weakness. She knew the story of Tier perfectly well. Most people knew it. She had to learn not to react so violently every time a mention of the magic Staff or the Hungry Isle took her by surprise.

Opening her eyes again, she forced herself to read on.

☀ **A tribe that reverences the sorcerer Tier exists in the deepest part of the Two Moons swamplands to this day. The symbol of the tribe is a turtle, and its leader is said to be heir to Tier's magic.**

☀ **The "turtle people," as they are known, are the chief suppliers of sunrise pearls to the traders of Two Moons. They are feared by other swamp dwellers, who believe that they use Tier's sorcery to collect the pearls safely.**

☀ **Few who enter the turtle people's territory ever return, and those who do never speak of what they have seen. Even the pirate Bar-Enoch, who is said to have spent several days in the depths of the swamp, did not boast of his time there.**

☀ **According to his crew, Bar-Enoch went into the swamplands alone, with precious goods to trade, and returned mud stained and apparently empty-handed. It is worth noting, however, that from Two**

Moons Bar-Enoch sailed directly to the Hungry Isle, where he claimed the Staff of Tier for himself. It seems likely that the turtle people gave him secret knowledge that allowed him to take the Staff from its creator's dead hand without being struck down by the famous curse.

Britta felt sick. This was something she had never heard or read before. Was this why her father had paid such a high price for the book? Because it told of Bar-Enoch's visit to Two Moons, and guessed at the reason?

Certainly, Larsett had followed in the pirate's footsteps. He had also visited Two Moons shortly before becoming the new Master of the Staff of Tier.

Britta snapped the book shut, forcing away the unwelcome thoughts and feelings it had roused in her. Keeping her mind blank, she jumped up, darted to the shelves and thrust the book back into its hiding place, telling herself to forget she had ever seen it.

★

The long days that followed as the ship forged south, on course for Two Moons, were very different from those that had gone before.

On the surface, little had changed. Good weather and fair winds continued to bless them. Flying fish still jumped in the spangled waves. Now and then a sea serpent seeking easy prey would follow the ship for a time before giving up and vanishing into the depths. Salted meat and pickled greens appeared on the dinner table all too often. Mab and Captain Hara ordered no search, and behaved exactly as they had before. And despite Jewel's fears, day succeeded day with no sign of the shadow sensed by the Keeper.

Yet below the surface, all was not well. Dark undercurrents were pulling the mood of the ship down, growing stronger with every sunset.

The crew was increasingly restless. As Hara had feared, his efforts to make little of the failed landing in Maris had not been successful. Those men who had seen Perlain arrive had done their utmost to catch at least a few of his words. What they had not heard for themselves, they guessed, and the tale that the *Star of Deltora* was cursed had quickly spread.

Bosun Crow suddenly recalled hearing that Zoolah, Senior Managing Officer of the Rosalyn Trust, had died suddenly the night before the ship sailed. His story fanned the flames of rumor. The death of a middle-aged woman with a weak heart would have meant nothing to the crew before, but now it was seen as a dread warning.

Rumors swelled and multiplied, fueled by fear. Those who knew the history of the *Star of Deltora* wasted no time in whispering the gruesome details of her first, ill-fated voyage to those who did not.

Soon everyone from Grubb the ship's cook to Davvie the cabin boy knew that the *Star* had been built for Dare Larsett, the famous Del trader who had become the sorcerer king of the dreaded Hungry Isle. They knew that Larsett had used his ship to find the fabled Staff of Tier and carry it back to the haunted place where it had been created, and where it would be most powerful. They knew that the *Star of Deltora* had later been found drifting in the Silver Sea, her crew slaughtered and the skeleton of Zoolah's brother, the gallant Captain Mikah, tied to the wheel.

All this made a mixture powerful enough to convince every seaman aboard that the *Star of Deltora* was at best unlucky, and at worst haunted by the vengeful dead. The fact that for eight years the ship had sailed safely under the flag of the Rosalyn fleet, and had never been forbidden a landing in Maris before, made no difference.

It was torment for Britta to overhear the furtive mutterings that had now replaced songs, rough jokes and raucous laughter when the crew worked on deck. She had her own reasons for wanting to forget Zoolah's wretched death. And every mention of her father caused a pang of guilt that, try as she might, she could not ignore.

I am not my father! she told herself, as she had told herself so often before. I am not responsible for what my father did!

But in her heart she knew that it was not so easy. If Zoolah had lived long enough to tell Mab who Britta really was, Britta would have been disgraced and left behind in Del. If the troubled crewmen were to discover that their ship was carrying the daughter of Dare Larsett, they would very likely mutiny, and throw her into the sea.

But they do not know it, Britta told herself, lying sleepless in her cabin while Jewel snored softly in the bunk below. They need never know it. I must not let their talk upset me. I must forget I am anything but what Captain Gripp said I was. I must forget Zoolah, forget my father, my mother, my sister. I must forget everything but that I am Britta, a poor orphan, Gripp's distant relation—and a finalist in the contest to become Apprentice to the Trader Rosalyn!

She did her best. She shut her ears to the whispers she overheard on deck. She lost herself in work on her new trading plan. She did not react when Captain Hara gloomed over his dinner, murmuring to Mab of the latest rumor he had tried and failed to suppress.

The men went about their work sulky, fearful and muttering. They jumped at shadows, bickered with one another, neglected their duties and made mistakes. Accidents became common, and every accident, from burned rice in the galley to an arm broken by a carelessly tied water barrel, was taken to be proof of the curse.

Captain Hara tried to quell the rising discontent by sharp orders and at last by threatening to throw the worst of the troublemakers into the lockup. But still the muttering, brawling and mishaps continued.

"It was a mistake to sign on a gang of strangers instead of keeping to our usual crew," Britta heard Hara growl to Mab at dinner one night. "I will be surprised if half of them do not jump ship at Two Moons."

Mab looked up from her plate. "Offer them double pay," she said crisply.

"*Double* … ?" Hara raised his eyebrows. "By the heavens, Mab, have you any idea how much—?"

"I can multiply by two as well as you can, Hara!" Mab interrupted. "Tell the crew that I have offered double pay to every man who is still with the ship on its return to Del. Greed goes a long way towards conquering fear—especially fear that is based only on foolish whispers in the dark."

The next morning Hara did as she asked, and after that the crew became less troublesome, though the brooding atmosphere remained.

The finalists, too, were not as relaxed as they had been during the first leg of the voyage. The events in Maris waters had left their mark. Troubled as she was, Britta was well aware that she was not the only one whose mood had changed.

Now that the contest had shrunk to two trades on islands about which they knew little, all the finalists had become more secretive. Britta was still angry with Sky. Sky behaved as if Britta did not exist. Jewel was unnaturally silent and watchful. Vashti, her sweet smile firmly back in place, took every opportunity to upset them all.

Between meals, the candidates spent their time alone. Vashti kept to her cabin. Britta haunted the reading room. Jewel and Sky spent hours on deck, Jewel pacing the rail like a caged beast, Sky sitting cross-legged in the sun practicing tricks with a battered deck of cards.

Jewel and Britta still talked a little when they were alone in their cabin at night, but their conversations were more awkward than before. This was because they could not speak of the two things that were uppermost in both their minds—Two Moons and the Keeper's warning.

Neither cared to mention Two Moons, in case she let slip some useful detail her companion did not know, and so lose an advantage. And Jewel refused point blank to discuss the warning.

At dinner, the night after leaving Maris, Jewel had bluntly asked Mab what plans had been made to unmask whoever was harboring the evil felt by the Keeper. The sharp snub she had received had silenced her, and from that moment she had kept her thoughts on the matter to herself, even when Mab was not present. The others assumed, perhaps, that her fears had subsided. Only Britta, who climbed past Jewel into the top bunk every night, knew that her cabin-mate now slept with her knife by her side.

7 - Two Moons

The weather warmed as they moved steadily south. Sea serpents became rare. Great schools of small golden fish, spotted and striped with black and equipped with needle teeth, surged up from the deep to fight over the scraps thrown overboard by the cooks. Huge turtles basked on the white shores of tiny, deserted islands.

The sun gained strength. The ship began to smell of warm tar, harsh soap and sweat. Mab stalked the deck in flapping cotton trousers and a loose, lavishly embroidered tunic of scarlet silk. Healer Kay appeared in a long, tentlike garment striped in purple and silver. Jewel and Sky discarded their boots and went barefoot.

After a few days of stifling discomfort, Britta thrust aside visions of her mother's horror and left off her flannel petticoat. The next morning she unfastened the two top buttons of her tight white shirt and rolled up her sleeves to the elbow. And the following day, wrestling with hairpins in the stuffy cabin, she lost patience and simply tied her hair back in a bunch with the scrap of red ribbon she used as a bookmark in *A Trader's Life*.

"Oh, Britta, have you lost all your hairpins?" cooed Vashti at breakfast that morning. "What a pity you did not bring spares, as I did!"

Britta merely smiled. She felt so comfortable that she was wondering why she had not abandoned the tight knot at the nape of her neck before. Vashti, of course, had not loosened a single button of her shirt, despite the heat, and her hair was as rigidly confined as ever.

Finding that taunting Britta was of no use, Vashti chose another target.

"Only think, in three days we will reach Two Moons, safe and sound!" she said, with a sideways glance at Jewel, who was wolfing down rice sweetened with dried fruit. "*Some* people feared we would never survive the voyage. But then, ignorant folk panic so easily."

Britta held her breath, but Jewel refused to rise to the bait. She went on chewing stolidly without even looking up.

"I would change my tactics if I were you, Vashti," drawled Sky, speaking for the first time since entering the room. "We all know your little game by now."

Vashti blinked, and widened her blue eyes.

"What can you mean, Sky of Rithmere?"

Sky's face split into a mocking grin, her teeth gleaming very white against her olive skin. She pushed back her chair, stood up and swung out of the dining room, the little ornaments tied to her braids jingling merrily.

Vashti forced a silvery laugh. "That girl is so *odd!*" she murmured. "But I suppose we have to make allowances for her. Poor, plain creature, she is sadly out of her depth among us, and naturally she is jealous."

Jewel scraped her plate clean, swallowed her last mouthful of rice and threw down her spoon. She wiped her mouth with the back of her hand and then she, too, stood up.

"I will make no allowances for Sky," she said genially. "That would be foolish. Sky is as slippery as a fish and as cunning as a messenger bird."

She bent, leaning her hands on the table. Her eyes narrowed. "But you, Vashti, are as sly as a snake! From the beginning you have done your best to lure the rest of us into trouble that will put us out of the contest."

"That is insulting and absurd!" hissed Vashti, paling with anger.

"Insulting, yes!" Jewel replied calmly. "Absurd, no! And in my opinion this shows that you are far from being as confident as you wish to appear. You fear you cannot win in a fair fight."

Then she too left the room. After a moment, Britta followed. She had not finished her breakfast, but the look on Vashti's face had spoiled her appetite.

★

Three days later, just before sunrise, the *Star of Deltora* sailed into Two Moons harbor. Washed, brushed and buttoned, hair carefully knotted and pinned, Britta stood at the prow with the other finalists, her heart beating very fast, her eyes drinking in the scene before her.

She had read that the island was shaped like a crescent moon. She had read that its large, calm bay could provide safe harbor for a dozen ships. But nothing she had read had prepared her for this beauty.

The long, curving spits of land that were the arms of the crescent seemed to embrace the *Star of Deltora* as she passed between them. The smooth water of the bay was mauve beneath a sky flooded with glorious pink. The arc of the shore ahead was spangled with small, glowing lights. The center lay dark and mysterious beyond, shrouded in a shining, rose-tinted haze.

Wrapped in the dimness of the silent ship, Britta gazed, spellbound, as the land drew closer. It came to her that, win or lose, the whole voyage, her whole, mad attempt to become the Trader Rosalyn Apprentice, had been worthwhile just for this moment.

She became aware of a scent drifting on the air. It was the breath of the island—a mixture of spices, sodden earth and still, dank water, with the faintest trace of something almost unbearably rich and sweet.

Without warning, the strangest feeling swept over her. Two Moons was unlike any place she had ever seen before, yet something was telling her that it was not merely beautiful, but familiar and beloved. The island was tugging at her heart as if somehow it reminded her of home, and a great yearning to reach it swept over her, bringing tears to her eyes.

The feeling was so strong that Britta was frightened. It seemed—almost—to be coming not from her, but from something outside her. The very air, the shadows around her, seemed thick with longing.

Familiar words from *A Trader's Life* flashed into her mind.

Once, long ago, a monster called Tier, said to be half man, half turtle, was born to a sorceress who lived on the island of Two Moons in the Silver Sea ...

Of course I am moved, Britta told herself. There is no mystery about it! I have read Trader Sven's tale of the sorcerer Tier so often that I almost know it by heart. I saw the same tale in the *Mysteries* book just a few days ago. And now I am in the place where the story began!

But Trader Sven also wrote of Maris, the small, cold voice of reason argued in her mind. *You have read those stories time and again. Yet you did not feel like this in Maris waters. You felt fear and awe when you saw the Keeper's isle, but no longing when you looked upon Maris itself.*

Britta frowned, but the small voice went on remorselessly: *Two Moons is different, because Tier's story is so closely linked with your father's. Tier created the enchanted isle your father now rules and the magic Staff your father now wields. Your father came to Two Moons on his last voyage. The seeds of your family's disgrace lie here.*

Gritting her teeth, Britta pushed the unwelcome thoughts away. She fixed her eyes on the dreamlike shore, willing it to cast its spell over her once more.

"Do not be too impressed. Two Moons always looks its best at dawn and dusk."

Britta jumped and turned. Mab was standing behind her. The old trader looked haggard, but she was as vividly painted as always and dressed splendidly for shore. Her loose trousers were brilliantly white and her floating silk coat glimmered with all the colors of the sea. From her earlobes swung long silver hoops, the base of each hoop set with a single, blush-pink pearl.

"I first saw Two Moons on a morning very like this one," Mab said. "I was just a girl then, serving my first year as the Trader Rosalyn Apprentice. I will never forget that moment. I thought I had come to paradise!"

She smiled wryly. "But the vision did not last. The rising sun burned away the beauty as quickly and surely as the years since have worn away my youth and strength. Sadly, time does not stand still."

Her lips tightened and abruptly she turned away. "Unless," she added, her voice hardening, "you are willing to sacrifice anyone and anything to defy the course of nature, and cheat death."

As Dare Larsett was. The words had not been spoken aloud, but Britta felt as hollow as if they had.

Mab stalked off to join Captain Hara and Crow, and in an instant Jewel was by Britta's side, her eyes alight with curiosity.

"By the stars, you are favored, Britta!" Jewel whispered. "A private chat with Mab! Vashti is sick with envy, and I am feeling rather green myself. What did the old witch say to you?"

Britta swallowed. "It was hardly a chat. She might as well have been talking to herself. She was just—remembering her past."

"Oh, yes?" Jewel spoke with perfect good humor, but she withdrew a little. Plainly she thought Britta was keeping something to herself—a shred of advice from Mab, perhaps—some words of wisdom that her rival did not want to share.

Suddenly Britta felt intensely lonely. A wave of homesickness washed over her, dulling the beauty of the dawn.

She thought of Jantsy, sliding his last batch of fragrant, crusty bread out of the great oven in his family's bakery as the sun rose in Del. Jantsy's face would be flushed with heat beneath the white cap that covered his honey-colored hair. After a time, he would open the shutters and unlock the bakery door, ready to greet early customers with his usual friendly grin.

Captain Gripp was an early riser, too. Every morning before it was light he settled himself at the window of his cottage by the shore to watch Del harbor come alive with the dawn. Safe in his chair, he would shout orders to Bosun the polypan, who would be clattering about at the stove, making the first brew of strong black tea for the day.

At daybreak, Margareth was usually still asleep in their bedroom above the shop, curled up on her side as always, with one hand beneath her cheek. When she woke, her gentle eyes might sadden at the sight of her younger sister's tidy, empty bed on the other side of the cramped little room. Then she would sigh, and smile, and get up to begin another day working in the shop with their mother.

The thought of her mother made Britta wince. How often over the past weeks had the dawn found Maarie ill and fretful after a sleepless night spent thinking of the daughter who had left her, betrayed her, to chase a dangerous dream?

Furiously Britta swallowed the burning lump that had risen in her throat. "Truly, Jewel!" she insisted. "Mab told me nothing of importance—nothing at all!"

"Very well," said Jewel, eyeing her curiously. "I believe you. Do not upset yourself."

"I am not upset!" Britta hissed, all too aware that her face must be giving the lie to her words. "I am just sick of—of not being trusted!"

Jewel shrugged. "None of us can afford to trust

too far. We are rivals for a great prize, and we all want to win."

The calm good sense was like a splash of cool water. Britta bit her lip and nodded, very ashamed of her outburst. What had she been thinking of? This was no time to lose her nerve! Deliberately she straightened her shoulders and raised her chin to look ahead once more at the land that had so enchanted her.

But in the last few minutes, without her noticing, the sun had risen higher in the sky. The pastel dawn had given way to the bright, clear light of early morning. And as Mab had predicted, the dreamlike beauty of Two Moons had vanished as if it had never been.

The mist rising from the center had turned from luminous pink to dull white. At the shoreline, the muddy water of the bay lapped sluggishly against great, slimy posts supporting a long line of jetties, each jetty bearing a large, bright-yellow number. And between center and shore lay the narrow band of the town, no longer veiled in gentle dimness but revealed all too plainly by the merciless sun.

Lining the paved streets, shops, stores and warehouses of every shape and size jostled together, their roofs and sides plastered with garish signs, most written in several languages. *Two Moons Trading Post*, Britta read. *Sunrise Stores—Finest Quality! Bargains! ... Xen's Prices Cannot be Beaten—Make an Offer! ... Genuine Sunrise Pearls Here! Beware Imitations! ...*

In the harsh light of day, Two Moons no longer

looked like a place of legend and mystery. It had been shown for what it was—a bustling, thrusting trading port where the business of buying and selling was all that mattered.

The change was startling, but in Britta's present mood it was very welcome. Now she was dealing with something she could understand.

Nervous excitement thrilled through her body, banishing the shadows that had clouded her mind, burning away fear and doubt. She turned to pick up her shore bag and pack away the snack meal and water flask that Davvie had dumped beside it. She could almost feel the blood rushing through her veins. Now, at last, it was time to show what she was made of. Now the real test was about to begin.

8 - Word of Honor

The landing at Two Moons began well. Numbered flags raised on the shore directed the ship to moor at Jetty 3, right opposite the main part of the town. As the *Star of Deltora* slid gently into place, as the anchor was dropped and ropes were tied, dozens of eager people, all with something to sell, gathered to wave, sing, and call words of welcome. But by the time Mab, Healer Kay, Sky, Jewel, Vashti and Britta moved down the gangplank stretching from the ship's deck to the jetty, things had clearly changed.

The singing welcomers had fallen silent and retreated from the jetty. A man and two women stood in their places. The three wore vividly colored robes that swept the ground, and their heads were swathed in turbans of bright-yellow silk. They were all smiling, but the smiles did not reach their eyes.

"We are honored, Chief Trader Xen," Mab said to

the older of the two women, bowing slightly. "I did not expect an official welcome at this early hour."

"It is we who are honored," the woman replied, returning the bow. "It is always a pleasure to greet the Trader Rosalyn. You know Council members Traders Lau and Bool, of course?"

"Of course," said Mab courteously, as Xen's companions bowed in their turn. "They are both old friends."

There was a slight, awkward pause.

"We are surprised to see you out of season," said the second woman. She was shorter and slighter than Xen, and her voice was thin, with an unpleasant, slightly whining note.

"It is not a usual trading voyage, Trader Lau, though of course I hope to do a little business while I am here," Mab replied smoothly. She gestured at the finalists behind her. "These young people are in training, and what better place for them to test their skills than Two Moons, home of the wiliest traders in the Silver Sea?"

Xen, Lau and Bool nodded and smiled at the compliment, but there was a tension about them that showed they had more to say. As Britta looked at them more closely she could see signs that they had dressed very hastily. A trail of yellow silk hung untidily from the back of Xen's turban. Bool's chin sprouted gingery stubble above his braided orange beard. Lau was wearing odd shoes. The shoes were both the same style, but the left was black, the right, dark blue.

The three had rushed from their homes to meet Mab as if the arrival of the *Star of Deltora* was some sort of emergency! The sober face of Perlain, the Maris man, flashed into Britta's mind, but she did her best not to let her anxiety show.

"If this visit is merely for training purposes, then I daresay it will be a very short one," said the woman Xen, with only a hint of a question in her voice.

"We had planned on three days, as usual," said Mab. "It is hardly possible to do justice to Two Moons in less."

Xen hesitated, glancing at her companions.

"Do I gather there is a problem?" Mab asked pleasantly.

Bool cleared his throat. "A slight problem, Trader Rosalyn. Very slight—more of an embarrassment than a problem, really. And not, of course, anything to do with the traders of our little island, who I can assure you are always more than delighted to—ah ... " He trailed off, having lost the thread of what he had been intending to say.

"It is the swamp dwellers, Mab," Xen said, suddenly abandoning any attempt at formal politeness. "Somehow they have got it into their heads that the *Star of Deltora* is *ishk*—unlucky."

Britta's stomach turned over. She felt Jewel stiffen and heard Sky draw a quick breath.

Mab did not flinch. "Indeed!" she said in a light,

amused tone. "A little too much orchid wine last night, perhaps?"

"Perhaps." Xen sighed. "But you know what they are when it comes to omens and curses and such like—the turtle people of the center in particular. They will not listen to reason. A group of them came to me at first light. They said they sensed bad luck entering the harbor on a *batak* ship—excuse me, a foreign ship, I mean—and insisted that the vessel must be turned away. Naturally I refused, but ..." She spread her hands in a gesture of helplessness.

"But you depend on them to gather sunrise pearls for you, so you cannot test them too far," Mab said, with a faint smile.

"In my view, we should have put the savages in their place long ago!" the woman Lao declared. "They think too much of themselves as it is, and the part-swampies on the fringes of town are almost as bad. If we start allowing them to dictate to us—"

"There is no question of that, Lao!" Xen broke in crossly. "The *Star of Deltora* was not turned away. What is more, we have resolved that all those on board who wish to land may do so."

She turned back to Mab. "But—but to keep the peace, Mab, we would be in your debt if on this occasion you finished your business here in one day—and left before sunset. As you know, the swamp dwellers have ... beliefs about dawn and dusk."

"They think the spirits of the dead are strongest

and more visible then, you see," Bool hastened to add, clearly wanting to make up for his previous poor showing. "It is a very ancient superstition."

"One I have often been tempted to believe myself, entering Two Moons harbor at sunrise," said Mab, with every appearance of calm good humor, though Britta could imagine how differently she must be feeling. "Well, if we are to have only one day here, so be it, Councillors. The turtle people in particular must not be upset. We must keep them working. There have been all too few sunrise pearls on the market in recent years."

She held out her hand to Trader Xen. "You have my word that my trainees and crew will be back on board the ship in good time, and that my ship will have left the harbor by sunset. Will that suit you?"

"Indeed it will," exclaimed Xen, shaking the offered hand eagerly.

Mab smiled. "And in return," she suggested, "perhaps you could spread the word that my young trainees are to be treated fairly—or at least not duped too thoroughly—and that the old Two Moons trick of drugging new traders and robbing them of their purchases will be suspended for today."

Bool spluttered indignantly. Lao bristled. But Xen gave a snort of laughter and shrugged her plump shoulders.

"I admit nothing, but you will not have to worry about your chicks, Mab, I am sure," she said. She nodded gaily at the finalists, looking at them properly for the first time. Suddenly her brow wrinkled.

"Do I not know you, my lovely?" she asked, staring at Britta. "You have been in Two Moons before, have you not?"

"N-no, Trader Xen," Britta stammered, blushing hotly and lowering her eyes. Perhaps Xen had seen her resemblance to her father. On his last visit, in the *Star of Deltora*, Dare Larsett had stayed in Two Moons only a day and a night, it was said. But before that, when he was working for Mab and the Rosalyn fleet, he had visited the island many, many times.

"This is Britta's first voyage away from Del, I believe," Mab murmured.

Xen shook her head. "Strange," she said. "I could have sworn … Ah well, I am getting old, I daresay. My old nanna used to see familiar faces wherever she went, I remember. It came from living so long, she said. Everyone starts to look the same."

She laughed heartily, took Mab's arm, and led the landing party along the jetty and into the town.

✬

Half an hour later, Britta was walking the narrow backstreets of Two Moons, her shore bag slung over her shoulder, her hand pressed firmly to the bulging pocket of her skirt where the coin purse Margareth had made her hung heavy with ten gold pieces. Grubby children swarmed about her, and she was sure that some among them were expert pickpockets.

The children had come from nowhere, gathering around her like a flock of hungry, chattering birds as soon as she left the main streets.

"Sunrise pearls, Trader Lady!" a sharp-faced boy cried, breaking from the throng to dance in front of Britta, waving a flimsy strand of shiny pink beads. "Famous sunrise pearls! Cheap! Very Cheap!"

"You come to my uncle's shop, Lady?" lisped a girl who had lost her two front teeth, tugging at Britta's hand. "Come! I show you! Best shop in Two Moons!"

Britta shook her head and strode on as fast as her skirt would allow. It crossed her mind that perhaps it had been a mistake to move immediately to the backstreets of the town, instead of settling herself by spending a little time in the larger stores at the harbor's edge. There were guards at the doors of the big stores, to keep traders from being pestered.

But the less popular backstreets had proved lucky for her in Del, so she had decided to try them first in Two Moons. And after what had been said on the jetty, she knew that time was too short to be wasted.

Mab had not bothered to warn Britta, Jewel, Sky and Vashti to return to the ship in good time. They had all heard her promise that the *Star of Deltora* would leave the harbor before sunset. They all knew that she would be furious with anyone who made her break her word.

Britta moved on, vainly trying to focus on her

surroundings. It was hard to think with the children gabbling around her, plucking at her skirt, every one of them determined to get her attention.

The street was a bewildering blur of color and noise. The shops and storehouses all looked alike. Their wide entrances gaped beneath canvas awnings that were fluttering with little flags and plastered with signs. Baskets and tables heaped with a huge variety of cheap goods spilled heedlessly out into the roadway, as if intended to trip and trap unwary passers-by.

Racks of vivid clothes flared in the sunlight. Shopkeepers shouted and beckoned, flourishing silk shawls and jewelry, gesturing at trays of dolls and animal figures made of molded clay.

Britta dodged through the clutter, turning her head from one side of the street to the other, seeing nothing that tempted her to stop and look more closely. Now and then she would try to shoo her noisy followers away, but they would laugh and skip back only for a moment before closing in again.

This is no use, she told herself. They are treating me as if I am an ordinary visitor to Two Moons, and no wonder! I am acting like one!

She stopped abruptly and turned to face the children, summoning up a serious frown. Taken by surprise, they stopped too, and fell silent. For the first time Britta looked at them closely one by one, noting the intelligence in the faces of even the youngest. Taking her time, she dug from her shore bag the packet of nuts and dried fruit that she had been given on the ship, and held it out.

"I have important work to do, and your chatter bothers me," she said slowly and clearly. "So I offer you a trade. This food from Deltora, the Land of Dragons, is yours to share if you go away and leave me in peace."

The children eyed the packet in her hand then glanced at one another uncertainly.

"It is your choice," said Britta, shrugging her shoulders. "You can waste your time following me about and miss out on the food, if you wish. But you will get nothing else from me."

There was a short pause, and then the girl with the missing teeth nodded, stepped forward and took the packet. Gravely she showed it to the others. Then she said something Britta could not understand, and the whole troublesome gang turned and ran off, weaving through the crowd like a little school of fish and at last vanishing from sight.

Britta did not linger. She was pleased at her success, but she knew better than to trust her luck too far. Bargain or no bargain, it was quite likely that some of the children at least would return as soon as the food was gone. She was a Del trader, and for her a trading promise was binding, but they might not feel the same way.

She walked quickly on, turning down the first laneway she saw and hurrying to the end.

Emerging from the lane, she found herself in a street narrower and dingier than any she had seen before. Lined on both sides by shabby stone and timber buildings, most of which looked like small warehouses, it stretched away to her left and right like a ragged cord threaded with dull, square beads. It was completely deserted. Directly behind it, the mists of the swamp rose, staining the sky.

Britta realized she had reached the edge of the town, and felt a prickle of uneasiness. Perhaps this was not a safe place to be. She half turned, intending to return the way she had come. And then, out of the corner of her eye, she saw a sign that made her heart leap.

Two Moons Treasure House

9 - Master Mull

The sign hung over the door of a narrow shop sandwiched between two much larger buildings. Britta did not hesitate. She crossed the road and made straight for the dull-looking place as if it was what she had been looking for all along. And of course, she realized with almost guilty surprise, she *had* been looking for it. Without admitting to herself what she was doing, she had been scanning every shop she passed, hoping to see the name that had headed the receipt she had found in her father's book.

The shop's cracked door was shut, and its one small window was covered by a heavy curtain. There was no sign that it was open for business. Indeed, by the look of the spiderwebs, dead flies and dust balls caught between the curtain and the window glass, the place had closed down years ago.

Britta felt a stab of bitter disappointment, quickly

followed by a small, surprising wave of relief. She pressed her lips together in irritation, tracking down the source of the relief, and soon found it. She had felt compelled to follow in her father's footsteps, to stand where he had stood, to meet the shopkeeper who had sold him *Cladda's Mysteries of the Silver Sea*. But if the shop had closed, she was spared that. She was free to put her father out of her mind and go her way.

Furious at her own cowardice, she seized the tarnished knob of the door and twisted it. She had not expected success, but there was no resistance. The knob turned with a rattle, and the door creaked open. Before she could think about it, she had pushed through the gap and the door was swinging shut behind her.

After the bright sunshine of the street, the shop seemed very dark, despite the glow of a few lanterns hanging from the walls. It was stuffy, too. The stale smells of dust, old metal and aged wood hung thick in the dead air.

Britta hesitated, coughing a little, then shuffled forward, willing her eyes to adjust to the dimness. She had only taken a step or two, however, when she found her way barred by a heavy wooden counter. It appeared to stretch from one side of the narrow room to the other, and nothing stood upon it except a jar of round pink sweets.

She stared across the counter into darkness. It was hard to see anything clearly, but she had the impression of a vast clutter of objects, stacked so high that they reached the shadowy ceiling.

It occurred to her that the Two Moons Treasure House was more like a lair than a place of business. She shivered—with excitement or nervousness she could not tell.

"How may I be of service?"

The voice came to Britta out of the dark, and the next moment a head appeared on the other side of the counter, apparently floating in thin air. The head was as round, bald, pale and shining as the full moon—a full moon with a face that had been drawn by a child, with orange dots for eyes, a curving pink squiggle for a mouth, and no nose to speak of.

The illusion only lasted for an instant, but it was an instant of pure terror. By the time Britta realized that she was merely facing a grossly fat man whose body had been invisible in the darkness because of the long black robe he wore, she was shaking all over.

"I fear I startled you," the shopkeeper said. "I do apologize!"

He did not sound sorry at all, and in fact his tiny eyes were sparkling with malicious pleasure. Britta became convinced that he played this trick on every stranger who entered his shop. No doubt he had played it on her father in his time.

And how would Dare Larsett have reacted? Remembering some of his tales, Britta could guess, and without any difficulty she did the same.

She burst out laughing.

If the shopkeeper was disappointed, he did not show it. He laughed too, in fact, his pale cheeks wobbling, his eyes disappearing completely between folds of fat, his small mouth stretched into a tight, round "O."

"Ah!" he gasped, when his laughter died at last. "I do like a good sport! Have a *tuppi!*"

He flipped the sweet jar open and shook it invitingly. A sharp, tingling scent filled the air. Britta smiled and, feeling she could not refuse, took one of the small pink balls and tasted it cautiously. It was strangely refreshing, a little like mint.

"Thank you," she said. "I have never had one of these before."

The man helped himself to a huge handful of *tuppi* and crammed them into his mouth.

"Very good for the digestion," he mumbled, chewing rapidly. "Hard to get, though. The swamp dwellers can only make them when the orchids are blooming, and they keep most of every season's batch for themselves. I am favored because I am half swampie myself. Ha! One of the many advantages, I assure you!"

He swallowed, and licked his sticky fingers. "So, young trader, you have laughed in Mull's ugly face, and he has laughed in your pretty one. Now, back to business! What brings you to the Treasure House? So few outsiders know of me, and that is how I like it. I like to keep my dealings quite ... private and discreet, you understand. I have regular customers enough, and do not advertise."

"I came to you because I am looking to buy something rare and strange, Master Mull," Britta said, abruptly deciding that frankness would serve her best in this situation. "I want something that I can trade at a very good profit in Illica."

"Illica," Mull repeated thoughtfully, nodding his great round head. "Yes, indeed—you are wise, for one so young. Something *kaja*, as the swamp dwellers say, is what is needed to trade well in that place, to be sure."

He made the "k" sound of the foreign word in a harsh, grating way, as if he were clearing the back of his throat. It was like the sound that Councillor Xen had made when saying *"batak"*—the Two Moons word for "foreign."

Seeing that Mull was eyeing her curiously, Britta hastened to cover up her confusion.

"Kaja," she repeated, imitating the grating "k" as best she could. "That means ... unusual and interesting?"

"Quite so," Mull agreed, looking amused. "True *kaja* objects are powerful—sometimes because of how they were made, sometimes simply because they are one of a kind. I specialize in *kaja* items. The swamp dwellers will give sunrise pearls for them, you understand, if they like them well enough."

He rubbed his fat white hands together as if

relishing the thought of the riches the rare pearls could bring. "If you want *kaja*, my dear, you have come to the right place. I fear, however, that your pocket may not be deep enough to pay for what I have to sell."

"Oh, I am sure you will find something I can afford, Master Mull," Britta replied firmly, recognizing the first move in a familiar game.

"I only wish I was so sure," the shopkeeper said with a regretful smile. "Still, we must try our best."

He leaned across the counter to look more closely at Britta, and all of a sudden he froze. His smile grew fixed, and his face became even paler than it had been before, though Britta would have said that was impossible.

Her heart gave a great thud and she pulled back a little, feeling her face and neck grow hot.

She could not know that Mull, the part-swamp dweller, had seen the gray shadows of the wraiths writhing behind and around her. All she could think of was that he had seen her resemblance to her father and, unlike Trader Xen, had guessed who she was.

Dare Larsett had been one of Mull's "regular customers," she was sure. *Kaja* goods sounded exactly the sort of trade goods her father had loved to buy— so much more interesting, and often more profitable, than the ornaments, spices, tea and silks that usually filled a Del trading ship's hold.

What a bitter irony it would be if after all she had been through she were to be unmasked so far from home, in a place where she had been sure she was safe!

I will not let that happen, Britta told herself fiercely. If Mull challenges me, if he even mentions my father, I will act very surprised—even insulted. Yes, insulted, as any other girl of Del would be if someone accused her of being related to a man loathed from one end of the Silver Sea to the other.

She tried to catch Mull's eye, to stare him down. And only then did she notice that the man was not looking directly at her at all. He was gazing over her shoulder, into the darkness behind her.

Britta breathed out, but the relief she felt was mingled with uneasiness, and she turned quickly to assure herself that no one had crept after her into the shop without her knowledge.

There was nothing behind her—nothing but shadows and the pale outline of the closed door.

"Is something the matter, Master Mull?" she asked politely, turning back to the pallid, staring man.

The shopkeeper started violently. His long nails scrabbled on the counter top, making a rasping sound that set Britta's teeth on edge.

Drawing back, he pulled a handkerchief from the pocket of his robe and mopped his gleaming face.

"On second thoughts, I do not think I have anything that will suit you," he croaked. "I am sure I do not. You would do better to look elsewhere. I bid you good day."

10 - *Kaja*

Dismayed, Britta stared at the shopkeeper's twitching face. Why had he changed his mind about trading with her? *Had* he recognized her after all? Or had she said something to upset him? Rapidly she ran through what had happened just before his behavior changed. All she could remember was saying that she was sure Mull would have something she could afford.

Was that it? Had Mull become agitated because she had made it clear that she was determined to buy something? He was plainly very eccentric. Perhaps, despite his boasting of regular customers, he liked to hoard his *kaja* treasures, and the thought of letting one go to a stranger threw him into a panic.

The thought would never have crossed Britta's mind if it had not been for old Mistress Finlock.

Like Mull, Mistress Finlock had her own

business. She was a doll maker, whose tiny shop was not far from the bakery in the center of Del.

She lived quietly above her shop, and her clothes, though very worn, were always perfectly neat and clean. No one who did not know her would have guessed that she was in desperate need.

But she was. In her way, Mistress Finlock was as troubled as poor, ragged Sheevers, the once-famous Del potter Britta had found hiding in an underground den, guarding his collection of clay lanterns.

Mistress Finlock's dolls were beautifully made and dressed, it was said, but she did not display them in her shop window. She scraped out a living mending broken dolls that were brought to her, but she would not sell the dolls she had created. What was more, she spent any money she had left after paying her rent on buying materials to make more dolls!

Far too proud to ask the palace for aid, she might well have starved if Jantsy and his family had not given her leftover bread from the bakery at the end of every day.

"She lost her husband and children during the Shadowlands invasion," Jantsy had told Britta when she shook her head in wonder at the doll maker's strangeness. "The dolls are the poor soul's family now. She cannot bear to part with a single one."

Britta thought quickly. If Mull were as disturbed as Sheevers and Mistress Finlock, it would be best to leave his shop at once and stop wasting time. Yet …

could the man have laughed as he had if his mind had been shattered by grief and loss? Would he have talked of *kaja* goods, and his dealings with the swamp dwellers, so freely? And after all, he *had* sold her father that book.

She smiled sweetly, just as she had often smiled at customers across the counter of her mother's shop in Del.

"Oh, no, Master Mull," she cried playfully. "You cannot get rid of me so easily! I am staying right here until you sell me something wonderful! And I have gold to give in payment, if the item pleases me."

With satisfaction, she saw Mull's small eyes flash, and a pink tongue dart out to lick the thin, curving lips. That book about the islands of the Silver Sea was right, she thought. Gold is king in Two Moons.

"Very well, " Mull said, speaking very fast and low. "I understand you. I will show you the best I have—a thing that I swear will dazzle the Collectors of Illica. And then I beg you will leave me in peace. Wait! One moment!"

He hurried away into the darkness. Britta heard him moving things, opening a drawer …

And then he was back, carrying a bright lantern. Under his arm was what looked like a roll of soft, yellowed paper tied up with ribbon. An old map or chart, by the look of it, Britta thought, very disappointed and more than a little annoyed.

Mull was still playing games with her. The

bookstall near her home in Del was always stacked with tattered, out-of-date maps. Sometimes the lettering on them was quite beautiful, but she knew perfectly well that they were not valuable. There were too many of them about. Captain Gripp had bundles of them, and with her own eyes Britta had seen him use strips torn from their edges to light his stove

Still, she waited calmly while the shopkeeper hung the lantern from a hook dangling above his head and placed the paper roll on the counter. She did not say a word as he untied the ribbon. But when Mull cast the paper aside and she saw what it had been protecting, her heart jumped into her throat.

It was a roll of embroidered silk, a wall hanging fastened top and bottom to polished wooden rods. It looked very old and delicate. Gently Mull unrolled it, holding it up for Britta to see.

"There," he said thickly. "There … "

Britta gazed at the exquisitely embroidered silk. She saw a bird's-eye view of an emerald island, ringed with black sand and set in a rippling silver sea. She saw a soft haze rising from the island into a sky of cloudless blue. She saw circling seabirds, and could almost hear their mournful cries.

Cool breezes seemed to be caressing her skin, raising the hairs on her arms and the back of her neck. A hollow whispering filled her mind, like the echoing sea sound she heard when she pressed one of Gripp's giant shells to her ear.

Britta swallowed. She knew that by all the rules of trading she should be nodding and smiling faintly as if the offering was pleasant enough, but not worth whatever the seller was about to demand for it.

She could not do it. She could only gaze. The work of art hanging from Mull's sausage-like fingers, its colors glimmering in the lantern light, was like a dream captured in silk. She longed to own it—longed for it with every fiber of her being. She leaned forward, and had the strangest feeling that the darkness behind her moved too, hanging about her shoulders like a muffling cloak.

"What island is this?" she heard herself ask faintly.

Mull shrugged, his thick eyelids dropping briefly over his tiny amber eyes. He had shrunk back a little. His hands were trembling, and sweat was beading his forehead again. Suddenly Britta sensed that the man was staying where he was by pure effort of will. At any moment he might turn and escape into the darkness at the back of his lair, taking the embroidery with him.

He is like Mistress Finlock after all, Britta thought, seizing on the only explanation she could think of. He was tempted by the idea of gold, but now he sees that I long for his treasure, he does not want to give it up. I must say something! I must keep him with me!

"How much do you want for it?" she asked quickly, and held her breath.

A hoarse, barking sound burst from Mull's lips.

It could have been a laugh, but it sounded more like a sob. "It is more a matter of what you will pay, is it not?" he mumbled.

"I can offer seven gold coins," said Britta, and waited for him to laugh again.

But this time Mull did not laugh. He merely groaned softly.

Britta waited.

"Make it eight, and the hanging is yours," Mull said, as if he had just remembered he was supposed to haggle. "I—I will add a necklace of sunrise pearls to sweeten the bargain. Not genuine sunrise pearls, you understand, but good copies—very good copies indeed!"

Five minutes later, Britta was back on the quiet street, the sweet-sour odor of the swamp wafting around her, the taste of Mull's *tuppi* still faintly refreshing in her mouth. The rolled embroidery, again wrapped in its protective layer of paper, was in her shore bag. The strand of false pearls was in her pocket—the perfect gift for Margareth. Two gold coins still remained in her purse.

And it was only then, thinking of those gold coins and marveling at her good fortune, that she remembered the burning look in the shopkeeper's eyes as he stood behind his counter, watching her leave.

Mull thought she had cheated him—Britta felt it in her bones. And that was all wrong. Trader Sven always said that for a successful trade both parties in the bargain should be well satisfied.

But Mull did not have to accept my offer, Britta told herself irritably. I would have given him all my gold if he had asked for it! And if he did not want to sell me the embroidery at all, why did he show it to me in the first place?

She realized that she was very thirsty, and took a drink from the flask in her shore bag. Then she wandered on, without paying much attention to her surroundings. The sun beat down on her unprotected head, and after a time she started to feel dizzy with heat.

She felt very tired, too. Terribly tired. No wonder, she thought hazily. She had woken long before dawn.

She came to a place where there was a gap between two warehouses. The vacant land was littered with empty boxes, broken baskets and drums stuffed with discarded packing straw. Behind the rubbish loomed the swampland, green, dim and secret.

A great desire for that green shade swept over Britta. The longing was even stronger than the yearning she had felt looking at Two Moons from the ship at dawn, but she did not wonder at that. She did not even think about it—could not, in that moment, think of anything but her need. She stumbled off the road, and it was as if some invisible force was at her back, urging her on, as she wove unsteadily towards the beckoning green.

She had almost reached her goal when her ankle

cracked against something hard. The pain brought her to her senses. She rubbed her forehead in dull confusion. What was the matter with her? How could she have thought the swampland was a refuge? The swampland was perilous!

She found that she was leaning for support on the thing that had saved her by standing in her way. It was a long wooden box with a stretched canvas cover—an abandoned storage box for a large piece of furniture, perhaps. It was lying so close to the swamp that its far end was hidden, shrouded in murky green.

Britta shuddered to think how nearly she had staggered like a sleepwalker into danger. At the same moment she realized that all was not well with her. She was swaying where she stood. Her head felt thick. Her eyelids were so heavy that they kept closing.

I have been too long in the sun, Britta thought slowly. And looking around vaguely for shelter she saw that the answer was right there, beneath her hand. The end of the big wooden box on which she was leaning gaped open like the entrance to a shadowy cave. Britta sank to the ground and crawled gratefully into the blessed shade.

The bulging sacks piled at her head did not trouble her, though the one closest to her face smelled strongly of onions. She did not even think about what they might mean. All she cared about was that she was out of the burning sun, and there was enough room for her to curl up and rest a while, to sleep ...

And sleep she did, almost instantly. The drug that had spread through her system had done its work well. The rasping sound as a heavy flagon was pushed into the shadows beside her barely entered her dreams. When the wooden flap at the end of her refuge was lifted and bolted shut, she heard nothing. And when there was a low whistle, and the shelter began to move, she did not stir.

11 - Fear

Britta woke slowly, and for a few moments lay with her eyes closed, quite relaxed, hazily assuming that the soft, gurgling sounds she could hear, the gentle, rocking movement she could feel, meant that she was in her bunk on the *Star of Deltora*. She might easily, indeed, have drifted peacefully back to sleep if she had not drawn a long, contented breath and become aware that something was not as it should be.

Her nose twitched. There was a strange smell in the air—a heavy, sweet and sour odor that was nothing like the smell of the ship.

Britta's eyes flew open. She saw a dark covering not far above her head. She stretched out her hands and felt hard wooden walls rising on both sides of her. She tried to flex her legs, and felt her feet strike more wood.

Gurgling, rippling sounds filled her ears. Into her confused mind flew the nightmarish certainty that she was trapped in a coffin that had been thrown into the sea, and pure terror thrilled through her.

She tried to scream, but her throat had closed with horror, and the scream died in a strangled gulp. Darkness closed in around her. Frantic to escape, refusing to accept that there was nothing she could do to save herself, she raised her arms and beat at the shadow lowering above her head …

And as soon as she touched it, she realized that it was not a coffin lid, but merely some rough fabric, like canvas, stretched tightly over the wooden sides of her prison.

And the fabric was not wet. It was warm and dry.

As the nightmare faded, Britta began to breathe again. She was not in the sea. She was not about to drown, trapped in a locked wooden box. Her panic subsided and the darkness enfolding her seemed to sigh and warm.

Slowly she began to think rationally. She began to think about what the gurgling, watery sounds, the rocking movement, might mean. Perhaps she was in a boat—being taken somewhere in a boat! But why? How?

She forced herself to think back, step by painful step.

She remembered walking along the narrow street beside the swamp, away from Mull's Treasure House.

She remembered the sun beating down, and how tired, how very tired, she had felt. She remembered that her eyelids had been so heavy that she had hardly been able to keep them open. She vaguely remembered crawling into a storage box at the back of some vacant land, and curling up in its shade …

And that was all.

I was drugged, Britta thought blankly.

The memory of Mull's great round face, the way his tiny eyes had burned as he watched her leave his shop, came back to her. She remembered Mab's comment about Two Moons shopkeepers who drugged their customers and took back what had been honestly bought. She remembered the taste of the pink sweet Mull had called *tuppi* and her stomach roiled with nausea.

Her mind was still working sluggishly. It did not occur to her to look and see if her shore bag was missing, the *kaja* embroidery gone. All she could think about was that she had been drugged and kidnapped, and was now being carried away from the spot where she had fallen asleep. Every moment, she was moving farther from safety. She had to get out—had to escape—even if it meant throwing herself into the sea and swimming for her life.

Clumsily she rolled onto her stomach and crawled onto her hands and knees. Her prison tilted slightly as her weight shifted. Something beside her—a large, heavy jar, by the sound of it—toppled over and rolled noisily. Outside there was a heavy splashing sound, a high-pitched voice cried out in warning or complaint, and the sweet-sour smell that Britta had noticed before was suddenly much stronger.

Britta gagged, but fought the sickness down and remained perfectly still, waiting tensely for what might happen next, bracing herself to fight.

But nothing did happen. The base of her prison steadied, became level again. The heavy splashing ceased, and the smooth, gurgling sound began once more.

She found herself staring at a pile of bulging sacks and baskets. A few had fallen over when the craft tilted, and one bag had split so that small brown onions had begun spilling from its corner. Pale light glimmered through gaps in the clutter of bags, and with it came air, puffing into Britta's face like warm, foul-smelling breath. That was her way out.

She squirmed forward like a burrowing animal, squeezing between the sacks, pushing towards the light. And in no time at all she was peering through a gap into the open—gaping, thunderstruck, at a scene that was nothing at all as she had imagined.

She was not in the bay, beneath the open sky. She was in a dim, green-tinted place that was almost completely overhung by trees. The trees' gnarled branches and forked trunks were thick with flowers that looked like fleshy, freckled spiders, and their twisting roots sank deep in soupy gray mud.

The swamplands, Britta thought dully. I am in the swamplands. The smell ... of course!

Her idea that she was in a boat had been quite wrong. From what she could see, she was in some sort of sled—a long, covered sled that was sliding over the glossy mud like the sleds that skimmed over snow in pictures she had seen of Deltora's north.

Mull must have paid swamp dwellers to take her away, to make her disappear so she could not tell anyone what he had done! What could be more natural? Mull traded with swamp dwellers, he knew the language—he was half swamp dweller himself!

She pushed herself forward a little more, craning her neck to see the sled's driver.

A small, hooded figure was hunched on the driver's seat, shaking a set of woven reins and looking warily from side to side as if keeping watch for danger. And the reins were—Britta's teeth began to chatter. The reins were attached to the creature pulling the sled—a creature of nightmare.

It looked like a slug—a vast, gray, glistening slug—except for the two great black-spotted humps that rose in the middle of its back. Its waving eyestalks were as thick as Britta's arm. Its bloated body rippled horribly as it slithered over the mud, threading its way between the trees, dragging its burden behind it with no apparent effort. The simple woven harness that circled its body between the two humps was thick with silvery slime.

"*So-so-so, Zrath,*" crooned the driver, leaning forward. "*So-so-so* ... "

Shuddering with horror, Britta jerked back. Her knee hit the split sack and onions tumbled around her, bouncing and rolling. She slid a little farther back, and the next moment her groping hand had touched something unexpected but very familiar.

Her shore bag! It was still with her—and it was still firmly strapped. Bewildered, Britta pulled the bag open. To her astonishment she saw that the wall hanging she had bought from Mull was still inside, wrapped and tied with ribbon exactly as it had been when she left the shop.

The embroidery had not been taken! It was there, as real as the water flask that lay beside it.

What did this mean? Bewildered, Britta clutched the bag to her chest. The spilled onions rolled around her feet, their strong smell mingling with the odor of the swamp.

Onions ... A faint memory crept into Britta's mind—the memory of curling up to sleep with the smell of onions in her nose. And all at once, with a sickening jolt, she saw the truth.

She had not been abducted and bundled into the sled. She had been inside it all along! She had crept into it thinking it was just a storage box, barely registering the fact that part of it lay in the swamp, failing to see what the sacks of supplies meant. While she slept, the sled's owner had returned, closed the tailgate and set off for home, probably without the faintest idea that a stowaway was on board.

She *had* been drugged, she was certain of that. And Mull must have been responsible, because the *tuppi* sweet was the only thing she had eaten since leaving the ship. But the plan to rob her had failed—because she had been whisked away into the swamp before Mull had the chance to get to her!

Relief, shame and horror warred in Britta's mind. Her thoughts raced, each new thought tumbling over the one before. The obvious thing to do was to hail the driver of the sled, to beg the driver to stop and let her get down. That was what she would have done at home, in Del.

But it would be a very risky thing to do here. The swamp dwellers were hostile to strangers. Intruders had been known to vanish without trace, and the traders of the coast turned a blind eye to anything that happened beyond the area of their control. Britta could not speak the swamp dwellers' language. She would never be able to explain how she came to be where she was.

She could try to escape without the driver's knowing—loosen the canvas covering somehow, and jump for her life from the speeding sled. But if by some miracle she managed to do that without injuring herself or plunging over the side of the path into mud that would suck her down to certain death, how in the Silver Sea was she to find her way back to the town?

Yet if she did nothing, she would at last be discovered—and what would happen then?

Her plight was appalling—impossible!

And as this last, despairing thought slammed into Britta's mind, taking the place of all the others, she heard the driver give an urgent, husky cry, and felt the sled skidding rapidly to a halt.

Her heart leaped. This was her chance! She might be hopelessly lost, but anything was better, surely, than being carried even farther from safety. She slung her shore bag over her shoulder and again wriggled forward through the sacks of supplies.

The driver of the sled was standing up, the reins held tightly in his hands. His hood had fallen back, showing him to be not a short adult, as Britta had thought, but a thin, mud-smeared boy who looked to be no more than ten years old.

He was looking intently at something to the right of the sled. Britta followed his gaze.

There, floating in a broad patch of pale mud, not far away, was a circle of round green leaves surrounding a single, bright pink flower with many pointed petals.

And in the center of the flower was a perfect pink pearl.

12 - The Battle of the Giants

B ritta's whole body stiffened. Her pulse began to race. She had discovered the swamp dwellers' great secret—the thing that no outsider had ever seen and lived to tell the tale. She was witnessing a sunrise pearl in its natural setting! Not created by shellfish, as other pearls were, but borne like bizarre fruit by a plant that lived in this one place—the swamps of Two Moons, where long ago the turtle man Tier had worked his magic.

She gazed in greedy wonder at the treasure glimmering in the green dimness. It was the color of the pink clouds she had seen over the bay at sunrise. It was flawless—perfect! And it was big—bigger by far than the pearls on Mab's earrings. It was a prize any trader would die for!

For a wild moment Britta thought of leaping onto the driver's seat, pushing the boy aside and plunging into the mud. She imagined herself plucking the pearl from its nest of petals. She could almost feel its smooth, round hardness safe in the palm of her hand …

Then she came to her senses. She saw that the distance between the sled and the circle of green leaves that surrounded the pearl flower was more than a body length. She saw how the pale mud on which the leaves floated moved and wrinkled like thick soup. She knew that before she could reach the pearl, that mud would have closed over her head and sucked her down.

She had been wrong. No prize was worth dying for.

The creature that the boy in the driver's seat had called "Zrath," was moving uneasily, making harsh, complaining, coughing sounds. Plainly it was not happy about being forced to stop. The black spots on its humps were darkening and spreading. Murmuring to it soothingly, the boy looked nervously from side to side and then bent and felt for something lying at his feet. When he straightened, Britta saw that he had picked up some sort of tool—a long, straight rod with a groove running all along its length.

Still holding the reins in one hand, the boy twisted his body and leaned over the side of the sled, pushing the rod forward till it almost touched the floating pink flower. Straining her eyes in the dimness, Britta thought she saw an amber shape sliding along the groove in the rod, towards the pearl in the flower's center.

She watched, holding her breath. Then, all of a sudden, with a ghastly, gurgling sound, another giant slug reared up from the ooze right beside the rod. The boy yelled, and jerked the tip of the rod upward. As the amber shape streaked back along the groove and vanished beneath his hand, he shrieked and shook the reins urgently.

But it was too late to flee. The second slug had lunged at the beast tethered to the sled, and already the monsters were fighting, rising on their tails and wrestling with terrible ferocity. The tethered beast was doing its best to defend itself, but the wild slug was larger by far, and it was angry—vicious!

Great folds of stinking mud rose and fell around the huge, twisting bodies. The sled pitched and rolled violently. The boy had thrown down the reins. He was clinging to the driver's seat, his high-pitched cries rising shrilly over the grating snarls of the wallowing beasts.

"*Zrath!*" he wailed. "*Ah, Zrath!*"

Paralyzed with horror, Britta clung to the side of the sled as sacks and baskets of supplies slid about her and the rolling flagon cracked open, disgorging a flood of cooking oil. The tame beast was still upright, but it was weakening. Slime tinged with dull green bubbled from great bruises all over its body. It had drawn back its eyestalks, and its blunt head was bobbing blindly.

It was nearly finished. Its enemy knew it. As Britta watched helplessly, the giant reared up, higher than it had ever done before, then slammed itself down with tremendous force, crushing its rival deep into the mud.

The sled tipped sideways. The boy was thrown off, into the patch of pale, heaving mud where the pearl lily floated. He screamed as the mud began to suck him down.

Without a thought, Britta shrugged off her shore bag, threw herself facedown and wriggled out onto the slippery, tilting driver's seat. Clutching the edge of the sled with her left hand, she reached desperately for the boy with her right.

As she stretched, the muscles of her arm and shoulder straining, she saw the boy's eyes, blank with terror, his mouth open in a soundless scream. Already the mud was creeping up to his chin. The tips of Britta's fingers brushed his flailing arm, but she could not quite catch hold.

The boy felt her touch. He turned his head slightly and saw her. His eyes bulged with shock then flamed with hope. His fingers clawed at the surface of the mud, straining towards Britta's groping hand.

But the slug tethered to the sled had thrown off its enemy. It had reared up again, and was battling valiantly for its life. The sled was pitching wildly in great, churning waves of mud. Britta tried again and again, but she could not grasp the boy's clutching fingers.

In agony she saw the hope in the dark eyes fade,

saw the boy close his mouth as mud lapped his bottom lip.

In seconds he would be gone. Britta could have wept! If only there was something she could throw to him! But there was no time to rip off her blouse with its tight cuffs and many firm little buttons, no time to turn and fossick for the shore bag she had so thoughtlessly discarded inside the sled.

There was only one thing to do. Britta tightened her grip on the side of the rolling sled and let herself slide into the swamp.

Liquid mud, stinking and faintly warm, closed in around her, flooding into her boots, soaking through her clothes, tugging at the pins in her hair. The feeling was loathsome. Britta tried to block it from her mind, tried not to think of what might be rising from the depths of that warm mud, wriggling stealthily around her ankles, creeping into the folds of her petticoat. Pushing herself as far from the sled as she dared, she reached out for the boy again.

She missed the first time, but on her second try she had him! Her heart leaped as her hand closed over his wrist. She felt the frail bones beneath her fingers and held tight, pulling with all her strength. She heaved till the child's mouth was above the surface of the mud, till his chin was clear ...

But she could do no more. The pale mud was holding the boy fast. She could not pull him to safety. She could only hold on, her hands stiffening, the muscles of her arms and back aching with strain, as the sled bucked, the mud heaved, and the harnessed slug fought desperately for its life.

Then she saw, floating beside the boy's shoulder, the muddy remains of the pink flower. It had broken from its stem, its petals were bruised and battered, but the sunrise pearl still gleamed in its center.

Britta stared at it longingly. With one move of her hand she could have reached it and plucked the pearl from its pink bed. But first she would have to release the boy's wrist, and let him sink.

That, she could not do. She did not even consider it. But it seemed to her that never had fate so cruelly laughed in her face. There, right in front of her, taunting her, was a prize that would win her the Rosalyn Apprenticeship, secure her future, give her the *Star of Deltora* ... and she could not have it.

She smiled wryly. So be it, she thought, and looked away, back to the boy.

He had spat out the mud that had seeped into his mouth, and begun screaming again. And suddenly, listening to those harsh, high-pitched cries, Britta realized that she was hearing words, the same words repeated again and again.

Kast! Kast! Imbuck! Kast! Kast! Imbuck!

The child was not just screaming in fear—he was calling for help! Britta added her voice to his, trying her best to imitate the sounds he was making, shouting as loudly as she could. The swamp echoed with their cries:

Kast! Kast! Imbuck!

Britta's throat was raw. Her arms were throbbing. Soon she could no longer hear the grunting of the fighting beasts. She could barely hear the child's voice, or her own. Her mind was filled with frantic, helpless, grieving whispers—her name, *Britta, Britta, Britta*, breathed over and over again.

She feared the whispers were a sign that the end of her life was near. What else could they mean? Her thoughts flew to Jantsy, who would miss her, to Margareth, who would weep for her, to old Captain Gripp, who would sorely grieve ... And to Maarie, who would no doubt see her reckless younger daughter's death as just another blow, another blight on a life that had already, surely, seen suffering enough.

There was a grating roar from the front of the sled. Painfully Britta turned her head. The giant slugs were twisting together, each trying to wrestle the other down. The wild, black-humped slug was on top of the other. As Britta watched, it arched its swollen body and bore down with tremendous force.

With a hoarse, coughing grunt, the tame slug vanished, struggling, beneath the body of its enemy. At the same moment the sled tilted, then flipped upside down, breaking Britta's grip, setting her adrift. Great waves of liquid mud hit her and the screaming boy, sweeping them farther from the sinking hulk. The boy's wrist slipped from her hand, but he clutched at her fingers and held on.

Britta felt the swamp sucking at her greedily, pulling her down. She felt warm mud lapping her neck. A few pink petals bobbed before her eyes. The last convulsion of the mud—even her desperate struggles and those of the boy, perhaps—had destroyed the pearl flower at last. The pearl was gone, to be lost in the depths of the swamp as so many other precious things had no doubt been lost before it.

The wild slug was bellowing its triumph, thrashing its tail again and again over the place where its rival still feebly struggled. The sled had vanished. Only fat bubbles of air rising to the surface showed where it had been. Britta thought briefly of the exquisite wall hanging from Mull's Treasure House, then forgot it.

"I am sorry!" she called to the boy she had tried to save. "I did what I could!"

She knew he could not understand her, but had felt impelled to say the words anyway. He still gripped her hand, but no longer could she hold him up. She was as helpless, now, as he was.

The boy gabbled something in his own language. And then, to Britta's astonishment, he spoke again, slowly and carefully, in words she could understand.

"I am Stassi," he said. "I thank you, *batak*. You risked your life for mine. I am yours now, till my life's end."

He spoke so gravely, so seriously, that Britta could not laugh wildly or shout at him as otherwise she might have done, with the stifling mud lapping at her chin and a horrifying death only moments away.

"Keep hold of my hand!" she called instead, then pressed her lips together as the mud rose higher.

13 - The Clearing

When Britta saw the flames, she thought she was dying. She thought she had slipped beneath the mud, and was experiencing the visions that some folk said always came at the end. But then she felt something touch the nape of her neck. She felt something sliding down her back. She felt cords looping under her arms, circling her chest. She saw orange flashes dancing in front of her eyes, felt pain as the cords tightened. And just before she lost consciousness, she heard the sucking, gurgling sounds of the swamp giving her body up, and knew she was saved.

When she woke, her head was bouncing against something that smelled of swamp mud, and the world was upside down. It took a moment before she realized that she had been slung like a sack of onions over the shoulder of someone who was loping along a dirt track at a slow, steady pace.

Every muscle in her body was aching. The taste of the swamp was sour in her mouth. Her hair was hanging down, slapping her rescuer's back in stiff, sodden clumps. She could see little, except that other people were jogging all around her—thin, mud-smeared people carrying torches that no longer flamed, but merely glowed and smoked.

I am alive, she thought. The swamp people heard our calls for help. They came.

She was too shocked to take it in, too exhausted to fear what might come next. Even relief was beyond her. Dimly she thought of the boy, Stassi. She tried to say his name, but her lips would not move. The bouncing of her head was making her feel sick. She shut her eyes and slept.

When she came to herself, she was lying on soft but solid ground. Someone was cleaning her face, dabbing it gently with a wet cloth. She opened her eyes and stared up at a leafy canopy that hid the sky.

The cloth was abruptly taken away. She heard a voice whisper something she could not understand, and another voice answer. Then there was a tense silence. Plainly, the next move was up to Britta.

Slowly and painfully, taking care to keep her swimming head as still as possible, she sat up.

A frightened-looking woman was kneeling in front of her, still clutching a cloth and a small bowl of dirty water. The woman's arms and legs were bare.

Her skin was so pale that it looked almost green in the dim light. The short, straight garment she wore was very plain, but her head was bound with brightly patterned fabric arranged in complicated folds. Many silver bracelets circled her wrists, and silver earrings winking with gems dangled almost to her shoulders.

Behind her stood a man so coated in dried mud that he looked like a stone statue. Only his amber eyes spoiled the illusion. His arms were folded across his chest. His face was very grave. Britta wondered if he was the one who had carried her to this place and, if so, where the other rescuers had gone.

Her hands shaking a little, the woman turned aside, picked up a jug and poured a little water into a cup. She lifted the cup to Britta's lips, but snatched it away as Britta grabbed for it eagerly.

With a cry of frustration, Britta leaned forward, but the woman was holding the cup well out of her reach.

"*Nak bess!*" The woman said in a low, trembling voice. "*Atta!*"

Seeing that Britta did not understand her, she pointed into her own mouth, swallowed, clutched her stomach and made a hideous face.

The man muttered something, barely opening his lips.

The woman frowned and shook her head. Leaning forward a little, holding up her first finger to claim Britta's attention, she carefully pretended to take a little water from the cup. She then puffed out her cheeks, made some harsh gargling sounds, bent over the basin and spat noisily.

"*Atta!*" she repeated, jabbing her finger at the muddy water. "*Nak bess!*"

Britta nodded. She understood. She had traces of swamp mud, *atta*, in her mouth. She had to rinse it out before she could drink. No doubt the mud was full of diseases, or the eggs of worms. Her stomach churned at the thought that some had surely gone down her throat already.

Cautiously, the woman offered the cup again. Keeping her hands folded in her lap to show that she was not intending to snatch and gulp, Britta took a small mouthful of what seemed to her to be the sweetest water she had ever tasted. She ached to swallow, but did not. She swilled the water round in her mouth, gargled as best she could, then spat into the basin the woman thrust under her chin.

The process was repeated twice before Britta was allowed to drink.

No life-giving nectar in an old tale could have tasted so delicious. Britta sighed with blissful relief.

The woman was watching her intently. "*Krest?*" she asked timidly, removing the empty cup and filling it again.

"*Krest,*" Britta repeated, nodding. She did not know if the word meant "good," "better" or "more," but reasoned that any one of those would do as an answer. Yes, the water was very good. Yes, it had made her feel much better. And yes, she certainly wanted more.

After the second cup of water, she had revived enough to take in her surroundings.

She and her two companions were at the edge of a small clearing screened from the sky by the overhanging branches of the trees that grew around it. In the center of the clearing, beside a swathe of glowing, amber-colored mud, there was a round hut with walls built of woven sticks and a roof thatched with bundles of reeds.

The hut looked very ordinary, except for one thing. Someone had used the amber mud to paint a strange decoration on its door—a large egg shape, patterned like a tiled floor, with six small, plain ovals spaced around it.

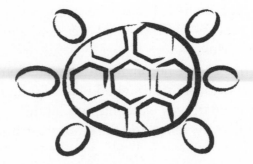

The mark gave Britta an odd, uncomfortable feeling. It reminded her of something, but she could not think what. Beneath the thick crust of drying mud her skin began to prickle in a way that had become all too familiar.

Why had she been brought to this eerie place? Where were all the other people who had helped in the rescue?

Britta curled her fingers, digging her nails into her palms, telling herself not to give way to her nerves. If the swamp dwellers wanted to kill her, they could have simply left her to die in the mud. They hated intruders, but surely the boy she had tried to save— Stassi—would speak for her?

If Stassi still lived. If he had not gone under before … The pattern on the hut door seemed to shift and waver before Britta's eyes.

She turned back to her companions and found that the woman had risen silently and was now standing beside the man, who had put his arm around her.

"Stassi?" Britta asked urgently.

In dismay she saw the woman's eyes darken, and a quiver of pain pass over the man's stony face. She scrambled awkwardly to her feet.

"I am sorry," she said, though she knew they could not understand her. "I tried—"

There was a small sound behind her. She spun round and saw that the hut door had opened. In the doorway stood a tiny but very upright woman wearing a plain gray robe that brushed the ground.

The woman's bare arms were white as bone. When she raised her left hand, it seemed to shine in the dimness.

She beckoned. The gesture was slight—just a slight crook of one glimmering finger—but it did not cross Britta's mind to disobey the summons. She moved instantly, without thought, as if impelled by some unseen force. Indeed, she had reached the hut before she realized she was moving at all.

The small woman stood waiting in the doorway. Britta met her faded eyes and saw with a shock that she was old—very old—though her pale skin was as smooth and unwrinkled as a girl's.

"*Ibik!*" the woman said softly. She opened the door a little wider and stood back, holding out one arm in a clear invitation to enter. And glancing at that bare, outstretched arm, Britta received her second shock. The woman's small, bony hands had a dull amber sheen, as if they had been dyed or painted to the wrist.

Britta glanced quickly over her shoulder. The man and the woman who had cleaned her face were standing where she had left them, watching her intently. There was a terrible tension in their stillness, as if they had been ordered to stay where they were against their will.

When Britta turned back to face the hut, the old woman was waiting with no sign of impatience. She was gazing straight ahead, past Britta's arm, into the clearing. Perhaps, Britta thought, she was looking at the two younger people standing so still at the clearing's edge, silently forbidding them to move.

"Ibik!" the old woman said again, in exactly the same tone. And Britta knew she had no choice but to enter the hut. The woman was plainly a leader—the authority in those faded eyes made that clear. The amber sheen on her hands, the loneliness of her dwelling, the mark on her door, were more signs that she was no ordinary swamp dweller. Britta had been brought to her for some sort of decision, and would not be allowed to leave until that decision had been made.

Ordering herself to seem calm and confident, but inwardly quaking, Britta stepped through the doorway.

As she passed the open door, she stole a glance at the mysterious gold symbol. One large oval, and six small ones …

Into her mind drifted the memory of shapes basking on the white beaches of deserted islands. Her heart gave a great thud as she suddenly understood what she was seeing.

A large plated shell. Four stubby legs. A head. A tail. The sign on the door was a picture of a turtle!

Britta's thoughts flew to the one chapter she had read in *Cladda's Mysteries of the Silver Sea*. Her throat dried and closed. If she was right, she was in the heart of the swamp. She was in the territory of the turtle people. And she was entering the home of their leader, heir to the magic of the tragic turtle man, Tier.

14 - The Bargain

Britta looked up, straight into the old woman's eyes, and saw something flicker there. She could have sworn it was fear, but it vanished so quickly that she could not be sure.

The woman gestured at the earth floor, where two woven mats faced each other over a faintly glowing oil burner. She waited while Britta sat down on one of the mats, then shut the door, plunging the small room into almost complete darkness.

Britta waited tensely as the old woman settled herself on the opposite mat. Then the woman leaned forward and turned up the burner so that bright flames flared up, lighting the circle where she and Britta sat, driving the darkness back to the walls.

The woman sat very upright, her legs crossed beneath her gray robe. She fixed Britta with her strange, amber eyes.

"Stassi," she said, pressing her stained hand to her heart. She lifted the hand to her forehead, then mimed cradling a baby in her arms. She put two fingers to her eyes and slid the tips down her cheeks, to mimic tears.

Without words, she had perfectly expressed her love and heartache for a child she had known since he was born. Britta's throat tightened.

"I am so very sorry—" she began, but the old woman shook her head. She had not finished.

"Stassi," she said again, holding up one hand. She pointed at Britta with her other hand. Then she gripped her hands together tightly.

She knows! Britta thought, hope flaring. She knows I tried to save him! The first rescuers to arrive must have seen that our hands were linked!

She nodded vigorously and clasped her own hands. The old woman watched her, expressionless, then abruptly turned away from the light and muttered something into the darkness behind her.

Britta thought she saw a movement in the shadows, near the floor. There was someone else in the hut, it seemed—someone who had stayed perfectly quiet and hidden till now.

The thought was not pleasant. Britta's uneasiness returned. She heard a thudding sound as something was placed by the old woman's side, just beyond the circle of light.

The old woman turned, picked up the object, and

set it down in front of her.

It was a glass ball on a low silver stand. Inside the ball, puffy white clouds drifted in a sky of dazzling blue. Seabirds soared and swooped below the clouds, their orange beaks opening and closing in silent cries.

Britta stared, transfixed.

"*Kaja,*" the old woman said, patting the ball with her amber fingertips.

Kaja—strange and unusual. Special. Unique ...

"*Kaja,*" Britta echoed faintly.

There was a roaring sound in her ears. She could not believe what she was seeing. There, on the earth floor of this hut in the middle of the Two Moons swamp, sat her father's sky sphere.

The old woman was pointing to the ball, then pointing upward, linking her thumbs and flapping her fingers to imitate the flight of birds, miming the rising and setting of the sun. She was trying to explain that the sphere showed the sky in miniature exactly as it was at this moment.

Those clouds were even now drifting across the blue above Two Moons. Those seabirds were wheeling and diving in the light breeze that was driving the clouds. Later the blue would dim, then all the colors of sunset would fill the sphere, and the birds flying to roost would be merely shapes and shadows.

Britta needed no explanation. How often in the old days had she sat on her father's knee at his desk, watching the colors inside the glass ball change as the real sky changed above the big house on Del harbor? It was one of the most vivid memories of her early childhood.

Once she had seen boiling storm clouds and thin, jagged streaks of lightning in the sphere, while thunder shook the house and rain beat on the study windows. Many times, snug in her night robe and slippers, she had seen a miniature moon rising in a velvety black sky pierced by tiny stars.

She had not seen the sky sphere since her father set sail in the *Star of Deltora* over eight years ago. She vividly remembered creeping into his study when she, Margareth and their mother returned from the farewell at the dock, and finding the sphere gone. She had known at once that her father had taken it, and supposed in her childish way that he thought it would bring him luck.

She had thought of the sky sphere sometimes, in the years of disgrace and poverty that had followed. Her father had loved it—and he had carried it with him on that fateful voyage. For Britta, that had been proof that he had known, or at least strongly suspected, that if he found the fabled Staff of Tier he would never return to his old life. So he had taken the sphere—the one thing he could not bear to leave behind.

The thought had given Britta many bitter moments. And now ... now it seemed that she had been quite wrong. Her father had not kept the sky sphere. It was not on the Isle of Tier with him. He had traded it for something he wanted more.

"Did you get this from Master Mull?" Britta burst out. She was too shocked to remember that her companion did not speak her language, but it did not matter. Recognizing the last word, the old woman guessed what the question had been, and shook her head.

"*Nak* Mull," she said. "*Batak.*"

Batak—a stranger from beyond the island.

Seeing Britta's frown of puzzlement, the woman lifted the glass ball and held it up to show the label fastened to the silver base.

This sky sphere, created on the Isle
of Dorne, was gained in fair trade
by Thurl of Two Moons.

Larsett

"Thurl!" the old woman said, ducking her head slightly as if to introduce herself.

Dumbfounded, Britta stared at the label. Her father had been here. He had, perhaps, sat in the very spot where she was sitting now. Her mind raced as she tried to make sense of what she was seeing.

"*Kaja,*" Thurl murmured, pushing the sphere forward a little as if she were urging Britta to take it.

"Krest kaja, per Stassi!"

Britta stared in amazement. Was it possible? Was Thurl offering her most precious possession in thanks because Britta had tried to save the boy?

It seemed she was. There was no other explanation for the way she was nodding and trying to thrust the sphere into Britta's hands.

Instinctively Britta shrank back a little, shaking her head. She did not need a gift of thanks. She had done only what she had felt impelled to do. She could not have allowed the boy to drown before her eyes without lifting a finger to help him.

Thurl looked aghast, and continued to push the sphere forward. Seeing how earnest she was, Britta was briefly tempted. The wall hanging she had bought from Mull was lost—sunk deep in the swamp. Most of her gold had been spent, and she had nothing to show for it.

Thurl's offer of the sky sphere should have been the answer to a prayer. The sphere was an object of great value—of far greater value than anything Sky, Jewel or Vashti could buy in Two Moons with ten gold coins. And, certainly, it was something that could be traded in Illica for a fortune!

But Britta knew she could not take it. The sky sphere would be familiar to anyone who had ever known Dare Larsett in the old days. If Mab saw it, she would instantly think of the man who had once been her favorite. It would make a link between Britta and

Larsett in Mab's mind, and that could be fatal. Mab might suddenly see Britta's likeness to her father, as others had done. She might begin to suspect …

And Britta could not risk that. Whatever else happened, she could not risk that. Smiling and shaking her head, she pushed the sphere gently away, and as she did she saw with a thrill of horror that the blue sky behind the glass was dimming.

It was far later than she had realized! She should be on the jetty waiting to board the *Star of Deltora* right now! How could she have wasted so much time wondering about her father, wishing she could accept the sky sphere, when she should have been thinking furiously about her own plight? Fear and shock had made her forget Trader Sven's golden rule:

The good trader always focuses on his or her main aim. All our intelligence and energy should be directed to gaining the result we want.

And what I want, Britta thought, is to get out of the swamp, and back to the ship. Things are bad enough for me as it is! Mab swore that the ship would leave the harbor before sunset. If I cause her to break her word …

She turned her attention to Thurl, who was looking downcast, the rejected sphere held limply between her hands. It seemed that Thurl believed she owed Britta a debt. Good! Now Britta had to make the old woman understand that guidance out of the swampland would pay the debt in full.

"Stassi!" Britta said, clasping her hands.

The old woman's eyes darkened. She waited.

Britta unclasped her hands. She touched the sky sphere, and shook her head. She touched her own chest. Then she lowered her right hand and made the first two fingers "walk" quickly along the earth floor. Finally, she pointed in what she hoped was the direction of the harbor.

The old woman groaned softly, and made a helpless gesture. She stood up and disappeared into the darkness.

Britta had hoped she would open the front door, call the man and woman waiting outside, and order them to guide the *batak* back to the coast.

That had not happened. The front door remained shut. By the sound of it, Thurl was rummaging around in another room at the back of the hut.

The blue inside the dome was slowly fading. Britta sat helplessly waiting, her heart in her mouth, very aware of the precious minutes slipping by.

At last she heard Thurl returning. The old woman reached the circle of light and knelt down. She was carrying a metal tray on which stood a crude little doll made of gleaming amber mud, like the mud in the pool outside the hut. No doubt she had made the figure herself, for its color matched the stains on her hands.

She placed the tray on the ground, held up the first finger of her left hand as if to command Britta's attention, and began muttering some words in her own language. Her grave face and manner seemed to indicate that this was some sort of ceremony.

Hoping that it was a ceremony that would end in her being released from the swamp, Britta controlled her impatience and waited respectfully. She did not even react when Thurl slowly extended the raised finger and tapped her lightly on the lips, though her every instinct urged her to recoil.

Apparently satisfied, Thurl folded her hands and soberly nodded at the doll, as if inviting her guest to take it.

Britta picked up the doll. The mud was still soft, and her fingertips sank a little into its sticky surface.

Thurl seemed to sigh. By signs she showed that Britta should put the doll first to her forehead, then to her heart.

Thinking grimly that more mud stains on her face and shirt would not hurt her, Britta did as she was told.

Thurl sat back on her heels, her face slack with relief. She looked, thought Britta in sudden panic, as if she felt that a bargain had been made—a hard bargain, but one that meant everything to her. Was it possible that Thurl now felt her debt had been paid in full— that she owed Britta nothing more?

Surely not! The little mud figure had some charm,

but it was more crudely made than the clay dolls and animals that Britta had seen for sale in the town, and it was nothing compared to the sky sphere. Yet ... who knew what the swamp dwellers valued? They were strange, secret people.

Cursing herself for blundering into a bargain she did not understand, Britta scrambled to her feet.

"Please let me go now!" she begged. "Please help me get back to my ship! Do you understand me, Thurl? Oh, Thurl, please understand!"

"I am taking you, *batak*, if no one else willing. Price paid now, with goozli, but still I am taking you."

The voice from the shadows was high and clear. And as Britta stood clutching the doll, speechless with amazement, the boy Stassi stepped into the circle of light.

15 - The Intruder

Her mind in turmoil, Britta stared at the boy she had believed to be dead. *"Nak, Stassi!"* hissed Thurl, waving him away urgently. *"Ishk! Ishk!"* But Stassi stood his ground, though his eyes were wide with what looked like fear. He ducked his head at the old woman, putting his hands together as if giving thanks, then mumbled in his own tongue, pointing to the door.

Thurl shook her head wildly.

Stassi wet his lips. "You risked your life for mine," he said to Britta. "So I am thinking that for me, your spirits not *ishk*."

Perhaps the second part of this speech was as much a question as a statement, but in any case Britta did not hear it. She was focusing on the boy's first words, the same strangely formal words he had recited in the swamp. The rest of what he had said as

134

she held him above the mud had come back to her, and suddenly it was as if her mind had been flooded with light.

Suddenly she understood the real reason for the grief of the man and woman waiting outside the hut. Suddenly she saw why Thurl had been so desperate for her to accept first the sphere, then the doll.

You risked your life for mine. I am yours now, till my life's end.

Britta had taken the words only as lavish thanks. Now she realized that Stassi had meant exactly what he said. By the law of the turtle people, it seemed, he had been bonded to Britta for life because she had saved him. Thurl had been bargaining for his freedom.

But the turtle people saved me in turn, Britta thought. Does that mean I am bonded to *them* for life?

But one look at Stassi's cheerful face told her it did not. The law applied only to turtle people saved by *batak*, strangers, it seemed. And that made a kind of sense. In this wild, treacherous place, turtle people must surely often fall into danger, and be rescued by other members of their tribe. If the law applied to that situation, there would be more slaves than free people in the heart of the swamplands.

"Thank you," Britta said to the boy. "Can we go quickly?"

He nodded and went to the door.

Weak with relief, Britta smiled and bowed to the silent Thurl. Carefully, making sure the old woman saw what she was doing, she pushed the little mud figure into her pocket and buttoned it safely inside.

She had just glanced at the sky sphere for the last time, and seen with dread the first faint glow of sunset tingeing the edges of the gathering clouds, when a great hubbub arose outside. The noise of angry voices grew louder, louder ...

Thurl muttered to Stassi, and stood up as the boy pulled the door open.

The clearing outside the hut was thronged with shouting people. There seemed to be a struggle going on in the center of the crowd. Gliding swiftly to the doorway, Thurl called a sharp order.

Instantly the tumult stilled. The crowd parted. Britta stared as three men dragged a mud-spattered figure to the doorway.

"My lady!" the bedraggled figure said huskily, catching sight of Thurl and realizing at once that she was a person in authority. "Have mercy on a poor, lost stranger, I beg you! These people have made a terrible mistake! I strayed into the swamp by purest accident, and was only trying to find my way out when they found me!"

And in astounded dismay, Britta recognized the voice, the long, tousled hair and the muddy face of Sky of Rithmere.

Thurl looked gravely at Sky, then glanced at Stassi, raising her eyebrows. Plainly she was asking the boy what the captured *batak* had said. Stassi stammered a few words. The men holding Sky jeered and shook their heads. One spoke rapidly, bending his head and shading his eyes with his free hand to show that Sky had been peering around, searching the ground.

Looking for sunrise pearls, no doubt, thought Britta. Oh, Sky, you fool!

In terror she saw Thurl's face grow stern. She saw Thurl raise an amber-stained hand, then lower it again.

"*Atta,*" the old woman said softly.

Atta—mud. It was a sentence of death—a terrible death by suffocation in the swamp.

"No!" Britta cried. She ran to Thurl's side, shaking her head, racking her brains for the few words of swamp dweller language that she knew. "*Nak atta!*"

At the sight of Britta, the men holding Sky shrank back, hissing the strange word *ishk* over and over again. The other swamp dwellers in the clearing were rigid with terror, all except two—the man and woman who had attended Britta when she first woke. They ran forward, calling Stassi's name, but Thurl had thrust the boy partly behind her, as if to protect him, and was holding him fast.

Britta could not see what the swamp dwellers could see—the wraiths swirling about her like gray mist as she stood framed in the doorway. She did not remember that *ishk* meant evil or unlucky. She assumed that the people feared her because of the power she had gained over Stassi by saving his life.

I daresay they all knew that Thurl was going to try to trade with me for Stassi's freedom, she thought. Thurl has not yet had the chance to tell them that she has been successful, and that Stassi is safe, despite their cruel law.

And suddenly, an idea came to her. She turned away from Thurl, and looked directly at Sky.

"You!" Sky croaked, staring in astonishment.

Sky could not see the wraiths. All Sky could see was the startling picture of Britta covered in dried mud, her hair tumbling over her shoulders in stiff, clotted clumps, a strange amber mark on her brow and her dark eyes burning with purpose.

So I have surprised you for once, Sky of Rithmere, Britta thought. The danger was very great, but it was impossible not to feel a trace of ill-natured satisfaction in seeing the smooth, confident Sky thrown so far off balance.

"They are planning to kill you by throwing you into the mud, Sky," she said bluntly. "I am going to try to persuade them otherwise. Unless … " She raised an eyebrow. "Unless you still feel you would prefer me to stay out of your affairs?"

"On this occasion, I give you permission to interfere as much as you like," replied Sky, with a feeble return to her usual manner. She even tried for a rueful grin, but Britta saw that she was very white around the lips.

"Do you have any gold left?" Britta demanded.

"No." Sky grimaced. "I spent it all. And the very fine clock I bought was lost in the mud with my shore bag when these dolts pounced on me. Why? Do you charge for your services as a lifesaver? Or do you fear you will fail, and hate to think of any gold I might have going down with me?"

"I am hoping to trade for you," snapped Britta. "I will have to make do with what I have. Meanwhile, say and do nothing to alarm them."

She turned to Thurl and Stassi, who had been watching the exchange in silence.

"*Nak atta,*" Britta repeated, pointing to Sky. She pressed her hand to her heart as the old woman had done when explaining her love for Stassi, then pointed at Sky again.

"This foolish one is dear to me," she went on slowly and clearly. "I wish to trade with you for her life, Thurl, as you traded with me for Stassi. As part of the trade, she must be taken with me to our ship. Then I swear we will sail far away and never trouble you again."

She waited, trying not to show how anxious she felt, as Stassi translated what she had said. The boy looked a little puzzled, and stumbled over some of the words. She fervently hoped that he had understood her.

Thurl frowned in thought, then nodded shortly and called something to the crowd. Britta's heart lifted, and fluttered only a little as the old woman silently gestured to her to return to her former place by the oil burner. It was hard to turn from the open doorway and move back to the pool of yellow light, but she had no choice. If the trading for Sky's life had to be done with ceremony, and in private, then that was how it had to be.

Thurl waited till Britta was settled on the woven mat, then muttered something to Stassi and pushed him out of the hut. Just before the door slammed behind him, Britta heard two voices crying out in joy and imagined the boy flying into the arms of the man and woman she had realized must be his father and mother.

She was glad for them, but wished all the same that Thurl had kept Stassi with her. Now the trade would have to be done without words.

I managed it before, Britta told herself. And at least this time we both know what is at stake. We only have to agree on the price. But her stomach felt queasy and her whole body was quivering with nerves as Thurl sat down on the other side of the oil burner and nodded at her to begin.

Britta unbuttoned her pocket and felt for the little mud doll Stassi had called a goozli. Except for two gold coins, the goozli was all she had to offer, but she was confident that it would be well received. Thurl had handed over the doll with so much ceremony that she plainly valued it highly. She would surely welcome the chance to get it back.

The doll still felt slightly soft beneath Britta's fingertips. She drew it gently out of hiding and placed it on the ground in front of her, pointing to it, then pointing to Thurl.

To her astonishment the old woman recoiled, shaking her head violently.

"But—but why not?" Britta burst out, forgetting in her panic the uselessness of words.

Staring as if she thought Britta had lost her mind, Thurl gestured at the doll, gestured at Britta, then stabbed at her own chest and forehead. Finally, seeing that her companion still looked baffled, she leaned forward and pointed to the small dents in the doll's sides, where Britta's fingertips had sunk into the soft mud.

Was she saying that the goozli was damaged, and now could not be returned? Or had Britta offered a grave insult by trying to give back an object that Thurl had crafted with her own hands? What did it matter? The fact was, the doll had been rejected.

Britta felt heat rush into her face. What was she going to do now? The goozli had been at the heart of her plan. She fumbled in her pocket, found the necklace of false sunrise pearls that Mull had given her, and without much hope, put it on the mat in front of Thurl.

Thurl barely looked at it before pushing it away. What use did the leader of the turtle people have for false pearls, her blank face seemed to say, when the real thing grew not far from her own doorstep?

Britta did not even try to offer her notebook, her pencil, her comb or her handkerchief. The sturdy lining of her pocket had shielded them from the mud, but all were worn, and none of them had been of high quality even when they were new. The two gold coins that remained in her coin purse were all she had left to give.

Trying not to show how anxious she felt, she placed the coins on the mat. Clean and bright, they winked temptingly in the yellow light of the oil burner.

Thurl looked down at them, expressionless. She held up two fingers, and shrugged. Then she raised the fingers and thumbs of both hands.

Britta felt a hot wave of despairing anger. I do not *have* ten coins, you wicked old bandit! she thought, shaking her head. See for yourself!

She turned her coin purse upside down and shook it to show that it was empty. Then she tossed it into Thurl's lap.

Thurl's eyes gleamed. She picked up the purse and turned it over in her hands, touching the delicate embroidery with gentle fingers.

"*Ah!*" she murmured. "*Kaja!*" And she pressed her hand to her heart.

Stunned, Britta focused on the purse. Her sister had sewn it for her, and given it to her on the night she left home. It was a pretty thing, and Britta valued it because Margareth had made it, but it was not particularly interesting or special. It was just a little coin purse embroidered with birds and flowers.

Then she remembered something Mull had said:

True kaja objects are powerful—sometimes because of how they were made, sometimes simply because they are one of a kind.

The little purse had been made with love, and Thurl could feel that love in every stitch. To her, this made the purse *kaja*.

And of course it is, Britta thought, a lump rising in her throat. I just did not realize it. And now I have to give it up. For Sky of Rithmere, who has never been a friend to me!

But there was no choice, of course. In moments the trade had been made, and Sky's life was spared for the price of a *kaja* purse and two gold coins.

Britta left the hut prickling with irritation. Sky's few, wry words of thanks on hearing of the bargain that had been made did nothing to soothe her. Nor did the way the crowd in the darkening clearing drew back from her as if she had the plague.

At least I am alive, Britta told herself. Stassi is alive, too. And I saved Sky, whether she is grateful for it or not.

These thoughts cheered her—and cheered her more than a little. But she could not help remembering that now there was the journey back to the shore to be faced—and at the end of it, Mab's fury.

16 - Moonlight

Thurl plainly wanted to rid herself of her visitors with all speed. Orders were given, people ran to obey, and in no time at all, it seemed, Britta and Sky were bouncing in the back of a sled that was speeding towards the town. The driver, an elderly, sour-looking man Britta had not seen before, clicked his tongue to urge on the giant slug pulling the sled, but did not speak. A woman sat stiffly beside him, armed with a flaming torch. She, too, was silent.

They did not look behind them. It was as if they were trying to pretend that Britta and Sky were not there.

"That thing is monstrous!" Sky exclaimed, peering out at the dim shape of the slug in fascinated disgust.

"The one pulling the sled that carried me into the swamp was even bigger," said Britta listlessly. "It was badly injured when the wild *imbuck* attacked, and I lost sight of it after the sled overturned. Poor creature, I hope the swamp dwellers managed to save it after they saved Stassi and me. It fought so bravely."

She saw that Sky was staring at her, and frowned. "What?" she demanded.

"Nothing," Sky muttered, and turned away, shaking her head.

They went on in silence after that, and this suited Britta very well. Images of the sky sphere kept swimming into her exhausted mind, and she was unable to force them back. Now that she was safe, the strangeness of finding her father's most precious possession in Thurl's hut had come back to her with full force.

She closed her eyes and tried to work out what must have happened, step by step.

Her father must have taken the sky sphere into the swamplands to trade. He would hardly have weighed himself down with such an awkward, delicate burden otherwise. The swamp was forbidden, but danger would not have worried Larsett. He was famous for taking risks—why else did people call him "Dare"?

And—Britta felt a rueful twinge of admiration for her father's cunning—the sky sphere was, of course, the perfect item to trade. What else in the nine seas could be so powerfully tempting to a swamp dweller like Thurl, from whom the real sky was always hidden?

The sled rocked. Mud swished and gurgled.

Britta kept her eyes closed and let her thoughts run on.

Larsett must have wanted something very badly—something only Thurl could provide. But on that last voyage he had had only one goal—to find the lost Staff of Tier.

Britta shivered, remembering the symbol on the hut door—the symbol declaring to all who knew how to read it that Thurl was in some way heir to the magic of the sorcerer Tier.

Had Dare Larsett discovered, or guessed, that in his last years the pirate Bar-Enoch had brought the Staff to the Two Moons swamplands, where Tier had been born? Had Thurl told Larsett where the pirate's body and the Staff lay hidden, receiving the sky sphere in return?

That would explain the oddness of the label on the base of the sphere. The label was a kind of receipt, proof that Thurl had come by the sphere honestly. Yet traders' receipts always stated both sides of a bargain, and this one had not done that. It had noted that Thurl had traded fairly for the sky sphere, but had not revealed what she had given in exchange.

And this could only be because Thurl's part of the bargain had to be kept secret—as of course it would, if she had allowed the Staff of Tier to be taken from its resting place.

It all made good sense. And yet … Britta shook her head. She could not quite believe it. There was something wrong. What was it?

She thought about all she had seen and done since coming into the Two Moons swamplands. She thought of the hut, and Thurl's shrewd, faded eyes. And then she knew what her problem was.

Thurl loved *kaja*, but as her trade with Britta for Stassi's freedom proved, she loved her people more. Britta could not believe that Thurl would have let a dangerous, powerful, magic object like the Staff loose on the world again, whatever she was offered in return.

And besides, was it really likely that Bar-Enoch would have chosen the unfriendly swamplands of Two Moons as his final refuge?

No, it was not. The back of her head bumping gently against the side of the sled, Britta frowned, more certain every moment that her first idea had been wrong. The Staff of Tier had not been hidden in the Two Moons swamp. But then ... what had her father received in exchange for the sky sphere? What else had he badly needed, that only the swamp could provide?

The obvious answer was a sunrise pearl. But why would that have to be kept secret?

"Britta, wake up!"

Sky's voice was low and the touch on Britta's arm was soft, but still Britta sat forward with a start.

"I was not asleep!" she snapped, shaking off Sky's hand.

"I am sorry," Sky said calmly. "You looked asleep. One minute shivering, the next frowning—as if you were having a bad dream, which would not be surprising after—"

"I was merely thinking," Britta retorted. "Leave me alone! You have caused me trouble enough."

"Now, are those the words of a friend?" Sky sighed gustily. "How fickle you are, Britta! It seems no time since you were putting your hand on your heart and swearing I was dear to you!"

Britta bit back a sharp reply, determined not to give Sky the satisfaction of making her lose her temper. At the same moment, she noticed that the sound of the sled had changed, and the jolting and bumping had grown less.

"We are slowing down!" she exclaimed.

"Indeed," Sky drawled. "And if you stop glaring at me for a moment and turn your head, you will see what I saw just before I roused you. We are almost out of the swamp. The lights of the town are ahead."

★

Set down at the town's edge and quickly left to themselves by the swamp dwellers, who were plainly only too glad to turn the sled and get away, Britta and Sky trudged alone and unnoticed towards the shore. The moon was hidden by a few slowly drifting clouds, and the stars shone small and cold. The streets they passed along were deserted, and for this Britta was very thankful. She could only imagine what a sight she must look—ten times worse than Sky, who was bedraggled enough.

She longed to be safely aboard her ship once more, but the thought of facing Mab made her feel sick.

"It is not far to the harbor now," Sky said casually, and Britta realized she must have sighed aloud.

"It is not that," she said drearily. "It is ... "

And suddenly she could keep her thoughts to herself no longer. Sky of Rithmere was the last person she would normally confide in, but she did not care. All she knew was that her heart was so full it seemed it would burst.

"I was drugged," she burst out. "I fell asleep, and was carried into the swamp by accident. It was not my fault, but I fear that Mab will not believe me. In Del I came back after the last test saying I had been attacked and locked up. She believed me then. But who would believe that I fell into the hands of an enemy for a second time here?"

"I believe you, if you say so," Sky said surprisingly. "Who drugged you?"

Britta glanced sideways. Sky's head was bent, and her dangling braids had swung forward, hiding her face, but her question had sounded quite serious.

"It was a shopkeeper called Mull," Britta said. "He gave me a sweet from a jar on his counter. He ate some of the sweets himself, so I did not think there could be any harm in them. But he must have become used to the drug so that it did not affect him. I have read of such things."

"I have too," Sky said slowly. "But I do not think

they happen often outside tall tales. Did Mull steal back what you had bought from him?"

"No," Britta admitted. "It is odd, but I suppose ... he did not have the chance."

Sky made no reply, and for a long, tense moment they walked on in silence.

"I *was* drugged, I swear it!" Britta burst out at last. "And Mull *must* have been the one who did it! I did not eat or drink anything else except—"

She broke off. A terrible thought had suddenly flashed into her mind.

"Except water from my flask," she finished slowly. And suddenly she was remembering the flask lying unprotected by her shore bag on the *Star*'s shadowy deck. Anyone could have meddled with it without being seen.

She had drunk deeply from the flask, walking along the road beside the swamp. The heavy sleepiness had come on very quickly afterward.

Had the enemy who had tried to spoil her chances before the *Star of Deltora* sailed tried again in Two Moons?

The still, sticky, swamp-scented air of the town was warm on Britta's face, but inside she felt cold. The thought of reaching the ship no longer made her feel safe. And no longer was it a relief to talk to Sky. Because Sky could easily have been the one ...

"I did not drug your flask, Britta, if that is what you are thinking," Sky said lightly. "Certainly, I have known for some time that you are far from being the prissy little trader's daughter I thought you at first. If I seriously wanted to win the Rosalyn contest, I would see you as a dangerous rival. But for one thing, I do not seriously want to win. And for another, while I do not have many scruples, I do draw the line at drugging my rivals."

Britta hardly knew whether to feel insulted or flattered. Nor did she know how far Sky was to be believed. She decided, after a moment's thought, that she was in no fit state to judge on either of these questions, so she said nothing and walked on.

Then, quite suddenly, just as a huge full moon emerged from behind the clouds, the harbor was before them. Small lanterns glowed along the curving shoreline. Beside Jetty 3, the *Star of Deltora* rocked gently at anchor. And beyond the jetties, beyond the ship, a pale moon floated in the calm black water of the bay, a rippling reflection of the real moon in the sky.

Two Moons …

"Mab waited for us!" Sky muttered. Hearing the relief in her husky voice, Britta glanced at her in surprise.

"I would not have put it past her to leave us stranded," Sky admitted, with a twisted smile. "I daresay if I had been the only one missing, she would have done it, too. But since her pet was missing as well—"

"I am not Mab's pet!" Britta protested heatedly.

"If anyone is her pet, it is you!"

"I amuse her, that is all," said Sky with a shrug. "You are a different matter. Mab watches you intently, when she thinks no one will notice. I have seen her."

"You cannot take me in, Sky!" Britta snapped. "Though what you think you will gain by trying to make me believe such a ridiculous lie, I cannot imagine!"

Sky merely raised her eyebrows and smiled knowingly.

There was a shout from the ship. Someone had seen them, just before the moon vanished behind a cloud once more. Lanterns swung wildly as dark figures began running towards them.

In moments they were stumbling up the gangplank of the *Star of Deltora*, and Mab, flanked by Captain Hara and Healer Kay, was scowling at them furiously. Behind Mab stood Vashti, very prim and disapproving, and Jewel, whose eyes were popping. In the background, Crow and other members of the crew were watching avidly. Chief Trader Xen, looking grim, stood a little apart with a group of glowering shoremen.

"Explain yourselves, wretches!" Mab thundered, as Britta and Sky came towards her. "Have you any idea of the trouble you have caused?"

She gestured at the shoremen. "These men have been combing the town for you since sunset! The entire crew searched for an hour before that! They could find no trace of you! We—"

She broke off with a startled curse. She had just seen Britta clearly.

"Britta was drugged and carried off into the swamplands, Mab," Sky said quickly. "I saw it happen, and went after her!"

Furious, Britta opened her mouth to say this was a lie, then shut it again. What did it matter? If Sky wanted to protect herself from Mab's fury by pretending she had entered the swamp for a noble purpose, then why not let her do it?

"If your young people had really been lost in the swamp, Mab, they would not be standing here now," Xen said curtly. "They would almost certainly be dead. No doubt they stumbled into a muddy ditch at the edge of town, but that is no excuse—"

"The girl has been in the swamplands without doubt," one of the shoremen declared loudly. "She has been in far—in deep—where the turtle people hide from the sun!"

He shuddered. "Do you not see? She has been marked! Only once before have I seen that on a *batak*, years ago, and that was the evil one—Larsett!"

Britta's stomach lurched as if she had plummeted from a very high place. Her ears were filled with a dull, growling sound, and it took a moment for her to realize that she was hearing the fearful muttering of the listening crew.

Mab's drawn face looked ghastly in the flickering

lantern light. *"What?"* she demanded, peering from Britta to Sky and back to Britta again. "What does he say, Xen? Who is he talking about?"

"The female!" the shoreman gabbled, tapping his forehead then pointing at Britta with a shaking finger. "The female bears the mark of Tier! The male is clean."

There was a thunderstruck silence. And suddenly everyone was staring at Sky. As if the clouds had been waiting their moment, they parted abruptly and again the ship was bathed in moonlight.

There stood Sky in the cold white glare, dark eyes alight with amused defiance, wide mouth curved into a rueful smile. The lean brown face had not changed. The lithe body had not changed. The long, braided hair had not changed. The tattered trousers and tunic had not changed.

But in an instant, thanks to a stranger's words, people were looking at Sky differently, and the disguise that was no disguise at all had dissolved. Gaping with all the rest, Britta suddenly realized that Sky had told her the truth about not aiming to win the Rosalyn Trust contest. The winner had to be female. And, without a shadow of doubt, Sky of Rithmere was male.

17 - Surprises

Jewel was still shouting with laughter as she and Britta hung over the rail, watching the *Star of Deltora* glide through the watery moon on her way out of the bay. "No wonder Sky kept himself so apart from everyone else!" Jewel hooted for the fifth time at least. "No wonder he was desperate not to share a cabin! By the stars, what fools we were not to see what he was! It was the hair that deceived us, I daresay. Did you hear him say that all men of the Mere let their hair grow long, for luck? Some folk have very strange customs."

"Indeed," Britta agreed mildly, eyeing Jewel's bald, painted skull. "But it was not just the hair. We believed Sky was female because he had entered the Rosalyn contest, and the Rosalyn contest is only open to females. It was as simple as that."

Jewel chuckled. "I daresay you are right. All he had to do was write a false sponsor's letter to go with

155

his entry paper. After that it was plain sailing. Oh, the clever rascal! He never tried to play a part. He dressed and acted in his normal way. He did not change his name. He did not even try to change his voice, except always to speak in low tones—and for all we know that comes naturally to him."

"I think it does," Britta murmured, remembering that Sky had not even raised his voice when he was struggling in the grip of the swamp dwellers outside Thurl's hut. At the same moment, she remembered how confused the boy Stassi had seemed when he was translating her plea for Sky's life. Like all the other swamp dwellers, no doubt, Stassi had known full well that the prisoner was a young man, so he could not understand why Britta kept referring to Sky as "she."

"I just cannot think why he entered the Rosalyn contest in the first place," Jewel said. "What if he had won? As he grew older his beard would have begun to grow in earnest and everyone would have seen—"

"He told me he did not want to win," Britta broke in. "I think he just wanted ... experience. And adventure. And a chance ... "

A chance to hunt fabled treasure and make his fortune, she finished to herself silently, thinking with a pang of sunrise pearls. She sighed and turned away from the rail.

"I daresay you are sorry for him," Jewel said. "So am I, in a way. It is hard for anyone outside Del, especially someone who has no powerful friends, to get a chance on a trading ship." She grinned. "Except, perhaps, as a very lowly sailor—and imagine Sky swabbing decks from dawn till dark under the eye of a pig rat like Crow!"

Britta felt a smile tweaking her own lips. She could not imagine it. Then her smile faded. Nor could she imagine Sky in the lockup below, being fed on bread and water. But that was where he was now.

"Mab will come round, never fear, little nodnap," said Jewel, with rare gentleness. "Just now she is fuming in her cabin, perhaps, but by tomorrow she will be feeling better, and will let Sky out. After all, she does owe him something. He saved your life!"

The sympathy in her voice irritated Britta beyond endurance. Jewel seemed to think that she cared what happened to Sky. But she did not! Why should she care what happened to someone so devious, so willful, so … so foolishly reckless!

"Sky did not save my life," she snapped. "I saved his!"

"Indeed?" Jewel's eyes widened with interest.

Already Britta was regretting her outburst. "But keep that to yourself, if you please, Jewel," she added. "He is in enough trouble already."

"And you do not want Mab enquiring too deeply into what actually happened while you and Sky were in the swamplands," Jewel guessed shrewdly. "Well, I can understand that, after what that shoreman said about you."

Britta did not know how to reply. The uproar about Sky had diverted everyone's attention from her. She had hoped that the shoreman's other statements would be forgotten—or taken merely as superstitious babbling. But that had been stupid. Jewel remembered them and so would everyone else, including Mab.

Jewel shrugged. "Plainly you are not ready to talk about it to me either, or you would have done so by now," she said briskly. "So I advise you to go below and do what you can to transform yourself from a mud monster into a human being. I will beg a bucket of warm water from Grubb and bring it to you. The first thing you should do is scrub that orange mark off your forehead. It looks—rather startling."

Britta raised her hand to her brow in surprise, and felt a small gritty patch beneath her fingertips. So this was the "mark of Tier" that the shoreman had talked about! She realized that it was only a smear of amber mud from the soft goozli doll, and felt reassured. She opened her mouth to tell Jewel, but the words seemed to dry in her throat. Her lips felt stiff, and her tongue suddenly seemed too big for her mouth.

It is as Jewel says, she thought. I am not ready to talk about the swamp yet. I am more shocked than I realize.

"You will have to cut off your hair, I think," Jewel said, regarding her critically. "It seems to have set in hard lumps, and I doubt that all the water in the Silver Sea will be enough to get it clean. Still—" She rubbed her own shaved scalp with satisfaction. "Hair is far more trouble than it is worth, in my opinion. It attracts nesting dragons, for a start! You will be better off without it."

★

Alone in her cabin, a bucket of hot water steaming at her feet, Britta stared into the mirror above the writing table. A pale, wild-eyed stranger with an amber brand in the center of her forehead and a muddy bird's nest for hair stared back at her. Mud monster, thought Britta, and saw the stranger's lips twitch, then open, as she gave a snort of laughter.

How can you laugh, you fool? she scolded herself. Look at the state you are in! Your best shirt and skirt are ruined—and that is not the worst of it. You have lost everything! Your gold has gone and you have nothing to show for it. You have no hope, now, of winning the contest. And because of that mark on your forehead, your name has been linked with your father's, which is the very thing you wished to avoid.

That last thought sobered her as nothing else had. She wet the edge of her face towel and rubbed at the amber mark. The surface mud vanished, but an orange stain remained on the skin where it had been. Peering at it, Britta remembered Thurl's hands—amber to the wrists.

"Perfect!" she said aloud. "Now I have a tattoo, right in the middle of my forehead!"

Telling herself that the color from one little dab of mud could not last forever and that the mark would fade in time, she began peeling off her clothes.

She had dropped her filthy shirt on the floor and was about to do the same with her skirt when she remembered the items in the skirt pocket.

She took out the notebook, the pencil stub, the handkerchief, the string of pink beads and the comb, and put them in a heap on the table. She thought of her coin purse, the *kaja* purse, and sighed. Right at the bottom of the other pocket was the goozli doll. When she pulled it out she saw that it had dried and hardened since she had last seen it, and its amber surface now had a dull sheen.

Britta put the doll on the table with the other things, balancing it on its feet so that it stood upright.

"I forgot," she said to it. "I have not lost everything. I still have you."

The goozli put its tiny hand to its forehead, then to its heart, and bowed.

Britta froze. I am dreaming, she thought dazedly.

The goozli put its hands on its hips, tilted its head to one side and regarded her solemnly. Then, like a streak of golden sunshine, it scampered up her arm, jumped onto her shoulder, and began drawing the few remaining hairpins from her clotted hair. Britta stifled a scream and tried to shake it off, but it clung to its perch and went on with its task as if nothing had happened.

She could see it clearly in the mirror—a moving, orange-gold manikin, standing on her shoulder. It had pulled out all the hairpins now, and was using them to tease out strands of her hair. Flakes of hard mud stuck through with fragments of leaves and sticks began showering onto the deck with a brisk, pattering sound.

Struggling to get her breath, Britta abruptly recalled several things at once.

She remembered the little amber-colored object that had slid down Stassi's grooved rod towards the sunrise pearl, during the ill-fated stop in the swamp. She remembered the dark-gold flashes she had seen as the life-saving rope was looped around her chest. She remembered the movement low in the shadows of Thurl's hut, as the sky sphere was brought for her inspection. She remembered the swathe of amber mud that lay beside the hut like a pool of dark honey.

And then she remembered some words from *A Trader's Life*:

Tier was a gentle soul who wished no one any harm. After his mother went to join her ancestors he lived on alone in the swamp that was his home. There he lived quietly, molding amber mud into strange, beautiful shapes that moved ...

Shapes that moved ... Britta had never really thought about those words before. They had seemed just part of the fable, without real meaning. Now she knew that they meant exactly what they said.

In ancient days, Tier had molded "strange, beautiful shapes" from the magic mud. In his time, no doubt, wonders had stalked the swamps. These days, Tier's heir used the same mud for more practical reasons. Thurl made goozlis, tiny servants who kept the turtle people's clothes and houses clean, fetched and carried for them and, most important of all, helped them harvest sunrise pearls.

Goozlis were one of the many deep secrets of the turtle people of the Two Moons swamplands. Most outsiders did not know they existed, and those who did know did not tell.

Could not tell, Britta thought, remembering how her throat had dried and her tongue stiffened when she was about to speak of the goozli to Jewel.

Fascinated, she stared at the reflection of the little amber creature laboring over her hair, patiently working it loose from the dried mud, strand by strand. The goozli was no bigger than her hand. Its tiny face was wrinkled in concentration. Its small, stout legs were no longer than her fingers ...

And suddenly Britta knew why Thurl had given the goozli to her. She remembered the signs she had made to try to tell Thurl that all she wanted in return for Stassi's freedom was to be taken back to the ship.

She had touched her heart. She had made her fingers walk quickly along the floor, like little legs. She had pointed in the direction of the harbor—which was also the side of the hut where the pool of amber mud lay.

Thurl had not understood. She had thought that Britta was demanding a goozli as her price. And for Stassi's sake, Thurl had given one.

Just as she had given Dare Larsett a goozli, in return for the sky sphere. Britta had never been so sure of anything in her life.

Britta sat, hands clasped, staring vacantly into the mirror. Why her father had wanted a goozli for himself, she did not know. But she was perfectly sure that, whatever the reason, it had something to do with his plan to find the lost Staff of Tier.

Forget Dare Larsett, she told herself angrily. Forget you have ever heard the name! What does it matter what Father wanted, or what his plan was? You have your own life to live!

But if that was true, why did she seem to be following in her father's footsteps?

Furiously, Britta pushed the unwelcome thought from her mind. She concentrated on the goozli, which had somehow managed to free most of the hair on one side of her head from mud, and was now working on the other side.

The little creature was a miracle! It would trade for a fortune in Illica, even without a receipt. From the little Britta had read, the Collectors of Illica were not fussy about proof of ownership.

But even as the thought crossed Britta's mind,

she knew it was base, and false, and impossible.

The goozli was not an item she could trade. It was hers—hers for life. She had touched it to her forehead and her chest, and it had marked her. Her fingertips had pressed into its sides when it was still soft and new. And … and somehow it warmed her heart.

The goozli was still wielding the hairpins vigorously. Dried mud was still showering the deck and powdering Britta's shoulders. Out of the corner of her eye Britta saw a few pink fragments fall with the brown ones, and remembered with a lurch of regret the ragged, broken swamp lily half submerged in pale, heaving mud.

Then the goozli paused. It bent, and plucked something from the tangled web of hair right beside it. The next moment, it had scuttled down Britta's arm and was presenting its find with a bow.

The thing looked like a gray river pebble. Britta's heart leaped. She looked at the goozli, which nodded knowingly. She took the pebble from its tiny hand, and dipped it into the bucket of water at her feet.

When she straightened, she was holding between her dripping fingers a perfect pink pearl.

"Caught in my hair when the wave of mud came, and it sank!" Britta breathed, holding up the pearl. "Smothered in mud, dried in the tangled hair, carried with me! Why, at any time it might have fallen out and been lost! Or Thurl might have seen it!"

But it had not fallen and been lost. Thurl had not

seen it. It was here, in Britta's hand, a sunrise pearl worth a king's ransom!

Britta did not know whether to laugh or sigh. In the end, she did a little of both.

She had no receipt for the pearl, so she could not use it to win the Rosalyn contest. But what might the Collectors of Illica trade for something so precious?

Suddenly, the future was stretching before her like a sunlit sea, the horizon glowing with mysterious, dazzling promise.

"You are very well worth having, my friend," she said to the goozli, after a while.

And the goozli touched its forehead, and then its heart, and smiled.

DON'T MISS THE NEXT THRILLING ADVENTURE IN
THE *STAR OF DELTORA* SERIES!

BOOK 3: THE TOWERS OF ILLICA

The *Star of Deltora* is making for Illica, home of the mysterious Collectors. Ahead is the most important trade of Britta's life—her last chance to defeat her rivals and win the Rosalyn contest. She knows she should be thinking of nothing else. But she is in danger. The ghostly shadows that haunt her are pressing closer. And though the terrors of Two Moons have been left behind, a cloud of fear still hangs over the *Star* like swamp mist.

Britta will need all her courage to face the shocking discoveries that are in store for her among the ancient towers of Illica.

BOOK 1: SHADOWS OF THE MASTER

Britta has always wanted to be trader like her father, sailing the nine seas and bringing precious cargo home to Del harbor. Her dreams seemed safe until her father's quest to find the fabled Staff of Tier ended in blood and horror. Now his shamed family is in hiding, and his ship, the *Star of Deltora*, belongs to the powerful Rosalyn fleet. But Britta's ambition burns as fiercely as ever. When she suddenly gets the chance to win back her future she knows she has to take it—whatever the cost.

She has no idea that shadows from a distant, haunted isle are watching her every move.

AUTHOR'S NOTE

Deltora is a place of magic and mystery, but the island it shares with the Shadowlands is only one of the many strange isles that dot the nine seas. Some of the nine seas islands are large, and some are small, but they all have their own rich history and their own stories. I have told a few of these stories already—perhaps you have read them, or will read them sometime in the future.

The five *Rowan of Rin* books are set on an island that lies west of Deltora, across the Silver Sea. Deltorans call Rowan's island "Maris," because for centuries they have traded with the fishlike Maris people who live on the coast.

One of Rowan's adventures also takes him on a quest to the nearby Land of the Zebak, a dangerous isle where trading ships never go. And somewhere beneath the waters of the Silver Sea is the lost Isle of the Four Sisters, where Flora, Viva, Aqua and Terra still sing to those who have ears to hear them.

The *Three Doors* trilogy is set on Dorne, a small, rich island in the Sea of Serpents, to Deltora's east. Dorne is not only a popular trading port, with many links to Deltora, but also the native land of the magical Fellan. Their mysterious forest surrounds the walled city of Weld, where Rye, the hero of the *Three Doors* story, begins his quest to find his lost brothers.

And then there is *Deltora Quest* itself—the tale of Lief, Barda and Jasmine's heroic struggle to free Deltora from the Shadow Lord's tyranny.

As those who have read *Tales of Deltora* will know, there are hundreds of islands in the nine seas. And there are thousands more stories to tell. I can't promise to tell them all, but sailing with Britta on the great trading ship *Star of Deltora* will certainly give me the chance to try.